AMERICAN INDUSTRY IN DEVELOPING ECONOMIES

AMERICAN INDUSTRY IN DEVELOPING ECONOMIES

The Management of
International Manufacturing

WICKHAM SKINNER

Harvard University
Graduate School of Business Administration

John Wiley & Sons, Inc.   New York • London • Sydney • Toronto

To
Robert deBoer
Pioneer in
International Manufacturing

Copyright © 1968 by John Wiley & Sons, Inc.

Library of Congress Catalog Card Number: 68-24799
GB 471 79525 9
Printed in the United States of America

PREFACE

This book is the product of research into the manufacturing operations of thirteen corporations of the United States with plants in six developing economies of the world. Its objective has been to identify the more important problems that are being encountered in managing such plants, to isolate key causes, and to suggest frameworks for thought that may be useful to managers at headquarters and abroad.

This work represents an initial exploratory probe into a management area that scarcely existed fifteen years ago. Although studies have been made of certain specialized aspects of international manufacturing — for example, labor relations in various countries — to my knowledge this is the first attempt at a broad look at the problems of international manufacturing management in underdeveloped countries. Therefore the book, although hopefully accurate in a descriptive sense and believed sound in its analysis of the facts observed, makes no attempt to set forth definitive conclusions. Instead, the research effort has been to explore new ground, in a sense by drawing outline maps that describe the type and nature of the problems involved, and to suggest ways of analyzing and handling them more effectively in the future.

The book is addressed primarily to men working in the field of international management. Although the emphasis is on manufacturing, the point of view is that of the general manager rather than the technical specialist. Managers in international business in the fields of marketing, finance, and control will, I believe, find grist for their own mills.

The focus is on plants in developing economies, an exciting field of increasing significance to Americans. The contributions of American enterprise are being felt in many ways in such locations — in producing needed products, supplying employment opportunities, developing managers and technicians, and exporting modern technologies. American industries often bring a new point of view to the country — the point of view of responsible management, enlightened labor relations, and high quality products.

But in this field all has not been "peaches and cream." In fact, as one goes from country to country talking to the managers engaged in these pioneering enterprises, it is impossible to avoid a sense of stress and strain. They have often been through a real struggle for survival, a series of difficult and often frustrating problems and events. Bureaucracy, paperwork, foreign exchange shortages, unfamiliar laws and social customs, uneducated and untrained workers, lack of experienced vendors, marginal quality of local materials and supplies, struggles with the training of foreign national managers, culture shock, and family adjustment make up a partial list of the frustrations in mounting this kind of enterprise. Another set of problems adds to the embattled manager's load: the uncertainties involved in determining whether to adopt American technology, equipment, and procedures and/or to adapt flexibly and innovate abroad. Yet another set of problems has to do with home-office demands, controls, reports, and communications.

The locus of this study is the overseas plant. Since the influence and ultimate responsibility of the corporate headquarters is all-pervasive, I have included discussion of the impact of the parent corporation's policies and managers. One chapter deals directly with the home office.

My point of view has necessarily been critical of present practices, stemming from the assumption that improvement is always possible and usually necessary. In fact, the research indicated that improvement in international production management is vital to growth, profits, and, in some cases, survival of our foreign subsidiaries. The problems, as stated before, have been enormous, but compounding them has been the clear fact that American industry had had little experience to learn from before the early 1960's. The urgency of our need may sometimes make my criticism seem unduly harsh. My observations, however, have led me to the conclusion that it is vitally important that we start to learn more from our experience. Hence this book.

Wickham Skinner

Managua, Nicaragua
February 1968

ACKNOWLEDGMENTS

In the process of twelve months of overseas research, spread over four years, I have developed a strong feeling of admiration for many of the overseas managers I have come to know. They have often gone abroad as risk-takers, giving up more comfortable and stable posts. They have struggled with decisions that resist easy solution and tangled with the complexities inherent in doing business with unfamiliar economic structures and the obstacles of long-distance communications with headquarters. Add to those obstacles the immersion in cultures that at first seem to provide few values and attitudes appropriate to industrial efficiency. These expatriate managers have often been lonely, criticized by the home office and foreign nationals alike. For the most part they have coped admirably with these conditions and they have represented company and country well, although for some of them the pressures and problems have simply been too much. Only a small fraction has been truly outstanding, a conclusion that I believe tells more about the scale of the problems than the inadequacies of American managers.

One American, Robert deBoer of Toledo, Ohio, stands out in my memory as particularly successful. This is true partly, I am sure, because he was one of the first I met who knew his business and knew it well. When I met him he had just returned after an absence of two years to the plant in Turkey he had helped to design, build, and start up. The warmth and sincerity of his reception was so evident that I began to ask about his earlier work. Separated from wife and family, he had worked as the lone American, shoulder to shoulder with Turks through a cold Turkish winter on the shore of the Sea of Marmara. He lived in a simple cottage, working against time and dwindling finances to get into production. The quality of his example, his wisdom, and his spirit are demonstrated in his relationships with Turkish workers and managers and in the practical efficiency of that plant. Bob deBoer set up similar plants all over the world. I met other American managers with similar accomplishments but I single out Bob deBoer, who died in 1966, as an example of what a courageous, practical, and goodwilled man has done for his country and the underdeveloped countries in which he worked. This book is dedicated to him.

I want to acknowledge the contributions of the following Harvard colleagues and the competent staff who helped me in this work. Professors Franklin Folts, Stephen Fuller, Arch Dooley, Philip Thurston, Maurice Kilbridge, Louis Barnes, Renato Tagiuri, Curtis Jones, Richard Rosenbloom, David Rogers, Raymond Vernon, Myles Mace, and Dan T. Smith read and commented on various parts of the manuscript. John Fox and Richard D. Robinson were instrumental in helping me get started in Turkey. Andrew Towl provided much valuable counsel. Mrs. Evelyn Howard typed from dozens of reels of tape, and Miss Constance Lussier typed redrafts, one after another. Miss Barbara Kinney and Miss Jenny Watson did much typing as well.

Though not included in this research, I am indebted to the Mobil Oil Company for a grant that provided some of my early work abroad. I am very grateful to the Harvard Business School for allowing me the time and travel funds necessary for research and writing. Special thanks go to Dean George Baker and Associate Dean George Lombard of the School and to Professor Bertrand Fox, Director of the Division of Research.

I am more grateful than words can convey for the interest and tolerance of my wife Alice, son Charles, and daughter Polly. To my wife goes the credit for patient, thoughtful, and creative editing and constant personal support during the long process of this effort.

I shall always remember the open receptions and the complete cooperation of the many companies I visited and studied in order to write this book. To preserve anonymity, however, I am regretfully forced to withhold the names of the companies and personnel. Nevertheless, to each of the managers and workers who helped me I send warm thanks, for their interest and willingness to talk with me made this book possible.

The accuracy of the facts and the validity of the conclusions that follow are my sole responsibility.

W. S.

CONTENTS

CONTENTS

1

MANAGEMENT PROBLEMS IN
INTERNATIONAL PRODUCTION

This book is a study of the management problems encountered by thirteen U.S. firms that set up production facilities in six developing countries. It examines these problems to determine their causes and to analyze management approaches used in dealing with them. The principal objective is to develop some insights into international production management by drawing on the experiences of companies that have responded to worldwide business opportunities.

The scope of these operations may be grasped by consideration of the spectacular increase in the number of U.S. manufacturing facilities established in relatively underdeveloped foreign countries over the past 15 years: close to 2000 plants in the nations of Asia, Africa, South and Central America, and of Spain, Greece, and Turkey in Europe. In the $5\frac{1}{2}$ years between July 1960 and December 1965 over 908 new manufacturing facilities were established by U.S. firms in these locations.[1]

Such moves have been made in response to new market opportunities that spring up as foreign economies develop and in response to the moves from competition in world markets.

Unfavorable trade balances and political pressures in developing economies have frequently forced U.S. companies to establish manufacturing facilities abroad under conditions that would otherwise have been more favorable toward exporting. Although overseas plants and divisions have been generally profitable, the pioneering

[1]*Sixty-six months (1960-1965) of new Foreign Business Activity of U.S. Firms,* Booz Allen & Hamilton, Inc., Management Research Department, New York, 1966.

1

managers involved have expended considerable effort and have been beset by uncertainties and tension. Interviews reveal a consistent sense of struggle in coping with problems that were typically seen as far more complex and demanding than those in domestic business.

Managers of companies which established manufacturing plants in the developing economies of the world found themselves attempting to cope with a different set of problems from those of domestic production management—problems arising from the facts of producing in unfamiliar environments. Some had to plan and construct a building while dealing with untested contractors and using materials and methods which were strange to them. Decisions had to be made regarding the equipment and processes to be used in the new plant; new labor forces, including a cadre of first line supervision and middle management personnel, had to be hired and trained; procedures had to be established for production control, cost control, quality control, and the movement and storage of parts and materials; arrangements had to be made for the purchasing of materials and components in the new country. Through all of this new relationships had to be created with government officials and recently hired managers. Expatriate managers had to learn to work within an intricate framework of governmental regulations in both the United States and the particular country involved.

Executives at headquarters needed to work out communications systems to exchange information with those in the overseas plants. Decisions had to be made about how the overseas operation would be planned, organized, controlled, and effectively integrated with the international corporation. Who would establish schedules, budgets, processes, and inventory levels? Who would decide whether the foreign plant would change its product or add new products? How much help would be provided by the home office in managing labor relations, working out new collective bargaining agreements, purchasing, and production control?

Investment in overseas manufacturing facilities posed other new problems for a domestic company, such as the creation of a new strategic dimension as it became clear the overseas plant could be used as a competitive weapon in other locations in the world besides the country in which the new plant is placed. The conditions of distance, cross-cultural administration, scarcity of trained managers, governmental restrictions and regulations, political undercurrents, developing economies, and a new economic cost mix could all be expected to pose management problems.

There have been few precedents on which to lean. The experience of such companies as National Cash Register, Corn Products, Singer, and the international oil and mining companies which have been operating abroad for many years is relevant. The combined total of their years of experience, however, is a drop in the bucket compared to the man-years of new experience of American industry abroad during the past 10 years.

Management problems of international manufacturing have attracted little attention. Much research in international business has been directed toward marketing, corporate policy, and financing overseas investments. There has also been a great deal of study of economic development, international trade, and balances of payments. In addition, much work has been done on the study of labor movements, the management elites, and power structures. Anthropologists have analyzed the values and assumptions and beliefs inherent in many of the world's cultures. But relatively little research has been done concerning the problems peculiar to manufacturing in underdeveloped areas or the ways in which they might be overcome.

Perhaps this lack of prior study is due to the relatively high profitability of many overseas ventures. Comfortable operating margins have tended to make management difficulties seem less traumatic when seen from home. And although they are painfully real to the men abroad, problems in work force management, local procurement, or developing managers, did not arouse much concern or incite keen interest of either the home office or, indeed, the profession of business administration. Low labor costs suggested that low factory costs were assured. And sometimes highly favorable results were obtained largely because the competition was relatively weak and operating margins were ample enough to cover many inefficiencies and falldowns. As long as the plants were profitable and growth, due in part to import substitution, was satisfactory, overseas managers were left to struggle alone.

Since my own first research in 1958 the rush of investments abroad has resulted not only in more international companies and plants but in less experienced companies and managers, more marginal operations, and more vigorous competition. The profit situation has also been changing. A McKinsey study[2] cited a one-third reduction in overseas pretax return on investment such that in spite of greater risk abroad, the profit incentive has fallen, so that it is, on the average, only slightly better than in domestic business. This

---

[2]*Overseas Performance of American Corporations*, McKinsey and Company, New York, 1963.

reason may help to explain my observation that many corporate officers are beginning to show more concern and to place more attention on the manufacturing end of international business. Continued contacts indicate that many companies can no longer accept poor productivity per machine or worker, high inventories, poor quality, and high scrap rates.

This research indicates that to many companies the early years in underdeveloped countries have proved vastly more frustrating and disappointing than is commonly realized. They have been beset with perplexing difficulties arising from strange economic, political, and cultural environments. Inventory control and maintenance approaches which have worked well in the United States were not successful in the new location. Elements of personnel policy and personnel management based on American values and industrial civilization sometimes led to conflicts abroad. Shortages of items which had been easily procured in the United States introduced problems which were further accentuated by shortages of foreign exchange and subsequent difficulties of importation. Increased governmental regulations and nationalistic pressures added further tension.

The following case example illustrates a problem perplexing to the American manager of a manufacturing company in a developing country.

Example 1

The American co-director of the California Farm Implement Turk plant in Istanbul, Turkey, walked through the machine shop and noted to his irritation that only four workers were actually producing parts. Thirty-five workers were employed in the machine shop, and, as Mr. deSalle looked around the area, they were to be found at such tasks as cleaning their machines, counting parts, carrying parts to other machines, waiting for tools at the tool crib, going and coming from the washrooms, and talking.

He noticed with further annoyance that the foreman and superintendent were in the foreman's office. On joining them he found that they were discussing various alternatives in machining a new job. They both seemed genuinely surprised to learn that only four machines were running and explained that they had been busy with the new job and "checking timecards, job tickets and other essentials." Mr. deSalle reminded them through an interpreter that he had repeatedly told them that one of them should be on the floor at all times to keep things going productively. The superintendent agreed but said that although they tried to follow Mr. deSalle's orders they were "so busy with paperwork and other managerial duties" that it was very difficult. The American replied that "nothing is more important than keeping the machines going" and left the office.

In recounting the incident he explained that his exasperation was due to "the fact that almost inevitably the superintendent and the foreman were never out in the shop supervising the men and their jobs. They give 1000 excuses every time and promise to do better, but they seem to gravitate right back to the office. They don't like to criticize the workers and make them change anything they're doing, and they feel, somehow, that the job of a manager is in an office."

In a U.S. plant in the Far East a problem of employee sabotage arose when the plant was already losing money and under pressure from the home office.

Example 2

Strange incidents of employee sabotage began to occur over weekends and at night. Cooling valves were turned off, overheating and often disabling equipment. Chalk was dropped into material being processed, ruining it. Expensive instruments were damaged or totally removed.

In attempting to find the cause of the sabotage, the U.S. managers were hindered by the language barrier. The Personnel Manager stated that "it is nearly impossible to know what is going on. All our information is filtered and garbled. Our employees seemed happy enough, but obviously they are not."

Procurement operations are a frequent source of delays and frustrations. At a plant in South Africa the manager discussed local vendors.

Example 3

Even in a relatively advanced country such as South Africa our ability to purchase satisfactorily is badly limited. We can't count on getting deliveries in time, and worse yet, the quality is unreliable. Our vendors won't invest in equipment and the necessary gear to improve quality. They have a short-term outlook about spending money. And there isn't enough competition to give us any leverage.

Many problems arise over issues of control and policy making.

Example 4

In a large, multiplant, international company headquarters a manager stated:

Many of our overseas managers are completely unaware of our job here in New York. We are held responsible at the top for the total performance of the international business. We must determine and direct policy so as to build and achieve a total strategy and coordination. And we must have more information from the field, not less.

But at the overseas plants of the same company, managers made such statements as this:

Every year we are required to spend more and more time filling out reports. It's taking half our time now. Most of the information isn't even used in New York. And every year New York adds to the list of actions which require home office approval. It indicates a lack of trust which is highly irritating.

The emphasis in this book is primarily on the overseas management, but, necessarily, the home office headquarters function plays a major role in the overseas plant management. For this reason many of the effects of the home office operation are cited throughout the book, and one chapter is devoted to the study of the contribution and role of the home office in the success of the overseas plant.

In visiting the overseas plants, American and foreign nationals were interviewed, using an interpreter when necessary, with the researcher's initial questions directed toward learning the history of policies, practices, problems, and results at the plant. As many executives as possible were interviewed at each plant to obtain a variety of viewpoints on the same problems. In the course of interviews I inquired into the systems, procedures, and operations throughout the plant; these included work force management, personnel management, labor relations, procurement, production control, quality control, choice of equipment and process, the middle management function, the interrelationship with the home office, the competitive position, the relationships with the government, and the local living, economic, and political conditions.

It became clear as the interviews progressed that several basic problems came up repeatedly. One such problem was the structure of the international organization and its interconnections and relationship with the overseas plant. Who was to make the decisions having to do with the new products, with expansions, with new equipment, for example? What home office services would be available to the overseas plants? How much control was reserved to the home office? How much authority was granted abroad? These questions preoccupied men in all the countries visited.

In addition, dealing with foreign managers and a foreign work force was a major preoccupation of Americans. It was evident that differences in values, standards, and cultural outlook made the supervision of foreign managers difficult for most Americans. What is the impact of culture on the operation of a manufacturing plant? On what occasions or in what circumstances is it appropriate to try to modify or go against the existing culture in order to improve productivity? For example, in Moslem countries should the workers be allowed to stop their machines and pray at specified times during the day?

Questions arose in dealing with the local politics and economic situations. Where the labor costs were low and cost of material and interest high by American standards, equipment or scheduling decisions might require a different approach from one used domestically. And an overseas plant manager and his staff had many times more contacts and dependence on relationships with the local government than his domestic counterparts, requiring skills not usually associated with manufacturing.

Another question that emerged early in this research had to do with the exportation of American "know-how." What U.S. systems and procedures and what approaches to quality control, equipment selection and maintenance, production control, and work force management are applicable abroad? Where a method or technique proved useful in the United States, how and when could it be "grafted" into another culture and economic environment? Managers usually assumed that they either could or could not adopt a system in any particular location and seldom questioned their assumptions. This area of management decision stood out to the researcher because of the stark contrasts of opinions from one company to another.

Following the interviews abroad, the home office of each of the U.S. companies was also visited. The home office executives were interviewed to see how they perceived the problems observed abroad and how they attempted to manage the overseas operations from their headquarters.

In dealing with the data it appeared logical to divide the functions of managing abroad into three parts: first, the manufacturing aspects of the decision to invest in a particular location. This is the subject of Chapter 2. Second, the process of managing overseas is divided into six decision areas commonly involved in the management of any manufacturing facility. These areas, which are discussed in Chapters 3 to 8, are work force management, labor relations, procurement, control of production, technological strategy, and manufacturing organization. The third part of the study examines three different sources of management decisions: the home office, the foreign manager, and the expatriate American manager. These three sources of management are discussed in Chapters 9 to 11. Overall conclusions of the study are presented in the final chapter.

Throughout this book the aim is to develop a useful framework for the international manufacturing manager, a framework which provides a convenient, realistic, and effective scheme for thinking about each area of management. Usually without prior expertise, overseas manufacturing managers must attempt to master not only the art of manufacturing—with its normal demands for technical, quantitative, and organizational understanding—but also implicitly draw on the disciplines of economics, history, anthropology, and political science as they attempt to understand their jobs in a foreign environment. The same demands are made on the reader and on the writer as well.

The aura of criticism which may seem to surround many examples in the forthcoming chapters requires an explanation. The men studied are pioneers. They work at a frontier. To learn from their achievements and their shortcomings requires unbiased analysis and, sometimes apparently, excess criticism from the researcher. Even so there is appreciation for the beleaguered subject of our attention, and apology for what appears at times as not only an analytical but also a critical point of view. The very nature of the job requires a breadth of talents beyond those commonly available. It is too much to expect the enormous breadth demanded of any one man in what is, in effect, a new branch of the still new profession of management. In the future an accumulation of experience may help develop more men who can approach the specifications built into the job by the realities of the situation.

To develop better international production managers we need to appraise results abroad and to search out fundamental causes of the problems met and identify key ingredients for future success. This has been a humbling task for this researcher. The reader may also share the feeling that the role of spectator and judge is far easier than that of participant.

2

MANUFACTURING
CONSIDERATIONS
IN THE DECISION TO INVEST
IN DEVELOPING ECONOMIES

When strategic factors prompt a company to consider manufacturing in a less developed nation, how can the company identify obstacles to profitable manufacturing and determine whether they are serious enough to undermine the investment? And after the decision to invest has been made, what preinvestment planning can help to avoid or minimize the problems that are likely to be encountered in the new location?

This chapter is concerned with analysis of the manufacturing situation before a final decision is made to manufacture in a particular location and with the preinvestment planning that leads to formulation of the manufacturing policies of the new plant.

The paper reports some of the findings of a study of the manufacturing operations of 13 U.S. corporations as observed in 24 plants in India, Nigeria, Pakistan, South Africa, Spain, and Turkey, and in their home offices. Industries represented were pharmaceuticals, automotive and agricultural vehicles, tire and rubber goods, construction equipment, food products, and consumer durables.

FINDINGS

Most of the companies in this study encountered serious problems in manufacturing abroad, which a more perceptive preinvestment analysis might have enabled them to handle more easily. Essentially, these firms slipped into one or more of three traps: (a) they focused on the wrong problems, projecting problems of an operating[1] nature to the neglect of fundamental structural factors; (b) they made erroneous assumptions about the manufacturing conditions in the developing nation; (c) they lacked the perspective necessary to recognize that the plant's products and processes, the company-country relationships, and the *modus operandi* of the international firm were all subject to change.

On examination these "traps," as we have called them, were difficult to avoid because they each are the result of extrapolating from one culture and environment to another. The following examples illustrate.

Example 1

The difficulty of focusing on the key problems in the preinvestment analysis is illustrated by a company which decided to set up a plant in Spain. After visiting factories in Spain and noting the many contrasts with United States manufacturing, they concluded that worker performance, product quality, and production scheduling would be their most critical problems. Elaborate procedures were designed to handle these potential difficulties. But after the plant opened, the company ran into serious trouble from quite a different, altogether unforeseen, source, namely, obtaining low-cost supplies of basic materials, available only at a high price from a competitor due to a cartel-like industry structure.

Impressed by obvious differences, they missed a more subtle yet fundamental problem.

Example 2

A vehicle manufacturer which set up a plant in Turkey, was concerned about the adequacy of foreign exchange for importing essential parts. After some difficulty they obtained the Turkish government's guarantee of sufficient foreign exchange, assuming that the government's written guarantee could be taken at face value.

---

[1] "Operating" problems are defined as the daily or short-term tasks of producing the product, including maintaining the equipment, the logistics of supply, personnel management, and record keeping.

Within one year their plant was virtually closed for lack of imported materials, and it floundered for four years. The government had not been insincere in making the promise, but the time came when no foreign exchange was available to dispense.

The company had misjudged a predictable condition in Turkey.

Example 3

Another company delayed its decision to accept a favorable opportunity to invest in India because of a vague fear that the government would not be cooperative. Later events showed that this belief was not justified, but after five years India had moved to a different stage in its industrialization and the opportunity to enter was effectively lost. Conditions changed more rapidly than had been anticipated.

Production managers heading overseas often hear of vexing problems in work force management, procurement, construction, maintenance, production planning, or quality control. They then concentrate their preparation in fearful intensity on those specific, tangible hurdles ahead. But although these problems are sometimes perplexing, expensive, and frustrating because of the cultural conflicts involved, they should be of secondary importance in the decision to invest. They require study and preparation, but they are seldom the critical problems that are going to "make or break" the new plant. Data from this study indicate that more fundamental and often less tangible and changing conditions are apt to be the eventual keys to the success of the plant.

This research suggests that there are four basic conditions that should be satisfied before a company decides to invest in a foreign location. These conditions are not absolutes in the sense of being precisely measurable. The satisfaction of each condition, as will be seen, is a matter of judgment. These conditions represent fundamental needs. When these needs have not been met, serious trouble has usually followed.

Four conditions to be satisfied before deciding to invest

1. The company's assumptions regarding the role of the foreign

government, the political climate, and the stage of economic development in the particular country are accurate and realistic.

2.   The local plant's objectives, plans, and needs are consistent with the corporation's strategic assets and plans.

3.   The company's objectives and plans for the manufacturing plant and its products are consistent with the economic interests of the host country.

4.   Company objectives and profit goals are consistent with realistic estimates of the conditions in the industry.

These four conditions bear on *whether* to invest. They should be distinguished from another set of preproduction considerations which relate to *how* to set up and manage the operation, anticipating which operating areas will present the more difficult problems. The "how to do it" considerations will be discussed following the "whether to do it" conditions.

Analysis of satisfactory experiences in investing in developing nations suggests that a sense of perspective about time is a vital ingredient. Hence these four conditions must be judged in the time dimension. For this purpose I believe it would be useful to recognize three kinds of typical chronological stages:

1.   Stages in the scope and development of an overseas manufacturing plant.

2.   Stages in the development of an international manufacturing corporation.

3.   Stages in company-country relationships.

Awareness of these typical stages can give a needed time dimension to both the "whether to" and the "how to" invest decisions. A "poor" condition that will probably be changing for the better is apt to be far less important than a "good" condition that is likely to deteriorate. These stages are described in more detail toward the end of this chapter.

WHETHER TO INVEST

Condition 1.   Accurate company assumptions of political and economic conditions

Some companies studied met unexpected trouble because they were unrealistic about the role of foreign governments in regulating the economy. These companies assumed that dealing with the foreign government was just an unpleasant chore, a nuisance factor to be tolerated but handled as expeditiously as possible. A corollary to this state of mind was that low-level clerks could handle government-imposed requirements. The local government, it was assumed, would be anxious to cooperate and assist in every way a company that invested in its country.

In retrospect, needless to say, this approach was not very effective. These firms were handicapped in their struggle with foreign exchange, customs regulations, government restrictions, and red tape. They were equipped with neither the expertise nor the attitude of accepting the validity of the problem.

Unrealistic assumptions about the political climate in the country in which the company is about to invest have been equally costly.

Example 4

An American auto manufacturer set up operations in a middle eastern location after being invited and extended considerable cooperation by the local government. Local auto production was needed to reduce import requirements. The company's first few years of assembly proceeded smoothly enough, based on importing 90 percent of parts requirements.

But the political climate was changing. The local government was nationalizing certain industries and expanding its involvement in business. A rigorous government policy was instituted requiring that the company manufacture a larger fraction of its parts. The company pointed out that the market was too small for economic production of most major parts. The government, under pressure from an increasingly strident opposition party, became militant in its edicts. The company threatened to close up rather than give in. After several years of deteriorating relationships, the U.S. company finally pulled out.

The researcher is left with the haunting question as to whether this political and industrial development climate might have been detected or predicted before the investment decision was made. If so, could the manufacturing policies have been adapted?

These examples illustrate the difficulty of making the necessary realistic appraisals of the governmental and political structural conditions before the commitment to invest.

Condition 2. The local plant's objectives, plans, and needs are consistent with the corporation's strategic assets and plans

Mention of this obvious condition seems to be gratuitous, for naturally the new operation must fit into the company's broad goals and international scheme. Nevertheless, this condition was violated several times in the situations studied, apparently because it involves some subtleties in interpreting company strategy and the implications of a new foreign enterprise.

Example 5

An American farm implement manufacturer set up a plant abroad in the midst of a domestic company crisis characterized by financial losses, declining sales, and a deteriorating competitive position. In fact, the prospective sale of excess domestic inventory abroad originally sparked the idea for the overseas plant.

But at that phase of the company's corporate life a foreign operation in an undeveloped location made no sense. The home company could not offer the needed logistics, credit, or high-level manpower support to the international operation. Things were going too badly at home to nurture an international venture in an underdeveloped economy, and the overseas subsidiary suffered from lack of support. While the new foreign operation offered an apparent short-term solution to a leftover-inventory problem, in the long term it created new crises and financial losses because the overseas venture was incompatible with the firm's needs and resources.

Example 6

An American manufacturer of motor vehicle parts and assemblies purchased a defunct truck company and subsequently established a joint enterprise in an overseas location to assemble trucks.

The truck had not been produced for five years. Most of the parts were purchased and vendors had gradually changed dimensions for other customers. The truck parts would no longer fit together when assembly was attempted abroad. But the U.S. company was not organized to quickly recognize and adequately handle the problem. The net results: 47 trucks built in $4\frac{1}{2}$ years, mountains of correspondence, and deep disappointments and accusations on both sides of the ocean.

In fact, the U.S. company was in a different business from that of the overseas plant; its goals and assumptions about its future success would not support the investments required to establish a viable international truck assembly operation. The enterprise was a mistake from the start because the home corporation's strategic assets and plans did not encompass the truck vehicle business.

Condition 3. The company's objectives and plans for the manufacturing plant and its products are consistent with the interests of the host country

Host countries have a set of conditions reflecting their particular economic needs and political interest which may emerge in some of the following forms:

1.   Requirements for increasing local manufacturing content.
2.   Requirements for increasing local procurement.
3.   Requirements for a certain percentage of local ownership.
4.   Requirements that a high proportion of the managers be indigenous foreign nationals.
5.   Requests for the company to diversify in its use of its manufacturing facilities to produce a wider variety of locally needed products.
6.   Requests for the company to work toward exporting its products.

Before investing, successful firms studied the nature of both the expressed and implicit local interests. They anticipated probable changes in the future. They then decided whether they could operate successfully, consistent with local needs and pressures.

Local national goals and policies often appeared unwise and unrealistic to managers in the investing company. However, managers in the companies that coped most adequately showed understanding of the pressures with which the foreign government was dealing. They studied the economy and analyzed the political situation. Even then they did not always agree with the approaches taken by the foreign government, but they attempted to understand the frame of mind, and the values that were incorporated in local government decisions.

In some instances companies have had to make drastic adjustments to the needs and interests of the host country. Often this change has come about only after long periods of wrangling and dissatisfaction. Some of the wrangling between host countries and American businesses can be traced to different concepts of what business is.

United States firms normally regard their establishment of corporate policies as their own unilateral prerogative. But in the developing economies, business is logically viewed by the government as an arm of economic development policy. Companies are required to assist in the local government's program, such as in providing technical training, enlightened labor relations, and fringe benefits, offering housing and other benefits which could not be provided in the United States, and occasionally even by taking large investment risks.

Condition 4.   Company objectives and profit goals must be consistent with industry conditions abroad

This stipulation has to do with the congruency between company plans, strategic assets, and costs and the competitive situation and operating margins in the industry market abroad. Perhaps this provision is the most important, because it pertains to the company's ability to compete in its new environment.

At any given time there is a set of critical determinants which structure the operating margins in an industry in a given locale. (Operating margin is defined here as the difference between the factory price of a product and its labor, material, and equipment costs.) The cost of basic raw material, parts, and supplies is largely beyond the influence of the producing company. The cost of labor and salaries is also a substantially determined factor. The economic scale of the plant, in combination with the technological requirements for equipment and process, complete the economic determinants of operating costs. The nature and extent of the competition, the characteristics of the market, and any government controls effectively establish the prices charged. The difference between these prices and the local cost of manufacturing must supply the marketing and administrative costs and any product development necessary and result in a satisfactory net profit. This "operating margin" is important in appraising an investment opportunity.

Making a thorough industry analysis in one's own economy is not an easy process. Industry and economic statistics must be gathered. Some facts are difficult to obtain, especially those concerning competition and how it is operating.

Overseas the problem is apt to be even more difficult. Industry and economic statistics must frequently be secured on a private basis because the government data are often either unavailable or unreliable. Industry is typically more secretive. Usually less public information exists. Contacts and personal sources are not likely to be at hand; it is a problem to know who to turn to and who to trust. A thorough analysis of the entire production process, a projection of the overhead structure, an establishment of basic systems and procedures, a forecast of the most difficult operating problems and the organization necessary to handle them are also needed. Finally, a study of conditions in the industry and government regulations affecting it is essential.

In obtaining and using these data an everpresent problem is that a study must discern trends. What is going to happen to the cost of labor? What is going to be the future size of the market? What may be the future action of the government in terms of allocations of foreign exchange, of price controls, and in industry regulations?

Hugo E. R. Uyterhoeven and Raphael W. Hodgson[2] point out that it is necessary to project beyond the present market in order to recognize opportunities before they become obvious and to avoid dangerous situations before a company invests. They point out that a company must recognize these elements:

1.   The limits[3] within which a firm operates abroad and plans its strategy.
2.   The means of competition in a foreign country.
3.   The critical elements of the industry in that particular country.

A McKinsey study[4] urges a study of the history of the industry in the United States in order to shed light on the present stage of the industry in the foreign country.

The whether to invest conditions will sometimes depend on the how to operate analysis. If, for example, low-cost tooling could be developed to offset an otherwise unfavorable operating margin due to too small a scale of operation, the investment decision could be tipped from a "No" to a "Yes." But such thinking requires a sharp pencil and a creative approach to technical problems.

[2] Hugo E. R. Uyterhoeven and Raphael W. Hodgson, "Analyzing Foreign Opportunities," *Harvard Business Review* (March-April 1962).
[3] This refers to the anticipated operating margins.
[4] J. G. MacDonald and Hugh Parker (of McKinsey and Company), "Creating a Strategy of International Growth," *International Enterprise* (1962).

Several of the companies studied demonstrated the advantages of being able to discern in advance particular industry conditions and local economic factors which would affect their operating margins. Their studies often indicated that conventional tooling and processes were not feasible in developing countries. In contrast to other firms studied, these companies learned to "think small" and to develop special tools and processes in order to establish a satisfactory operating margin. Equipment was designed to minimize capital investment and take advantage of low labor costs. Without such considerations in the preinvestment analysis, the operating margins forecast would have signalled a "No Go" decision.

PREINVESTMENT ANALYSIS FOR MANUFACTURING POLICY DECISIONS

Another area of preinvestment analysis is important, though usually not critical: identifying manufacturing problems that will be encountered and gauging the degree of each difficulty expected. If this is done accurately, manufacturing organizations, systems, processes, and personnel can be tailored to match organizational strength to the anticipated problem areas. This area of preinvestment analysis leads to decisions on what we called earlier "how to" manufacture.

When planning the manufacturing system, the firm needs to identify the operating problems the unique environment and local resources will maximize. Procurement, production planning and control, work force management, quality control, labor relations, choice of equipment and process, selection and training of managers—all these are functional areas of management subject to local environmental forces. In any of these areas unforeseen problems may depress profits.

Many major problems in these operating areas may be anticipated and planned for in the organization of the new business. Several examples of surmountable problems observed in the course of this research follow.

Foreign exchange and inflation

In many economies a chronic foreign exchange shortage and/or inflation had to be anticipated in organizing the manufacturing operation. At some U.S. companies in Turkey, even though the foreign exchange shortage was foreseen, the operation was not organized for profitable survival during a period of chronic inability to import.

When a chronic foreign exchange shortage is expected, self-sufficiency can be built into the operation. The equipment and the processes may be established for manufacturing items that would normally be imported. This calls for fresh technical thinking and ingenuity. An expanded and more versatile local procurement organization may be an additional or alternative arrangement to cope with import restrictions.

Creeping inflation was sometimes ignored in preinvestment planning. While voicing complaints about "poor government planning," the overseas managers were often slow to accept the reality of inflation and organize their production control, inventory management, and wage and salary systems to minimize costs and morale problems.

Procurement

Many companies have been irritated and frustrated by the problems of local procurement: late deliveries, marginal or unpredictable quality, limited variety, unfamiliar negotiation processes and terms. A pharmaceutical company's preliminary survey of conditions in Spain indicated many sources of glass bottles and apparently reliable vendors for packaging supplies. But after production began, it found the vendors unreliable in quality and delivery. The standards of vendors were far below those expected. Serious shortages and production line stoppages resulted.

In the less developed countries procurement problems were not surprising, but, strangely, few companies staffed their procurement sections to develop and assist local vendors to better meet their needs. Receiving inspection procedures, inventory levels, and procurement policies can be modified to counteract the effect of mediocre vendors. In companies where this was done, the effects of potentially serious procurement problems have been minimized.

Work force management

Experience shows that the initial problems of recruiting, selecting, and training a work force are not as serious as usually anticipated. More serious problems of developing first-line supervision, satisfactory pay systems, more advanced skills, and higher worker morale generally develop after the first six to twelve months. At many companies such work force management problems depressed operating profits because they were not foreseen and prepared for by adequate organization and procedures. Some companies successfully dealt with these problems by sending training personnel abroad and by giving home office staff assistance in the development of locally sound wage plans.

Labor relations problems

Caught in a major jurisdictional problem, rapidly changing local costs, and negative reactions to its wage plan and supervisory practices, a U.S. company in India suffered a series of walkouts and a major strike. In the United States a top executive stated, "We have been attempting to manage over there with too much of our own religion or philosophy. We are trying to learn to relax and adjust to conditions there. If we had conducted a more penetrating preinvestment analysis," this executive stated, "labor relations could have been handled better from the start."

These are examples of problems frequently met abroad which can be moderated if they are anticipated and the necessary organization is established. A thorough manufacturing survey in which the production team is well represented is a real advantage. But often production men have not been properly represented on the preinvestment analysis team. Marketing, financial, and top management representatives have predominated, even though a team should investigate a wide list of possible production areas and problems. Exhibit 1 provides suggestions for such a list.

AIDS IN ACQUIRING PERSPECTIVE

A manufacturing investment must be viable over the long run, for the passage of time will bring changes. Somehow a management must look ahead to envisage various conditions, pressures, opportunities, and resources at different future phases of the life of the organization. Company histories and intercompany comparisons suggest the existence of the following three different kinds of chronological stages, which, taken into account when planning a new facility, could help bring to light future eventualities.

Stages in the scope and development of the overseas manufacturing plant

The manufacturing subsidiary abroad revealed clearly definable stages in its growth (Exhibit 2). In the first stage, the operation is usually relatively simple. It concentrates on the end product and often only on its assembly; the scale of the operation is apt to be small, and it can be readily influenced and supported by a handful of American managers.

Typically, in a second stage the local manufacturing content is increased and foreign nationals take over virtually all of the management; labor relations mature (often with many more difficulties than experienced in the first few years); and the company becomes recognized as a continuing member of the local society.

In a third stage, after the company has been long established, the success and growth of its local manufacturing operation generally depends more on the development of the local economy than in the first two stages. With the passage of time a developing economy will probably offer better developed local resources and skills. Increasing competition means narrower profit margins. The operation is manned by foreign nationals for the most part, and it becomes an accepted element of the local economy.

Stages in the development of an international manufacturing corporation

Companies have also tended to pass through stages in their development as international businesses (Exhibit 3). At the business' start the emphasis has often been on exporting or selling parts abroad to be assembled. A second stage is characterized by increased activities abroad, with the establishing of more manufacturing operations. A third stage is marked by growth and diversification into a broader product line manufactured abroad. A fourth stage, which has emerged in several firms, is the establishment of a more "multinational" operation: each foreign plant makes certain parts and assemblies for the company's product line and there is a considerable interchange between the international plants.

In making the original manufacturing decision it is useful to recognize that these stages may be forthcoming. It is important for a company to perceive its present stage in its own international growth.

EXHIBIT 1
A Checklist of Production Management Areas

Work Force Management	Procurement	Production Control	Quality Control
Recruitment	Raw materials	Scheduling	Choice of
Selection	Supplies	Coordination	quality
Wage system	Equipment	Use of inven-	level
Job scope	Specifications-	tories	Specifica-
Training	design	Cost of in-	tions
Supervision	Vendors:	ventories	Receiving
Communications	Availability	Machine	inspection
methods	Skills	utilization	Inspection
Grievance	Attitudes	Internal	systems
procedure	Quality	scheduling	Inspectors
Labor relations	Delivery	Forecasting	Worker
Motivation	Equipment	Personnel and	training
incentives	Prices	training	Product
Fringe benefits	Procurement or-		design
Safety	ganization		
	follow-up,		
	contacts		
	Supervision		
	Vendor develop-		
	ment		
	Transportation		

Experience suggests that Stage Two often presents more difficult problems than Stage One. There will be political and economic pressures to increase local manufacturing content, to expand the operation, and to staff with foreign nationals. If this stage is expected, it may be easier to make the company's objectives coincide with the local needs and requirements, which typically become more critical when the Third Stage is reached.

Stages in company-country relationships

There also appear to be normal stages in the company's relationship with the local economy and the government (Exhibit 4). During the first several years, the company is a newcomer, often benefiting from special arrangements that have been made to induce investment. The local government is usually anxious to test its cooperation and the seriousness of its concern for local interests. This is the honeymoon stage in terms of labor relations and political rela-

EXHIBIT 1
A Checklist of Production Management Areas

Cost Control	Home Office	Choice of Equipment and Process	Foreign National Managers
Reports	Staff assistance, in which areas	Scale of production	Availability
Budgets-goals		Degree of mechanization	Knowledge
Cost accounting		Specifications-product design	Skills
	Controls	Materials handling	Attitudes
	Reports	Plant layout	Judgment
	Communications	Capacity planning	Recruitment
	Limits of delegated authority	New versus second-hand equipment	Selection
		Maintenance management	Salary system
		Spare parts, supplies	Motivation
		Construction	Communications
		Setup costs	Use of U. S. managers
		Running costs	
		Utilities	
		Tooling	
		Depreciation costs	
		Effects on quality, labor skills, supervision	

tionships with the labor sector of the society. The company may expect some government protection from competition in the early stages of a developing economy.

Following the early stage the company can expect increasing pressures to implement national policy through local laws, foreign exchange, permits, licenses, and so forth. Government pressures may develop for increased fringe benefits and stability of employment, or increased local manufacturing content, or even price and market controls and allocations.

A third stage comes about as a nation's industrial growth develops. In this period the economy is more mature and balanced, vendors are more plentiful, but competition may be pressing. There may be a higher degree of free, autonomous economic decision-making as part of a less controlled economy.

Some of the companies visited were surprised by the developments that took place over a short period. For example, in spite of American emphasis on free competition, several U.S. companies in

EXHIBIT 2
Typical Stages in an Overseas Manufacturing Plant

Stage	Typical Characteristics
1	Manufacturing operation relatively simple concentrates on end product assembly small scale import or buy percent is high—make percent is low Large U.S. overseas staff in top positions Heavy parent corporation support Duration about 2 to 3 years
2	Increasing local content—decreasing importation More complexity in manufacturing process Larger scale production Increasing foreign national management Greater dependence on local economy Duration about 2 to 7 years
3	Manufacture bulk of the product, including local procurement Import little Large scale operations Few, if any, American managers

developing economies have complained bitterly because, after the first stage, local governments have welcomed new competitors.

It is useful to keep these stages in mind when entering a new location. Conditions do not remain as they appear during the preinvestment study. Changes in the political atmosphere and the economic environment in which it operates may suggest company changes in scale, processes, products, and management which need to be appraised in advance.

As these stages are projected, they seldom suggest clear signals to go ahead or to stop. In fact, the projection of local operating problems is likely to reveal that there will be many hurdles both in the beginning and in the future. But if the four basic conditions look promising, then the company's strategy and plans can anticipate both the early problems and the long-range needs of the local plant, the local economy, and its own international organization. The production system can be set up to meet the problems forecast. The manufacturing function has a better chance to adjust successfully during the intermeshing stages of the company, the plant, and the economy if these stages are anticipated.

EXHIBIT 3
Typical Stages in the Development of an
International Manufacturing Operation

Characteristics	Stage			
	1	2	3	4
Number of plants	None	Few	More	Many
Amount of exporting from U.S. to overseas plants	Much, entire products	More parts, fewer complete products	Critical materials or sub-assemblies only	Little or none
Products manufactured abroad	None	Narrow line	Broader line	Diversified line
Material exchange between plants	None	Few	More	Highly planned and coordinated interchange
Experience and expertise in management of international manufacturing	Little or none	Limited	Growing	Extensive

EXHIBIT 4
Typical Stages in Company-Country Relationships

Factors	Stage		
	1	2	3
Company political status	Welcome newcomer	The foreign company is tested for its willingness to cooperate with national policies and aims	Long-time resident. Reputation established. Concerns about monopoly or control or competitive success versus local industry
Economic pressures	Privileges, exceptions, protection	Treatment as any local company subject to laws concerning foreign exchange, licenses, permits. No protection.	Pressures for increasing local manufacturing content, stability of employment, price controls or limitations to expansion of scope
Labor relations	Honeymoon — family style	Increasing pressures and demands Skirmishing	Maturing relationships

3

WORK FORCE MANAGEMENT

Management of an international manufacturing enterprise requires recruiting, selecting, training, compensating, and supervising a foreign work force. This chapter is concerned with such activities and discusses the various approaches taken by U.S. companies in this "people" area. Labor relations, dealing with the work force in a collective sense, will be treated in Chapter 4.

RECRUITING, SELECTING, AND TRAINING THE WORK FORCE

Recruiting and selecting

Creating a new work force in a strange environment presents problems that immediately appear formidable. Somehow the production manager and his team must recruit from the community men who are willing to work for the new company, and then they must select a work force which will ultimately prove to possess the appropriate level of capability.

Consider the steps involved: decisions must be made regarding the level of education, skill, and experience needed to properly man the factory. Some sort of appeal must be articulated and communicated to attract the necessary workers. When applicants begin to appear, a selection procedure must be established. How does one decide in a foreign country whether a worker is qualified, relative to other possible employees? In many countries there is a scarcity of workmen with the requisite skill and education. And in any country many qualified candidates will be reluctant to leave their present positions for an uncertain future with a foreign employer.

Language problems complicate the job. It is difficult enough to do a good job of employee selection in one's native culture; it is an even greater problem to make such a selection in a foreign country or to find an indigenous employee whose judgment can be trusted and to whom the choice may safely be delegated.

Considering these potential problems, it is surprising that the creation of an adequate work force by American subsidiaries abroad has generally not proven difficult. In the plants studied the American company has generally been able to attract sufficient workers with the necessary skills for development into a satisfactory working group. In no plant was there an immediate scarcity of men with at least minimum qualifications, nor was the start-up of any plant delayed by lack of an adequate work force. It was never considered necessary to change the recruiting and selection program in order to overcome difficulties hampering the start-up.

Clark Kerr and his associates corroborate this observation, stating that "Of all the processes of labor force development, recruitment is the easiest to handle. Managers generally are able, by one means or another, to recruit the number of bodies they need."[1]

This is not to say that recruiting and selection have not presented some unique difficulties. All of the hiring programs studied were fraught with uncertainty and lacked assurance that an adequate work force would be the eventual product. As one American manager in South Africa put it, "We still don't know whether or not we did a good job in the original selection of the work force."

Nearly every American manager interviewed stated that it was an uncomfortable experience, for with the differences in the culture and languages involved one had to use a good deal of "gut feel" or simply turn the job over to a new, local personnel manager, in whom one could feel limited confidence. From the standpoint of the American or third-country national, the selection process had to be based mostly on intuition. It was fortunate that the numbers of recruits attracted were normally sufficient to allow a broad selection.

The appeal of the American companies has apparently been due to several factors generally present in all of the countries visited. First, the reputation of America as an advanced industrial nation has evidently often carried with it the inference that the foreign

[1]Clark Kerr, John Dunlop, Frederick Harbison, and Charles A. Myers, *Industrialism and Industrial Management*, Harvard University Press, Cambridge, Mass., 1960, p. 169.

employees of an American company will be well paid, well taken care of, and, to an extent, will become "rich Americans." Workers' expectations at the moment of employment are perhaps unrealistic (an element which may subsequently affect labor relations), but this rosy aura at least appeared to help U.S. companies over the initial hurdle of establishing a work force.

In every country visited the management of indigenous companies often appeared to the researcher to be relatively "unenlightened" about the methods of modern personnel management. American personnel practices, supervisory methods, wages and fringe benefits, and working conditions were apt to appear more attractive to the prospective employee than in local industry. This reaction helped overcome any inherent reluctance to leave present employers and the sense of taking a chance with a new, foreign company. Evidently, too, new buildings and a modern plant were added attractions to many workers.

In many undeveloped countries a chronic state of underemployment has eased the recruitment of workers. In plants in Pakistan, India, Turkey, and Nigeria, for example, dozens of men waited daily outside the factory gates, hoping that they might gain a chance for an interview. In Turkey I talked to several such hopeful workers through interpreters. They said that they traveled each day to one of several American plants outside the city in hopes of obtaining "a good job with an American company."

A final factor in the relative ease of attracting workers has been that American subsidiaries abroad have usually been content to hire and train men with relatively low skills rather than insisting on employees with a higher present skill level. This policy was followed to avoid hiring men with "ingrained bad habits." American managers typically felt that it would be easier to train men without prior experience than to retrain already-skilled workers in "good industrial work habits."

Since establishment of an overseas manufacturing subsidiary is usually on a relatively tight time schedule and the investment in plant facilities places pressure on the operating manager to get into production, there is a subsequent pressure for the manager to hire his work force without delay once the machinery and equipment are ready for use. The emphasis therefore was often on time rather than on that uncertain ingredient, quality.

But the quality of a work force turned out to be more important than was realized by many companies. "Quality" is a consequence of not only initial skills of the men but even more of their potential for development. When a relatively unskilled work force is hired and further skill development is necessary, the management is "betting on the come." They have gambled that those whom they have hired will be able to absorb training and, within a reasonable time, develop the additional skills, knowledge, and attitudes necessary to become efficient employees.

In this sense the finer points of employee selection and a discerning initial analysis can become more important than has been recognized. Perhaps most important are the attitudes and personality traits of the workers. The abilities of a worker which enable him to adjust to the disciplined routine and the occasional disappointments that are part of normal industrial life become important after he begins his employment. As an original "honeymoon" period's unrealistic expectations are replaced by a more sober understanding of life in industry, labor relation tensions often emerge.

The need for expanded skills and the ability to perform more demanding jobs generally increase over time, for the typical plant begins its operation on a relatively limited scale. Vehicle manufacturers, for example, are apt to start out with only final assembly operations. Later they move into manufacturing some parts. Building on latent skills, sound attitudes, and cooperative behavior patterns of initial employees is apt to increase in importance over the long run. For this reason problems inherent in an intuitive or essentially random selection of employees are likely to rear their heads as the jobs grow more exacting. Further, there is some evidence that a random selection inherently skews the hiring toward the low end of the distribution curve of the total worker population because of the tendency for castoffs, misfits, and transients to flock to the gates of the new company.

For these reasons the mere ability to hire sufficient numbers to get the wheels turning and to operate with at least a minimum of success in the first year is an inefficient criterion for judging the process of recruiting and selection. The experiences of several companies in different countries illustrate some problems and better possibilities in employee selection. All companies referred to in this book are, unless otherwise specified, foreign manufacturing subsidiaries of American international corporations.

In Turkey the California Farm Implement Company simply turned the hiring over to the Turk supervisors:

Example 1

The company first hired foremen and supervisors through the Turkish plant manager. . . . Using newspaper advertisements

which stressed unusually liberal benefits and the advancement
opportunities offered by a new organization, the plant manager
was able to attract applicants by the hundreds. The supervisors
invited other previous employees, friends, relatives and acquaint-
ances to apply. The selection among applicants was handled by
the Turkish supervisors, basing their choices on the experience
and over-all impression of the applicant and previous personal
knowledge about him. The original nucleus of 95 acceptable
employees was hired with little difficulty.[2]
An American handled the job of selecting men for a vehicle assembly plant in Turkey with equally satisfactory results:

Example 2

Robert DeBoer, the American who assisted the majority owners, in starting up, appraised the task confronting the company by
visiting auto repair shops to size up the skill levels which might
be available. He then advertised specifically for auto repair men
and interviewed them himself through an interpreter. He hired
no supervisors.

In the interview Mr. DeBoer asked detailed questions such as,
"How do you assemble a clutch?" or "How do you weld no. 14
sheet metal?" and based his decision on the knowledge and attitudes indicated by the men's answers.[3]
A pharmaceutical firm in Turkey actively solicited its employees to
recommend applicants:

Example 3

A friend's recommendations were always a major factor in the
selection. During 1959 seven workers unknown to present employees were hired and then dismissed at the end of their 30 day
trial periods. They had to be criticized for not fitting in well or
talking too much. By comparison, the eight friends of employees
who were hired in 1959 were all retained.

Some of the companies' managers attempted to resist pressures
to hire friends and relatives.

At CFIT, after originally allowing many friends and relatives of
employees to be hired, the U.S. manager concluded that such

[2]California Farm Implement Turk, Harvard Business School case, p. 6.
[3]Turk Willys, Harvard Business School case, p. 3.

people tended to be extravagantly described and did not work out well. He cited the fact that frequently a supervisor went so far as to recommend that a new job should be created for a friend.[4]

A company in Pakistan making electrical mechanical products decided that it would be wise to hire only a few men at a time and to break these men in gradually:

Example 4

The company had no trouble in obtaining unskilled employees, but it was more difficult to find men who were able to operate simple machine tools. Advertising did not yield good results, perhaps because the general literacy level was too low. The company set up an employment office and because great numbers of men applied, they were able to find men who seemed to be able to run machine tools. The personnel manager did all of the screening and selecting. He was a Pakistani who had worked for eight years for an American pharmaceutical company. For the foundry they hired "green labor" because they felt that experienced workers would have bad habits. In the machine shop they hired relatively unskilled men and brought in two German machinists to train them. The personnel manager stated "We hire carefully and we have a three month probationary period to size the men up. We give them irritating, silly questions in the interview to see if they are easily irritated or are willing to subject themselves to industrial discipline. If the men are impatient, we simply don't hire them."

A tire company in India purposely did not hire men with prior factory experience:

Example 5

The American personnel manager had been told by other Americans in the area that the local labor force would have bad habits, be inefficient, poorly trained, and contain some communists. The company felt, therefore, that they would be wise to hire and train farmers with no previous factory experience. They chose farmers as their first selection step in sifting out the many applicants who came to the factory gates. The interviewing problem with language differences, however, proved to be very diff-

[4]California Farm Implement Turk, Harvard Business School case, p. 35.

cult. When asked how they picked out a good farmer, the answer was, "we don't know." Company supervisors stated, "You can't pick a good farmer; his past experience means nothing and his education means very little either."

Company personnel felt that they had made a number of mistakes in hiring. They had received "contradictory advice" on the subject of caste and the regional areas of India which produced the best factory men and finally decided that they should ignore the caste and the locale in making the selection. They felt that this "was not totally successful, it created problems, but at least we have not built too rigid a system." It was considered difficult to convert product specifications and process instructions from English into the local Indian language. When a man spoke any English whatsoever it helped him to obtain the job. The personnel manager felt that it was important not to hire a man who had greater ability than the job required. Indians frequently stated, however, that "all I want is a job, I will take anything." The man-job fit was therefore often a trial and error process and the probationary periods helped weed out poor men. They had some difficulties with caste in that they sometimes hired Brahmins and asked them to work under non Brahmins. In the first year the company had a 75 percent employee turnover. They found men, tried them out and fired them if they were "no good."

The actual selection was made by the department heads. The personnel department screened applicants and then the department heads made the selection, picking about one in five after talking with the men through interpreters. Reference checks were made with the police and former employers but it was found difficult to get useful information.

The company maintained a group of 15 American labor trainers in the country for the first year. In the craft area experienced electricians were hired, selected by asking simple arithmetic and some practical questions. The hiring of relatives was allowed but later the personnel director felt this was a bad mistake. Relatives resulted in cliques, lack of harmony and higher turnover, it was argued. One good job in a family was often felt to be enough and so the other family members would quit after pay checks started coming in.

At a pharmaceutical firm in Bombay, the hiring was done jointly by the production manager and the general manager, both Indians. In this researcher's opinion, these men did an unusually good job of hiring:

Example 6

They did not allow factory supervisors to do any interviewing because they felt that "they are not qualified." They felt that references were not usually very reliable, for former employers were too polite, but they checked out all references given. During the interviews they asked the applicant for an entire history of his employment. They dug into any statements which suggested some unfavorable traits or experiences which might be hidden. They asked such questions as "what is 40 percent of 40" in order to "judge mental ability." In hiring sales people, the applicant was told about two products, and asked to come back in 24 hours to repeat what he recalled. They felt they could see in this way what a man could learn and how well he responded under pressure.

Workers were hired on a six months' temporary basis for, under the law, a worker could be kept up to six months maximum before being made "permanent." During the first six months they purposely drove the new worker very hard, testing him in every way that they could devise before "permanently" hiring him. Even this testing was sometimes insufficient, they felt, for some workers would do well until the six months probationary period was over and then ease off.

The general manager stated that they had no problem of mixing groups from different geographical areas; in fact they encouraged heterogeneity as it "would discourage the formation of cliques." They asked a man where he came from, however, and on this basis developed a balanced labor force, consisting of Gujaratis, Sindhis, Punjabs, Bengalis and Southerners. They liked to hire younger people under age 35 because they were "easier to mold."

A chemical company had some similar experiences in South Africa:

Example 7

References did not mean very much but the interview was felt to be important, along with a three months' probationary period for Europeans. They were forced to hire all natives through a government labor pool arrangement and had to "take them as they came." One problem was the difficulty of communicating with the native workers at the time they were hiring them. It was

felt to be almost impossible to do very much in the way of interviewing natives.

The major problem in hiring in South Africa, however, resulted
from the lack of skilled employees for jobs which by law had to be
filled by whites. The scarcity of "European" employees was such
that those Europeans the companies were able to hire were often
low in their abilities, marginal in their attitudes, and unsatisfactory
in their performance. Several other companies were hampered by
the nonexistence of white employees in their part of South Africa.
As a result they gradually tended to shift jobs to use natives instead
of Europeans. The government did not interfere in this process, although technically apartheid demanded "job reservation."

In some locations overseas the recruiting and selection process is
complicated by choices that must be made regarding the birth location, caste, religion, or race of potential employees. The American
company needs a policy on this matter, but experience suggests no
simple general rule. Results have been good or bad with both seg-
regation and integration. For example, the drug firm in India just
mentioned preferred to mix the castes and regional origins of its
employees. In South Africa, a large auto firm employed large numbers of "colored" people but very few natives. They stated that the
reason for not hiring more "natives" was that they had an excessive
record of absenteeism and that the "coloreds" were more adaptable.
As a result 47 percent of their employees were Europeans, 45 percent colored, and only 8 percent were natives. They had some problems in getting the different groups to work together in assembly
operations, but by and large the different groups worked cooperatively in assembly line teams. A tire company, however, employed
no colored people but large numbers of "natives." Executives here
felt that the natives could do the work satisfactorily and save them
the cost of another set of complete washroom and eating facilities,
which the coloreds would require. The scarcity of Europeans for
jobs that were normally in the skilled category forced the company
to hire increasing numbers of natives. Very few problems were
experienced in getting the natives to adapt, even to team jobs. They
were paid considerably less than the Europeans.

At a pharmaceutical firm in South Africa the management moved
slowly and carefully in regard to hiring natives. They actually hired
relatively few, and the manager stated that there would be resentment from the packing girls if they hired a Chinese lab assistant.
They minimized the difficulties by avoiding the contacts between

the job assignments in every way possible. They had separate entrances for non-Europeans but these were not used.

In South Africa the so-called Europeans were scarce and were given a wage of about four times that of the natives, but on the other hand they were more educated and communication with them was much easier. Recently a U.S. food products company in South Africa has had increasingly good experience with non-Europeans, citing that under "job reservation" the non-Europeans had to obtain a permit to move, which the company felt encouraged employment stability.

The decision as to what race or caste or mixture to hire is a particularly difficult one for American managers, partly because we tend to give little thought or concern to this type of choice, and partly because there are complex questions of local culture involved. In South Africa, India, Pakistan, and Spain, those involved felt that there were no reliable rules to follow. Hence decisions on the make-up of the work force were usually made on the basis of a blanket rule, following local practice or a conservative pattern. Most overseas managers interviewed said in effect, "You can't go wrong doing what the other companies are doing but you can get into real trouble if you take some unorthodox approach, mixing races or castes or northerners and southerners. We play it safe."

This may be good advice in many circumstances, but it is not always so. By following such advice the tire company in South Africa would not have employed natives in skilled tire-making jobs. Yet their results were excellent, not only in a low hourly cost, but a high rate of quality and output.

There are other circumstances in which a conventional "play it safe" policy is open to question. Often social conditions are changing. What appears to be standard practice today may be outmoded tomorrow. Innovative leadership (such as the pharmaceutical plant in India cited previously, where different castes and regional origins were mixed) has sometimes proved successful enough to challenge the existing notions of safe or normal practice. Management-effected factors of training, discipline, supervision, and organization of work are probably more important elements in long-run productivity than the race, caste, or local origin of the individual worker.

Conclusions

1. Careful employee selection is important because it ultimately influences labor relations, productivity, and candidates for supervi-

sion. Results over a period of months or years show whether the selection process was successful.

The policy of selecting inexperienced employees and then training them, used by the majority of companies studied, was challenged by others. The latter stated that the approach should depend on the job and the availability of different experience and skill levels. Clark Kerr, John Dunlop, Frederick Harbison, and Charles A. Meyers make the following point in *Industrialism and Industrial Man:*[5] management overseas is often more interested in hiring a docile labor force which can be controlled easily than a skilled or educated labor force. This purpose may explain the researcher's observations that most companies prefer to hire a relatively untrained labor force and train it. Kerr et al. state: "Managers want above all else a well subordinated work force. They are prone to hire and retain the kind of workers who do not 'talk back,' and they will insist upon the right to discharge any persons who question in any way the authority of their superiors."

The statement that experienced employees will have bad attitudes and bad habits was heard often. But my research indicates that this assumption has not proven consistently valid. Until more information is obtained about the particular applicant's attitudes and backgrounds, it is no wiser to assume that their habits and training would be poor than it would be to assume that they may be good. Certain skills in some industries were found to be too important to tolerate several years without competent workers. For example, the skills in maintenance required at an equipment-oriented operation such as tire manufacturing were too critical to allow hiring inexperienced workers.

2. It is necessary to delegate most of the actual selection to local supervisors because Americans are unable to communicate directly with the applicants. When an interview is handled through an interpreter, he acts as a filter, making it difficult to judge how the individual is responding to questions. Every company visited stated that references and outside checks were virtually meaningless. Valid information on an employee and his performance, attitudes, and skills could be obtained only through the actual process of interviewing him.

In all but one of the companies visited, the selection of employees was done by either middle or top management. First line supervision was not considered qualified for the task. Generally, person-

[5] *Op. cit.,* p. 28.

nel departments were considered responsible for recruiting but not for actual selection.

However, at a plant in Pakistan an experienced personnel manager took over the hiring of employees and did a very fine job. He was realistic in his attitudes and probed with determination and skepticism in his interviewing.

3.   Although the American manager cannot control the selection process, it does not follow that he should completely delegate the responsibility and fail to exert his influence. His dilemma is obvious. He knows the company, its operation, its product, and the skills and attitudes needed by its employees, but he feels blocked, by language and cultural problems, from making good choices of personnel. Most Americans also feel that they cannot count on local nationals to do a good job, and they recognize that several critical years will pass before it is possible to appraise the results of their selections.

Most American managers seemed unaware of their own assumptions: (a) that the foreign national does not necessarily know what he is looking for and therefore cannot select with proper discrimination, and (b) that Americans are unable to do an effective job of hiring in an alien culture. The fact that both of these assumptions have been proven false in practice may offer a lead toward improved approaches in building a good work force.

The Pakistani personnel manager and the Indian manager who interviewed with painstaking persistence are examples of foreign nationals who appeared able to do a good job of interviewing because they took it seriously and were aware of its potential impact.

Asking basic questions through an interpreter, as one American, Robert DeBoer, did in Turkey, helped to reveal an applicant's ability to solve problems and his knowledge of the work he would be doing. DeBoer's approach and his results indicate that an American who is well trained in the process of interviewing can, in fact, predict with good reliability a potential employee's value by asking specific factual questions which require analytical responses that reveal the employee's knowledge, basic abilities, and often his attitudes toward employment, a job, and himself.

If this is true, it should not be necessary for the American to throw up his hands and say, "I cannot help in this process. I must delegate it completely to men I do not trust"—a typical reaction to problems of selection.

4.   The headquarters personnel office could help in analyzing the

effective skills, knowledge, and attitudes necessary for each job in the local company, and in training both the overseas American and foreign nationals in conducting interviews.

In no case was the home office personnel department used in the employment area—neither to offer insights, nor to perform actual employment interviews. The hiring process was considered a local one, in which the local labor market, the particular skills needed, the process of interviewing, and the local cultural and communications problems were seen as areas in which the U.S. companies and managers could not be of material assistance. Nor were U.S. tests or more advanced selection procedures experimented with or employed.

There has been a tendency to perceive this area as more mysterious and difficult than it needs to be. The apparent success of some companies in selection makes the aimless wanderings of other companies appear to be wasteful. Home office personnel groups are unnecessarily negligent when they remain aloof, missing the opportunities for services which they could provide.

Training

Managers in company after company have been pleasantly surprised to observe how quickly men learn new skills and new techniques in industrial life. The oil companies in the Middle East have taught Bedouins in a matter of months how to weld and how to run large caterpillar tractors. Indians have learned to set up and run automatic screw machines in four months with quality as high as men who have been doing it for years. United States tire companies have found that natives in South Africa or farmers in India who have never seen the inside of a factory can learn to make tires of excellent quality within about six months. In fact, Goodyear's world record for production in a 40-hour week in 1963 was held by a worker in a plant in India.

In industries in which the skill requirements are relatively low the preceding conclusion is even more true. Workers can be taught packaging operations in a pharmaceutical plant in several days. Auto and truck assembly operations can be learned with proficiency in less than a month, even some of the more complex operations such as assembling pistons and connecting rods in engine assembly.

Professor Fayerweather concurs: "The consensus of companies operating abroad is that people can learn industrial skills with surprising rapidity."[6] Men and women who are attracted to industrial plants are found to be eager to learn new skills and become successful in their new environment. In the Turkish plant of the CFIT company, workers were so eager to learn their new jobs that one new worker said, "I know, I know" and grabbed the wrench from a trainer and proceeded to turn the nut at full tilt in the wrong direction. But with this enthusiastic spirit the worker learned his job quickly.

For these reasons none of the managers of the overseas operations studied felt that the task of the initial training of their workers was difficult or a deterrent to early production output. Most companies expected that in the underdeveloped countries training would be a difficult step and for this reason planned training programs, occasionally bringing in Americans as trainers. In fact, many overseas managers tend to underestimate the natural adaptation of men and to overestimate the skills required in learning their plant's operations. One tire company sent 15 men to India for a year to train tire makers and other operatives in their plant. The same procedure had been followed years before in setting up tire-making operations in South Africa. CFIT sent to Turkey several individuals who were familiar with the operation of assembling a tractor, and these men stayed for approximately 10 months to train Turkish assemblers. International production managers seemed to recognize and even overprepare this phase of their start-up operation. We found no example of a company which failed to handle this early training adequately.

But it would be wrong to dismiss training at this point as being relatively elementary and providing no major problems. Three distinctions may illustrate the conclusion that training is more of a problem than first appears.

It is necessary to distinguish between training for knowledge, for specific skills, and for judgment. Learning to run an automatic screw machine requires certain knowledge and certain skills. Knowledge and skill can generally be assimilated more rapidly than typically expected by overseas managers. But the matter of developing judgment is more troublesome. Yet good judgment is required by a worker if he is to operate independently, require less aid and supervision, fix his own work stoppages, and handle a larger variety of tasks.

A second important distinction is that between different stages of

[6]John Fayerweather, *Management of International Operations*, McGraw-Hill, New York, 1960, p. 264.

a worker's development. In the early stage of his employment it is usually necessary for him simply to learn the basic knowledge and skills to perform the minimum mechanical or technical requirements of his job. Subsequently, however, to meet company needs for a larger, more integrated, and complete facility, many workers must learn to set up machines, sharpen tools, plan ahead, be resourceful in overcoming work stoppages, recognize problems in the maintenance of machinery and equipment, and be able to perform more complicated, precise, or difficult work. Growing complexity and expansion have been the pattern in nearly every overseas plant visited. The early stage requires relatively simple operations, but as nationalistic pressures mount, the company needs to become less dependent on imports. Most plants progress to more complex operations as competition increases. A cadre of workers needs to advance its skills over a period of time as the industrialization process proceeds.

A third distinction in training is the difference between acquiring knowledge, skills, and judgment and making the adjustment to factory life. Managements tend to overlook this adjustment and the lengthy time periods often necessary to bring about those changes in attitudes, values, and assumptions that are required of a work force as it adapts from agricultural to industrial life. Extensive training operations are typically carried on to equip workers in the necessary fundamental knowledge and skills, but managers generally reveal little awareness of the complex social and psychological process workers must go through to adjust to a new life in industry.

Some early writers described the adjustment to life in a factory in terms that may capture some of the feelings of workers entering industry in many countries today. "A new sense of time was one of the outstanding psychological features of industrial revolution.[7] . . . The discipline of the early factories was like the discipline of a prison.[8] . . . But to all the evils from which the domestic worker had suffered, the industrial revolution added discipline and the discipline of a power driven by a competition that seemed as inhuman as the machine that thundered in factory and shed. If he broke one of the long series of minute regulations he was fined.[9] . . . All I wish to prove is that the discovery and use of machinery may be injurious to the laboring class as some of their numbers may be thrown out of employment.[10] The operative is condemned to let his physical and mental powers decay in this utter monotony. It is his mission to be bored everyday and all day long. . . .[11]

[7-11] Op. cit., p. 28.

The most important changes a worker must make in going from a village or agricultural life to that of industry appear to involve: (a) a different concept of time; (b) the acceptance of authority and an industrial hierarchy; (c) the development of a personal sense of discipline, which makes him willing to follow directions, to report on time, to work every scheduled workday; (d) his social adjustment from being a part of a system of social responsibilities based on the family, tribe, or village typical of preindustrial situations to an urban life in which he and his immediate family unit live alone and unprotected; (e) the necessity for teamwork, working on crew or assembly operations, or as a part of a working group which must cooperate. This contrasts with the life of a farmer or a small businessman who is essentially his own boss and has only a minimum of cooperative effort required daily.

These changes in one's social and psychological adjustment appear to be as important in affecting a worker's morale and productivity in the long run as his technical knowledge, skill, and judgment are. The adjustment to industry is further complicated by the need to assimilate the factory culture to the point of acquiring an understanding of the total factory operation he is performing, as in the following example.

Example 8

Turkish workers who learned to run lathes quite well were generally lax in maintenance of their equipment. They appeared to feel that it was best to leave well enough alone and not make any adjustments or lubricate the lathe as long as it was running well. They tended to personify the machine and to see it as either in good health or in poor health, but if it was in poor health, little could be done about it. They were not sensitive to unusual sounds or vibrations as evidence of impending trouble, and as one superintendent put it, "They run a machine right into the ground. The attitude is that as long as the machine was running it need not be stopped for checking, greasing or adjusting."

The Co-Director at CFIT in Turkey observed that the men in the machine shops readily stopped production: While a machine was operating properly, they turned out production well, but if the parts started to fall out of dimension or if the machine suffered a minor failure, they did not know what to do. Often a group of five or six men would crowd around the machine to give advice and discuss the problem. Unless watched closely, a man could lose a whole morning over a broken tool or a poor setup.

He cited as an example a machinist who spent a large portion of his time removing a rat's nest tangle of unbroken chips from a lathe instead of mounting a simple chip breaker on the machine. Mr. DeSalle stated that "The Turks never measure anything. Their setups and quality levels must be under constant surveillance."

The superintendent of the repair and modification area at another plant mentioned the same need for close supervision. "My main problem is in checking the work. When you turn your back they do nothing. This is not laziness, they just need direction, parts or supplies. I trust the foreman, but still I must check on the work and the workers at all times."

Adaptation to new technical demands is often accompanied by an obedience to the technique without a full comprehension of its significance, which may lead to strange behavior. This researcher has seen many examples of this phenomenon. In pharmaceutical plants in the underdeveloped countries the workers followed to the letter the sterilization requirements that were established by quality control specialists from the home office. However, workers filling a bottle were seen to spill tablets onto the floor and then to pick up these tablets and put them back in the bottle. Or occasionally they licked the fingers in order to facilitate the handling of slippery labels. The operators had learned the specific technique but did not understand its full significance. Dr. Fi-Suner, a cultural anthropologist, and Mr. DeGregori, a developmental economist, also described this process of adapting to new technologies:

"Adoption whether it be of material elements, techniques, or idea systems, involves more than simple accretion. A new element must be congruent with the rest of the culture or subculture; the trait must be meaningfully integrated. It follows that the physical presence of a trait is not the most important consideration, for a simple dichotomy of present-absent does not cover the full range of possibilities. We must also consider adjustments, reinterpretation, and a phenomenon that may be termed "peripheral borrowing" where the potentialities of the new trait are not realized.

Cultures may well resist the innovations even where there is the acceptance of borrowed technology. The context of the culture will give it a different meaning, and the existing habits of mind and outlook of the people can inhibit its efficient use. From the point of view of production the use of new tools may be inadequately understood by the new users, thereby leading to an inferior product and again not giving us a meaningful index of Westernization. The problem then is to find ways to transfer or diffuse to underdeveloped countries what Dr. Peter Drucker calls the technologist's way of looking at work and tools.

Technological borrowing has often occurred when people see an element of their technological complex and associate it with a desirable consequence. They borrow this element but use it incorrectly since they do not understand the complex nor the habits of the mind associated with it.[12]

Quoting further from Pi-Sunyer and DeGregori:

Those of us who were born in an industrial culture unconsciously as a part of our learning process acquire a knowledge of machines and industrial habits of mind. These are the technologist's outlook, refined later by more formal training and constitute one of the bases for the scientific and inventive character of Western civilization in the course of the past few centuries. When we try to diffuse this technology outward into other areas we not only encounter cultural resistance to specific traits but also people lacking in the habits of mind which accompany Western technological development. To ignore these nontechnological factors is to limit our ability to improve the economic situation of the technologically less developed portions to the world.[13]

The problem of job commitment is another factor in worker development. During an early stage of industrialization and urbanization the workers often tend to go back and forth between agricultural village life and the job in industry. In the beginning the worker may only work for a number of months and go back to life in the village with the cash earned. As commitment further increases, the worker may spend most of his time working in industry but still take every possible occasion to go back to his village and to his family organization. The calls upon the worker for personal commitments to the family and to the village may be substantial, resulting in high absenteeism and unexpected departures. This worker is not fully committed to the factory job, for his own system of security and his basic self-concept of where his security comes from is apparently still based on the village and the family.

Many workers in both India and Nigeria show these symptoms: going back to the village, high absenteeism, sending money home,

[12]Pi-Sunyer and DeGregori, letter to the editor of *Technology and Culture* (Spring 1964), p. 249.
[13]*Ibid.*, p. 249.

abrupt and unexplained departures. Probably only when the worker finds life satisfying in the city and factory and feels that his eventual security is better served in the urban society and through the company will he gradually tend to cut the ties to the village.

Few plants had training programs for the development of workers who had been with the company more than six to twelve months. The typical assumption was that training was required only as a start-up function, but the failure to recognize cultural and psychological problems ultimately affected the efficiency of operations. Lack of training limited the ability of the workers in many plants to advance to handle the more complex jobs later stages of industrialization require. It also contributed, we believe, to attitudes of protest against life in industry. Protests against working conditions, low pay, lack of advancement, and supervision are often made by the worker who becomes dissatisfied with life in industry during the process of attempting to adjust to a new urban life.[14] Factory workers who have a relaxed, long-term view of *time,* for instance, reacted negatively toward time clocks, schedules, and production controls.

This is a concept of training *for industry,* rather than training for a particular job. It has little precedent in the more developed countries. Because this is a new concept, techniques for carrying it out are yet to be developed. The following suggestions emerge from this research.

1. Training should usually go beyond original training for skills and knowledge into developing an understanding of industry and the company's production operations. For instance, courses that deal with the requirements of the worker in industry as he fits into the total industrial complex may be useful. Courses that deal with the problems of time, scheduling, coordination, downtime, and use of equipment can also help the worker toward an understanding of the total industrial society in which he lives and the part he plays in it.

These are experimental notions, but it will be seen in Chapter 4 that the protest against life in industry is often substantial and sometimes violent. This protest tends to occur after a worker has been in industry from one to two or three years. Training of the type described may increase the worker's eventual usefulness in the factory and help him to make a psychological and cultural adaptation to industry with less protest.

[14]See Edward T. Hall, *The Silent Language* (Fawcett Publications, Greenwich, Conn., 1961) for examples of this phenomenon.

2.   After the better workers have begun to perform adequately on their present jobs, training may be directed toward their next jobs. The assumption that training should cease when a worker is performing adequately is shortsighted. In training workers for increased responsibility, the workers should be given the opportunity to increase their cultural understanding as well as their technical understanding. Specifically, the job of the lathe operator must go beyond the operation of the lathe to its setup, maintenance, repair. He can thereby become a better lathe operator and eventually the company would have men who are ready to be setup men, maintenance men, and foremen.

In summary, our research indicated that the initial task of recruiting, selecting, and training a work force was generally disarmingly easy. Sufficient applicants, selected by indigenous supervisors and trained to perform the relatively elementary tasks characteristic of the early years of overseas operations (e.g., assembly instead of parts-making), usually resulted in a starting work force of at least minimum competence. But when production operations grew in complexity or competition reduced operating margins and workers' adjustments to an ongoing life in industry were not easy—then the character of the work force and its quality had a more obvious impact. Worker's knowledge, skills, and attitudes took on a more cogent meaning. The unseen demand for more careful selection and subsequent need for more advanced training, both in job requirements and for making a satisfactory cultural and mental adjustment to industry, are more critical than apparent.

WAGE ADMINISTRATION

Wage administration is a meeting place of ideas, and hence a confrontation of culturally derived values. The administration of local wages by a U.S. manufacturing subsidiary is a loaded subject. It is a sensitive issue to workers because it involves their pay. It is a sensitive issue to managers because it involves their concepts of "proper and sensible wage systems"—their notions of "what makes Sammy run."

Wage administration decisions abroad are made in a highly charged atmosphere, which is further fueled in some cultures and economies where there is more emphasis on job security, automatic progression, automatic bonus than exists in the United States. The typical American manager's idea of policies that will result in the best individual motivation may be quite different from those of managers abroad. For example, when American companies have taken over small foreign companies previously dominated by a family dynasty, the American concept of a uniform wage system has run head-on into long established practices of treating workers' wages on a highly individual basis.

The management of wages is sensitive, too, because it involves financial control and the felt need of home offices for control to prevent "giving the company away." Home office managers logically treat wage administration as a key element in both financial control and achieving efficient production. In the companies studied the operation of the wage system was typically perceived as an important decision-making area for the home office to influence. Wage administration has thus become a battleground in many overseas plants, a struggle over local autonomy and home office control in which skirmishing is not only between home office managers and foreign nationals, but between home office managers and overseas executives.

Often this struggle is expressed in debates over how formal the wage administration should be. Local plant managers often feel that a relatively informal system is adequate, whereas the home office is more inclined to advocate a more "rational" system, perhaps involving job evaluation, point systems, community wage surveys, merit ratings, and regular wage reviews. Local managers tend to reply that individual treatment of the workers is enough of a system and is more equitable than more "fancy" systems. Yet the lack of a "rational" system is disturbing to home office managers as they look for a sense of order and a degree of control.

For these reasons it is not surprising that different companies handle the wage area quite differently. Three main differences stand out.

1.   Systems differ considerably in formality and informality, complexity, and refinement.

2.   Differences exist in the extent of home office control and influence.

3.   Differences are evident in the degree of focus on the individual worker in the system as contrasted to more collective approaches.

Which stances on these three issues make sense? When? Under what circumstances? In arriving at some suggestions it is useful to look for a moment at wage administration in general.

Wage administration begins with the fact that workers must be paid. From the production management standpoint the question is simply how much each worker should be paid, and to what extent the pay system is to be an incentive or a control. Essentially, wage administration divides itself into five basic decisions.

1. How should the work be divided into different jobs? For example, should the assembling of an automobile be done by one man or divided into 50 or 75 jobs?

2. How much should be paid for each job? Why should one job be paid more than another? What is the company paying for? Should skill be more important than experience? Should physical discomfort or strength required be recognized?

3. How should the total company job structure be related to the environment either in the community or in the larger geographical area? Does the company wish to pay more than the community or less?

4. How and when should the individual worker's wage be adjusted? Should adjustments be made as changes occur in the economy, cost of living, laws, job content, or in the worker's particular value to the company?

5. What fringe benefits are to be paid, directly or indirectly? Should there be sick pay, hospitalization, paid holidays, and the like?

American foreign subsidiaries have varied in their handling of these five basic decisions. Analysis of their experiences can help in sorting out useful approaches to wage administration in international manufacturing.

The division of labor

The experience of a U.S. tire company in India emphasizes a number of the problems involved in deciding how the work should be divided into different jobs. Because the company had decided to employ farmers and no skilled tire makers were available, the scope of tire making and other operating jobs was narrowed relative to the job content in Akron and the other company overseas plants. For example, the job of removing tread stock from a belt was limited to simply removing it and stacking it, whereas in Akron, the job involved adjusting the equipment, removing the tread, stacking it, counting it, and making checks on its quality. These jobs were given to other individuals in India.

After the company observed that crew operations sometimes resulted in bottlenecks because of a lack of cooperation among workers, they cut down crews and divided jobs more individually. They also found that clerical workers were not willing to dust off their own desks or move typewriters or office equipment from one table to another. There was considerable pressure in the office to have helpers. This was also true in the maintenance area, where each maintenance man felt that he needed someone to help him carry his tools and do the menial tasks. The management resisted this pressure in the office but went along with maintenance helpers.

At another U.S. company in India, however, workers were required to carry the packaging supplies and bottles rather than the company's employing special helpers to do it. As the Indian General Manager put it, "Here, in an industrial plant, the workers must learn to do their own carrying. Certainly at home they do it. They can learn to behave differently in public."

Generally job classifications in India were more rigid and job scope was more narrow because skills were less developed. The caste system and workers' reluctance to perform tasks they felt were below them added further pressure toward a finer division of labor.

In a plant in Turkey, however, where secondhand equipment was being used, it was often necessary for a worker to handle a relatively broader job because the equipment was less mechanized than in the United States. To this extent job content is often broadened when the process is less mechanized and demands more manual steps from the worker.

These examples attest to the fact that job scope even within one company cannot be the same from country to country and from plant to plant. Job scope must depend on the local culture and conditions to some extent; it must also depend on the ability, skill, training, and interest of the workers, and on the equipment and tools that are available.

Development of the internal structure

Approaches to the decision of how much to pay for different jobs also varied considerably from company to company. For example, a U.S. food products firm in Spain broke down their factory jobs into only three categories, each with its own wage scale. These categories were:

1. Specialized workers who earned from 60,000 to 70,000 pesetas per year.

2. Assistants to specialists who earned from 40,000 to 50,000 pesetas.

3. Peons who earned 30,000 to 40,000 pesetas per year.

The bulk of the workers were classified as peons, and there were only a few assistants for the handful of specialists. This structure had been established by the indigenous company prior to its merger with the U.S. company.

The American advisor felt that the three job scales were too few. He said that there was not enough incentive for a man to work toward promotion. This would seem to be a reasonable criticism, for the specialists were limited in terms of numbers and restricted by educational requirements. Thus those workers who were peons had virtually no future to look forward to. But no change was planned for the immediate future.

Contrasts also exist in the pharmaceutical industry. One company in India had only two job grades. Another company in South Africa had only three grades, and nearly every employee was in the first grade. In India they used 13 grades for generally similar work.

General Electric used virtually the same job grades in their new plant near Bombay as they used in the United States. At a U.S. food products plant in India the structure was simpler than at home: all packers, sweepers, cleaners, and other factory workers (with the exception of porters) were classified in one job grade.

In addition to the number of job grades set up in different companies and locations, there were also contrasts between the salary ranges tied to the different grades and the overlap between grades. For instance, a U.S. pharmaceutical company in Pakistan had 13 different grades in the factory and 9 different grades among office people. The 13 grades in the factory all overlapped each other considerably. For instance, grade 1 ran from 96 to 136 rupees per month and grade 2 ran from 100 to 140. This is the opposite extreme from the company that had only one grade. The amount of overlap meant that a worker had only a moderate incentive for promotion from one grade to another.

Two companies side by side at a remote industrial estate in India provide a good contrast of the different approaches used. At an indigenous chemical plant owned and operated by Indians, there were 12 grades, and each worker within each grade was rated as *A*, *B*, *C*, or *D*. Workers advanced by a minimum automatic progression, with the possibility of merit increases in addition. At a U.S. pharmaceutical plant next door, however, there were only seven different grades in the factory and the overlap was about 40 percent. The U.S. company stated, "We pay according to jobs." The Indian company professed that "We pay according to individual qualifications."

Differences in the number of different job grades and wage ranges are more than academic. For in spite of the fact that there is no right or wrong and the way that a system is administered is usually as important as the system concept itself, the wage structure has considerable impact. A structure which has an excessive number of grades is apt to be needlessly complex and the grades mean little to workers. A large overlap is apt to offer little incentive. The larger the number of grades, the larger the overlap or the smaller spread for each job. Conversely, the smaller the number of grades, the less overlap and a larger incentive between grades. But as the grades grow in range and shrink in number, the worker may perceive barriers to future promotion. The general tendency is that the companies which had only one, two, or three job grades in the factory tended to offer their workers relatively little advancement. These systems marked situations where there was less social mobility and the workers tended to be less educated. The assumption was made that they would not be able to move up.

Relating the structure to the environment

When a structure is established, a company has to make a further decision: How should it set the level of the entire system so that it will attract and hold workers and still not be too expensive? This involves some sort of a community wage survey.

It was interesting how few companies had a mechanism for handling this step. For example, a tire company in South Africa did not make a survey for four years, and when they finally did so, they found that it was necessary to make a drastic salary change. Most companies obtained the community picture in an informal fashion simply by occasionally talking to managers from other companies. In many cases this appeared satisfactory. When a company was more isolated, however, it was often found that the company's wage scale tended to lag far behind the community as a whole. Further, an informal comparison was not always sufficient to equitably set rates for the many jobs involved.

Adjustment for changes

Once a wage system is established, it is never possible to freeze it indefinitely. For example, changes are necessary to reward workers' improved performance. Changes in the process and tools may also require wage changes. Movements in the cost of living, legal changes, and basic adjustments in the economy may also force the company to make changes in wage structure.

Companies differ in change mechanisms even more than in other facets of wage administration. For example, a tire firm established a system of piece rates to apply worldwide, regardless of the country. Top management felt as a matter of principle that workers should be given an opportunity to work as hard as they wished and that they should be paid to reward their production. Unfortunately, this did not always work out well. In India the workers tended to relax at a certain level of take-home pay and the crew workers did not always respond well to incentives when output was limited by their ability and willingness to cooperate. Further, the tire company's rather complex system of crew rates sometimes resulted in less than "one for one payment" (e.g., a 15 percent increase in production resulted in less than a 15 percent increase in pay above a certain level).

Other companies fumbled a good deal in their attempts to set up incentives. At a vehicle assembly plant the management wished to have an incentive pay system to stimulate production. They finally set up a plan that in effect resulted in a very large bonus for producing over a certain number of cars per day (x), but offered only a small incentive to produce beyond that level. This tended to insure production of about x cars a day but offered little incentive to get over x plus one or two. At a pharmaceutical plant in Turkey the company set up an incentive system which offered a large fund for producing over a certain minimum. But it too offered little inducement to the worker to go beyond this minimum level.

Incentives were nearly always left to the local management to work out. Few incentive plans were developed to offer piece rates or incentives to the workers in proportion to their production.

At a food products firm in Spain an apparently intelligent system was developed. A bonus was paid to the entire crew based on a percentage of machine downtime. This system worked well, for the total production depended on the machinery and equipment. As long as it was kept running, production was good. Downtime was the most critical variable.

At an indigenous chemical and pharmaceutical plant in India, a system of classifying workers as A, B, C, or D, within their job, worked well. Each job had a grade number and each worker in that job received a grade (A for best performance and D the lowest). This recognized the ability of a worker to be better than a similarly classed worker yet stay within the range, with pay advancement based on merit. In addition, an automatic progression guaranteed all workers a slow but steady advancement based on experience. Each job had a set ceiling.

Some companies, particularly those where the cost of living was moving up, did not set up maximums; they attempted to pay for performance and to handle the workers pay on an individual basis. The system worked best where the cultural tradition is to recognize individuals separately for their contribution. In South Africa, for example, the managements often believed that they got the best performance out of workers by treating them individually even in relatively large plants. At an auto plant in South Africa the company paid over the stated maximums on the salary ranges simply because white European employees were very difficult to obtain. It was noted that there was some confusion, and individual inequities occurred when the grade ranges were ignored.

The problem of handling wages during a period of inflation is common and difficult. If workers are given percentage increases, the ranges are held constant in relationship but the higher-paid workers get larger amounts and the total spread increases. Yet if each worker is given the same increments when the cost of living increases, grades tend to overlap one another and the low grades catch up to the high ones. This is a persistent problem in many countries where unstable currency and creeping inflation are endemic. Some companies have linked cost of living adjustments with merit increases. They increase the entire work force by a percentage sufficient to match inflation but deal the money out individually in accordance with merit. This brings about change in their whole structure but offers an opportunity to recognize different people differently.

These problems are given a large amount of time by local managements but, again, they receive relatively little help from the home office. This area of wage administration is often fought over by the three separate groups of managers. Strong feelings and opinions frequently become involved. The U.S. home office management's tendency to moralize is hard to miss. In contrast, U.S. managers abroad generally tend to feel that it is better to adjust the group as a whole than to attempt to make wage changes individually. A third point of view is expressed by foreign national managers, who often are aligned with the individual approach for a different reason: they frequently distrust wage systems and are reluctant to organize them.

Fringe benefits

Fringe benefits offered tend to vary more by country than by company or industry. American companies tend to adopt the basic fringe benefits package typical of the environment in which they are located. In many locations certain fringe benefits are compulsory, for example, a compulsory pension plan in India. In nearly every country there are compulsory insurance and workmen's compensation schemes and in many countries lunches must be provided, along with paid vacations and certain paid holidays. By and large, most managers felt that fringe benefits already common in the area should be offered, for "These side benefits here are as important as the salary. We've got to pay according to local customs." Often managers did not agree with the necessity for all of the fringe benefits offered in their particular country. For instance, in India and Pakistan there were as many as 20 paid holidays. Several foreign national and American production managers objected to these holidays and the overall national emphasis on indirect benefits. In other instances U.S. managers felt that fringe benefits in their locale were niggardly (e.g., Turkey and South Africa), but they did not wish to "upset the apple cart."

In no case did an American company studied take community leadership in making changes in fringe benefits, either to increase or decrease the total package. This is contrary to the recommendations of one writer, Elizabeth E. Hoyt. She states that businessmen underestimate the strains on workers in making an adjustment to industry and that American business should take the lead in setting up better conditions and offering benefits that may make the adjustments to industry come more easily.[15]

Milton C. Hagen[16] contends that the public's acceptance of a foreign company as a local asset depends in part on the company's reputation in regard to employee relations. He recommended that worker compensation plans should not only meet local requirements but that American companies should improve their image and move out in front of local competition to set the pace by offering new and advanced fringe benefits.

Much of the conventional and conservative practice in this area appears appropriate and understandable to the researcher. American

[15]Elizabeth E. Hoyt, "A New Diplomacy for Underdeveloped Areas," *Quarterly Review of Economics and Business* (August 1961).

[16]Milton C. Hagen, "Role of Employee Relations in the Free Enterprise Image," *Export Trade* (December 4 and 7, 1961).

companies must "feel their way" into the local culture and economic environment. A fringe benefit offered in the United States may be of less benefit than a direct wage payment, or vice versa. "Social leadership" would require a rare expertise in understanding the local culture and economy. Hiding behind local practice is easy to criticize, but it is prudent to do so until the company can formulate a sound long-range fringe benefit policy of its own.

In conclusion, the wage area tends to be poorly administered in U.S. foreign manufacturing subsidiaries. The tendency is to leave important decisions to U.S. managers abroad; however, they usually have relatively little experience or insight into personnel management. Their own values often influence wage decisions, whereas wage administration is necessarily involved with the customs, mores, and expectations of the workers.

American managers are "born and bred" on certain principles — the recognition of individual effort, treating each individual differently, monetary incentives, and so on. It is natural that Americans view these principles as prerequisites to productivity. Silently and implicitly they have crept into the wage system of American international subsidiaries; but analysis of local values is necessary. What seems fair and acceptable to the worker varies from culture to culture. The success of a system depends on meeting personal expectations.

Many companies tend to abdicate the derivation and appraisal of wage systems to local management because they perceive it as a local problem. Yet they simultaneously attempt to control from the home office any changes that cost money or violate home office wage "philosophy." As a result of this approach wage administration policies and procedures employed in the overseas plants studied were often either too complex and involved or they operated with virtually no system whatsoever. The excessively informal approaches of some companies contrasted with elaborate and overcontrolled systems of others.

Transplanting of American values abroad often caused unnecessary problems. For example, the home office of a company in India insisted upon using merit rating forms identical to those used in the United States. In this case an American value (e.g., "A man is responsible for his own performance. He should be rewarded or punished appropriately by his superiors.") was superimposed on a different culture. This value may be a basis for policy in the context of the American cultural heritage of the independence of the individual (though this is debatable), but in many countries it is virtually impossible for this principle to be understood and accepted as fair on the part of workers. If there is chronic underemployment, job security tends to be more important to the worker than freedom to advance or opportunity to increase his pay via merit rating or incentive wages. Where jobs must be divided so that they are relatively simple, it is difficult—if not impossible—to rate the performance of an individual employee. In fact, in most situations where this has been attempted the results are similar to those found at a U.S. plant in Turkey where a foreman rated every one of his workers as "excellent."

As might be expected, when managers and foremen of foreign origin were unable to fully understand and assimilate a U.S. personnel principle or a practice espoused by the home company, the practice in question was not intelligently applied. The control which the company desired and felt it had accomplished did not exist in fact.

In wage administration "control" and "good practice" can come only from intelligent local administration. Contrary to home office assumptions, commanding a local administrator to be "fair" and only giving wage increases to those who "deserve it" and then controlling the total practice at headquarters through overall percentages does not insure good wage administration. Inquiry usually revealed that the local supervisor's concept of "fairness" was quite different from that of the American evaluator.

Improved wage administration is therefore dependent on better understanding of the particular system by those who must administer it. Foreign (U.S.) derived principles, concepts, and techniques can seldom be used intelligently by local supervisors without training, for in the final analysis the local supervisor must be the one to decide who gets an increase. He makes the wage system work by his administration of it, or he ruins it.

This reasoning could lead one to conclude that wage systems should be entirely turned over to local managers, which would usually be an unfortunate error. We have observed that this function is frequently so loosely delegated that wage systems tend to be either overly complex or altogether too simple. One conclusion was clear: each plant needed some sort of a system to help make certain that the work was divided into jobs sensibly, that the internal structure was consistent and fair, that the company's total structure was competitive with the community, and that the system provided for renewal over a period of time. Further, experience indicates that it is a bad error to blindly accept local customs which may not be consistent with achieving better productivity.

Thus overseas manufacturers face a dilemma: it is "wrong" to blindly accept local customs; it is "wrong" to insist on an American wage system; it is "wrong" to have an overly complex system; but it is necessary to have some sort of a system.

One way out of this dilemma is to tailor the system carefully to the economics, the customs, and the norms of the particular situation. But to do this requires some time and a certain degree of expertise. Where may this management input be obtained?

It is almost too easy to suggest "Get yourself a good local personnel manager. He would be very valuable." Indeed, in many companies there were no personnel managers—"We do not need a personnel manager; we manage our personnel ourselves." The degree of breadth and wisdom needed makes the "good personnel manager" a rare commodity. In several cases, local personnel managers tended to be theoretical, impractical, and unrealistic. They sometimes identified too much with the workers; more often they tended to identify too closely with a hierarchical elite of top management. Our evidence suggests that local personnel managers need considerable help, which in most cases they do not receive.

Results from the Atul Chemical Company, a large indigenous Indian firm in Bulsar, India, are illuminating. Here is a company in which the managing director was close to personnel and wage administration. He had played a major part in deriving the wage structure and its concepts, and he supervised administration. His company had explored some "modern personnel practices," which he had applied to be consistent with the local customs and values. No foreigners were involved. The managing director personally maintained control charts to oversee the percentage of the workers classified in the various categories of performance in the promotional system. He insisted that his supervisors be trained to understand the system. He recognized the tendencies supervisors would have toward giving too many workers high ratings and insisted on a realistic distribution of grades. Atul had a system of small automatic progressions intended to induce among the workers a feeling that they could look forward to higher pay. In combination with this Atul offered a merit increase for improved performance. The system was relatively simple, and yet it provided an internal consistency and an apparently intelligent method for individual recognition and advancement.

The point of this example is that it appeared to the researcher that Atul had bridged "the gap" between the Indian culture and modern personnel practices and procedures. This indigenous company had not been in the prejudice-producing role of either fighting off or fighting for a "foreign" concept of wage administration. They had been able to identify and analyze the problems involved in wage administration; they were concerned with the treatment of individual workers, yet they perceived the necessity for a consistent system; the top man was able to talk over wage administration with intelligence and sophistication.

"Modern" or "advanced" personnel concepts can be genuinely useful in a variety of foreign cultures. These concepts bring a certain order and system to the inevitable problems of compensating people in organizations. But developing appropriate systems has been a genuine and persistent problem abroad.

Confusion and resistance occur when managements attempt to export the values behind a system, for cultural values are inevitably involved in compensation. "What we are paying for" is at the root of any system. The treatment of individual workers must be fair to be acceptable and motivating.

The critical ingredients appear to be (a) to have a system, (b) to have it simple and understandable, (c) to have it seem reasonable and acceptable to workers and supervisors, (d) to have it offer some rewards for individual performance which are appropriate within the local context.

Wage administration ordinarily should not be delegated solely to the overseas plant as "a local problem." Home office help is usually needed and it has often been fruitful in establishing sound systems and in training local personnel managers who must administer them. But home office control in details of wage system operation was generally fatal to high overseas morale. Instead, home office "control" can be based on mutually derived overall percentages, costs, and objectives after the wage system has also been mutually derived and is understood and accepted.

SUPERVISION

Probably few ingredients of production management have more long-run effect on productivity and labor relations than first-line supervision, the level of management which deals directly with the workers. For the purpose of this discussion we include "straw bosses," "leader men," and "working foremen," for in many parts of the world there is not a comparable position to that of the American "foreman."

In a factory someone must assign men to jobs, instruct them, and train them to do the work. Someone must schedule the work, follow progress, make sure that due dates are met, assign necessary priorities, and oversee quality. Someone must be responsible for elementary equipment maintenance and the proper use of equipment, obtain supplies and tools in order that workers are not delayed, and overcome work stoppages as quickly as possible. Someone must handle grievances and personnel problems. All of these activities affect labor productivity. The first-line supervisor is important, too, as a communication link with the management. He can pass along company policies and objectives to the workers, and he may keep managers aware of workers' feelings and problems. The first-line supervisor's effect on labor relations is equally sensitive.

First-line supervision was usually found to be a weak link in overseas production management. Even where English was spoken, the communications with and through first-line supervision was inadequate, thus making it difficult for higher management to know the situation on the factory floor. A vicious cycle is set up when middle management does not understand what is going on on the floor nor recognize the weaknesses in their first-line supervision. There are formidable problems in developing effective first-line supervision. For this reason there was a tendency on the part of management to accept existing performance of supervisors and, by the same token, to also downgrade the job, delegate little responsibility to foremen, fill in for the foremen, answer the foremen's questions instead of making them answer for themselves, and become discouraged over the possibilities of training good first-line supervision.

The communications problems stem, of course, not only from different language but from different cultural backgrounds and educational levels, social and cultural barriers between management people and those working on the factory floor. By and large there is a greater social gap between the management and the workers than in the United States. There is nearly always less mobility through first-line supervision ranks to higher management levels than is experienced in this country.

As a result of difficulty in communications, many U.S. and foreign national production managers tended to attempt to work around first-line supervision and to accomplish production through hiring masses of employees and dividing jobs into more specialized functions requiring less training and less supervision. The necessity for close scheduling was often eliminated by deluging the factory floors with in-process inventory; labor relations were handled at higher levels; and the attempt to achieve high individual worker productivity was frequently abandoned.

On a short-range basis, these practices actually overpowered the problem of weak supervision to an extent. But in the long run (as will be discussed in Chapter 4) problems of morale and communication in labor relations generally tended to grow. And as labor costs gradually rise, it may be predicted that developing better first-line supervision will be essential to accomplishing higher productivity.

Several examples of these problems in a variety of countries and plants may illustrate this conclusion.

Example 9

At a chemical plant in South Africa the production manager stated that it was very difficult to get a good supervisor. Ordinarily they must be promoted from the cadre of European employees. The plant manager said, "I pray that we do not have a vacancy and I will not have to promote one of our lower men. We train the men from the beginning on the technical part of the job, but some are not trainable; they are simply not able to handle emergencies. One man we promoted to be a supervisor the operators did not like from the beginning. The natives finally revolted and refused to work for him. We investigated and finally learned that he was not handling the men carefully. He had never learned the word "please." We found this clue by looking at his instructions in the log book, which were excessively rough. He was inclined to issue orders abruptly. Once we learned what the problem was, he has become one of our more reliable supervisors. Many of the white people did not pass beyond an eighth grade education but they continue on in school in the same grade until they get to be 16 and can legally drop out. Most of the supervisors are fairly considerate and they remember their own reaction to supervision. The black man is easy to get along with as long as you show him normal courtesy. One supervisor, however, became so frustrated with the natives that he hit one of them and we had to ask him to resign. All supervisors have to sign a form agreeing that hitting a black man will be tantamount to being fired. We had to fire him to prevent the blacks from a sitdown strike for they would certainly have reacted in one way or another.

In a case study of a Javanese factory, Ann Ruth Willner showed some problems of supervision in Asia. She noted that supervision is a new, intermediate role, which is unknown in the traditional village. In the village life individuals tend to work on their own, subject to tribal rules and regulations and those of the family. The group of foremen and supervisors appointed in the Javanese factory studies were faced with jobs that were without precedent in the local culture. Problems arise in promoting supervision from the ranks or from the outside. When promoted from the ranks, supervisors tended to be close to and identify with the workers. In merit rating, for example, they rated almost all workers as "satisfactory." When brought in from the outside, foremen often encountered resentment. Javenese foremen did not perform the task of discipline well, hesitating to reprimand or keep after employees who were not performing their jobs well. They did divide the work and parcel it out to the various employees, but they did not do a good job in seeing that the work was done on time or in following it up.[17]

At a tire plant in India first-line supervision problems unique in the company's broad international experience emerged. Supervisors had been promoted from within on the basis of their ability as workers and general evidence of intelligence. But after a supervisor was appointed, workers often did not cooperate with him. In fact, there were many instances of mysterious sabotage taking place after a new supervisor was appointed. It became clear, finally, that the workers resented anyone within their group who was appointed supervisor. It became necessary to obtain supervisors from the outside or at least from other departments or sections. This solution caused subsequent problems because the new supervisor did not know the work as well as the workers themselves.

In India the resentment of foremen was manifested outside the plant as well as at work. As supervisors, under management pressure, attempted to improve productivity, they were occasionally set upon in the darkness and beaten. Acts of physical violence against a supervisor attempting to do his job as his managers wanted it done undermined much training. It was clear that the workers did not accept the notion of one of their own group giving them orders.

The rigid hierarchical structure and lack of vertical mobility in India is clearly a factor in supervisory behavior. Supervisors did not identify closely with the workers and seemed to have little concern for them as human beings. They acted as if they felt they were in an entirely different social category than the workers.

[17]Ann Ruth Willner, *Human Organization.* Published by the Society for Applied Anthropology, Inc., Boston, Mass. (Summer 1963).

Professor Lambert in *Workers, Factories and Social Change in India*,[18] points out that in India there are especially strong feelings of hierarchy and status. In most of the plants he visited in Poona, India, the worker mobility, that is the movement of the workers from one job to another, was quite limited. A worker's status was difficult to change. A supervisor or a clerk was typically a Brahmin, a higher caste than the workers. There was virtually no chance for a worker to become a supervisor or for a worker to even learn new skills and undertake larger responsibilities. The few exceptions to this rule noted by Professor Lambert were in an engine plant where a higher gradient of skills was necessary.

The same type of reaction to status-leadership incongruencies was observed in several other cultures. In Turkey, for example, it frequently was necessary to appoint as supervisors only individuals who had had a technical education from a trade school. Unless the new supervisor had more education than the workers, he would not be accepted as foreman.

Cultural factors not only develop for supervisors, but the cultural differences between Americans and foreigners cause them to react differently to these same problems. As an American manager in India stated:

Supervisors tend to lean too much and too long on our American trainers. Training these men to make good supervisors is a real problem. It is difficult to get them to keep their personalities out of decisions. Our system of management seems to be very different from the normal Indian fashion. They tend to tighten the reins on people and get very tough all the way up and down the line. We tend to be more relaxed and informal and this has caused a hell of a lot of problems. There have been language problems — it has been very difficult to find out exactly what is going on on the floor. We don't know what supervision is saying to the men. There are too many times we feel that they are being nasty to the men and there is nothing we can do about it. The Indian supervisors have to be allowed to do their jobs in their own way, of course, and it frightens us day in and day out. We are not sure whether our way (i.e., of treating people better) will actually work out. The supervisors are not rational or objective; they carry grudges, they are immature. We are looking for the organization to work as a team and they don't seem to work to-

[18]Richard D. Lambert, *Workers, Factories and Social Change in India*, Princeton, University Press, Princeton, N. J., 1963.

gether that way. We wonder how many years it will be before we're sure that our policies of treating workers better are actually being carried out. The supervisors bring on much of the treatment that they receive (i.e., sabotage) because of their own vindictiveness. Most of their problems are their own fault.

One Indian general manager stated that "the biggest problems in increasing productivity have to do with our supervisors. They are not close to the workers; they do not tend to understand the workers' problems; they tend to be unnecessarily harsh and severe, and they do not recognize instances of poor production when they see them."

In Pakistan, a British production manager stated

Pakistani supervisors are impossible. They have no sense whatsoever of quality. They say, "If customers will accept the product, why worry about it?" Our answer is to keep after them constantly. Twenty parts for the first twenty machines which were desperately needed were ruined by drilling a hole all the way through a part when it should have been drilled only halfway. The supervisors were not close enough to the work to check it. Even foremen who were sent to Germany for training tend to be inefficient.

For instance, one man was a great disappointment, because after his training in Germany he tended to be excessively precise and excessively engineering-oriented. He did not appear to be concerned about the productivity of his individual employees. He was falling down daily on his production, yet was more concerned with individual tools and setups than he was with meeting schedules. When finally threatened that he must "get out 100 sets of parts by the end of week or else," he remained absent for several days.

The production manager stated that "our supervisors can only keep one thought in their mind at once. They are not really interested in the work, they have no pride in it. They are excessively trusting, accept promises and never do any checking whatsoever."

In many countries it was difficult for supervisors to accept the need for doing things on time. They had quite a different concept of time than the management people who were concerned with schedules, output, and productivity.

In some countries personal relationships seemed more important to the supervisor than the "tough-minded" performance of a job. Supervisors would sometimes refuse to correct, change, or criticize a worker. Often it was necessary for the production manager to go out on the floor himself in an effort to bring a worker's performance up to a minimum level.

It was difficult in some countries to get the foremen to stay out on the factory floor. They tended to gravitate toward their desks and paperwork, apparently feeling that this was higher-status work and that it was beneath their dignity to go out in the plant, get their hands dirty, and closely supervise the workers. They felt that a manager's place was at his desk and those who were out on the floor were not really "managing."

At a plant in Spain the American management stated that it was impossible to give the foremen much responsibility because they were only a cut above the workers, had relatively little education, and could not understand the larger problems. Hence it was considered necessary to have many foremen and expect relatively little of each one.

These are examples of the many problems in recruiting, training, and supervising first-line supervision in developing economies of the world. Supervision tended to be generally weak and brought about almost as many problems as it prevented or cured. Considering the fact that in some cultures the role of a first-line supervisor is new and that in most cultures it represents an unfamiliar social position, it is nearly inevitable that first-line supervision is a major problem. The world over, the foreman is "the man in the middle."

Recommendations

Many companies tend to give up on the problem of supervision and have managers at higher levels try to fill in for the weak supervisors and perform some of their functions. But this approach compounds the difficulty and tends to prolong its duration.

Although there can be no universal formula for getting and training better supervision because of the cultural differences between locations, certain approaches and concepts appear useful in handling these problems. It is usually necessary for expatriates to accept the overseas culture rather than fight to overcome what appear to be strange points of view. This means, for instance, selecting supervisors on the basis of their acceptance to the group. This may mean that the man has to come from the outside or have a technical or trade school education. The norms of the work group would take precedence over such American values as "promoting from within."

If a company responds to the workers' notions of acceptability, the question of who to appoint is narrowed. Selection on the basis of certain personal characteristics is replaced by a program of supervisory development. The management must size up their supervisory development. The management must size up their supervisory inventory and begin to work out means of improving it. Far more complaining about poor supervision was observed than training activities. If the men are technically oriented, they may need training in understanding the broader aspects of their jobs, such as scheduling, personnel problems, quality control, and discipline.

Carefully analyzing the skills, attitudes, and customs prevailing in the particular plant and sizing these up in terms of their effect on supervisory performance is critical. The next step is designing programs (including training, personnel practices, and salary practices) that will help overcome weaknesses. In contrast, when managements attempt to bolster weak supervision by minimum delegation or mediocre training programs, the difficulty will be prolonged.

If men are promoted from within, there may be leadership problems due to their close identification with the working force. It is useful to appraise the supervisors' feelings and the prevailing social pattern to see if the supervisors can be stimulated to see possibilities of moving up in the organization.

It is noteworthy that the home office gave little help to any of the companies in selecting, developing, training, and improving their first-line supervision. In spite of all the work that has been done on supervisory training in the United States this researcher found no instances in which personnel departments have been useful in this problem abroad. There are splendid opportunities for the application of social research techniques in determining existing skills and attitudes and comparing them to those that are necessary. The expertise of experienced and flexible personnel training men in developing programs would be beneficial.

As one foreign manager put it, "We have an excellent man at headquarters to help us on production problems. But we do not talk with him about foremen development because he is supposed to help us with our technical problems and that is not a technical problem." This reflects excessive preoccupation with technical problems and an assumption that technical know-how can be exported but management skills and techniques cannot because they will not apply in a foreign location. Often they will not directly apply, but many concepts and ways of thinking about supervisory education developed in our industrial society are both exportable and needed overseas.

PERSONNEL PRACTICES AND PROCEDURES

It appears that considering personnel practices and policies as a local management function, which should therefore be delegated entirely to local managers, is a common source of problems. In only two of the companies visited could the local personnel office and personnel manager be called "strong." More typically, personnel departments had little influence on the industrial relations climate and productivity. For example, in a large U.S. plant in South Africa the personnel department appeared weak, and inept, and legalistic. In spite of the existence of a giant American corporate parent and its myriad skills and know-how, there was no evidence of substantial transference of knowledge or skills in personnel work abroad. The personnel department staff philosophized and pontificated, and the jovial personnel manager knew almost everyone by first name, but he and his department played a flabby role in contributing to personnel policies and practices.

At minimum someone was needed to establish and preserve some sort of equitable compensation system in most of the industrial organizations studied. Individual foremen and supervisors had a tendency to respond to pressures and make exceptions. There was usually a need for the interdepartmental coordination provided by either a strong personnel manager or some other individual whose concern was with people.

In many other companies the personnel managers also tended to be weak or nonexistent. At a food product firm in India the manager stated that "We do not need a personnel manager." This was repeated at a chemical facility in South Africa. In sharp contrast, the personnel manager at a U.S. plant in Pakistan understood the wage and salary system and preserved it by insistence on using similar practices and policies in each of the various departments.

Many major personnel policy decisions were handled on an *ad hoc* basis in the plants visited. For instance, while the economic ups and downs in many developing countries were frequent and severe, policies regarding what to do with the workers during times of low activity often temporized rather than dealing with the basic issues of costs, investment in training, and a company's obligations to its work force.

Certain tools of modern personnel administration could be used abroad far more than they are; for example, one company studied has made good use of manning charts; some companies have used personnel succession and management inventory appraisal procedures. In many cases sketchy personnel records, which provided little historical or current data on experience and educational background, could have been expanded by trained personnel managers to be more useful.

Although certain U.S. techniques may be employed abroad under appropriate circumstances, exporting specific practices is not nearly as important or generally useful as some of the basic precepts of human relations worked out by practitioners and researchers in U.S. industry. Milton Hagen[19] confirms this conclusion. He makes the point that although U.S. domestic practices are not generally exportable many of the basic human relations concepts of progressive corporations in the United States do have applications abroad. In agreement, Professor Charles Myers[20] asserts that the distinctive applicable American contribution is in managerial organization, personnel administration, and human relations. For example, the human relations concepts of recognizing the individual's feelings and making the basic assumption that men will respond positively to treatment they regard as fair are both exportable.

But the absence of workable mechanisms for transferring hard-earned knowledge and concepts from one country to another was notable. The tendency to consider "personnel" as a local problem appears to be the prime reason for this vacuum. A second factor may be the lack of versatile, high-stature, broadly competent men on the staffs of many international companies. It is a "chicken and egg problem," certainly, which requires a new point of view on the part of higher management. The new point of view would include three new assumptions about a home office personnel staff: (a) they *can* contribute to local plants, (b) their contributions are needed, (c) the payoff in productivity and long-range industrial relations would be worthwhile.

CONCLUSION

Work force management by an American subsidiary in a foreign location involves a confrontation of values. Not only do the values of one culture meet headlong with those of another, but the norms and goals of men in different roles and status levels are also brought face to face. This confrontation can be observed in the initial pro-

[19] *Op. cit.* page 54.
[20] Charles Myers, "Exportability of American Industrial Relations," *Monthly Labor Review* (March, 1963).

cess of recruiting and selecting workers, and it continues in the establishment and administration of wages and salaries, training, and first-line supervision.

Companies dealing with the effects of a differing value system in managing their work forces found themselves taking a stand — purposely or implicitly — on three basic issues involved not only in work force management but in nearly every other aspect of managing international production as well. These are:

1. *Environmental adjustment.* How should we adjust to a foreign cultural, economic, and political environment?

2. *Exporting U.S. know-how.* How much company technical and managerial expertise can and should be applied abroad?

3. *Organizing the international company.* How much control from the home office? What role should the home office play?

Research abroad suggests that companies tend to take extreme positions on the issue of environmental adjustment in the management of work forces, some saying, "The foreign subsidiary should do it our way," more saying, "Worker management must be localized. When in Rome . . . ." Our analysis is that more often than not U.S. companies leave useful U.S. know-how at home; home office personnel staffs offer little help; relatively new or inexperienced overseas middle management is left to work things out for themselves. But home offices frequently interfere in details when some of their own philosophy of how to manage people is violated.

Control from the home office as well as specific procedures or techniques are seldom needed. Often required and seldom given are basic insights and ways of thinking about personnel management problems and issues which some companies have developed over many years of wrestling with these same "people problems," although in a different environment. From the companies studied, the best solutions to problems of value confrontation are those in which the values and environmental differences involved have been precisely identified and evaluated as a prelude to a rational and creative set of decisions.

4

LABOR RELATIONS

Management of labor relations in the overseas manufacturing plants studied could be improved if those responsible were able to acquire a more adequate sense of perspective. History shouts that every industrial relations environment changes, but past and future are too often overlooked in formulating labor policy and practices.

Changes in labor organization and its political power, technological change, and a nation's current economic restraints combine with the evolution of relationships between a company and its workers to make up dynamic, ever-changing labor relations situations. A more precise feel for the factors involved, their histories, and recognizable trends would allow the manager to cope more perceptively with the present and prepare more realistically for the future.

There have been few major problems to date in the typical labor relations structure studied during the research for this book. However, study of many companies in a variety of environments and varying longevities of tenure in a country offered a basis for comparison. With this background, symptoms in a number of worker-company relationships suggested storm warnings, which the management seemed unaware of. In the troubled situations visited, longer-range analysis might have offered a source of strength, creative ideas, and hope to an embattled management group.

The absence of a big-picture, long-time span kind of understanding should be neither surprising nor a reason for criticism of the managers studied. A grasp of economic, social, and technological history is difficult to acquire and use in one's own country. Abroad, amidst cultural and language differences, it is an even more demanding task. The task is complicated by the fact that the overseas manager, either American or indigenous, must cope with the fluid relationships of a relatively new company. In newly industrializing economies with rapid environmental changes, he must deal with daily pressures for both production output and domestic tranquillity, which preoccupy managers everywhere. Without perspective the daily pressures dominate management action; a long-run point of view might modify this.

The purpose of this chapter is to propose a framework to help managers develop a better perspective. A framework was suggested by the data from the variety of foreign subsidiaries studied in different countries, different industries, and the various labor relationships observed abroad. The findings of this study are congruent with the conclusions of several labor relations analysts who have offered useful ways of looking at and understanding the broad sweep and change in labor relations. We begin by examining a summary of labor relations experiences in the companies visited in this study.

AN OVERALL VIEW OF LABOR RELATIONS IN THE COMPANIES STUDIED ABROAD

Relations between the typical U.S. overseas manufacturing subsidiary and the local labor force were laden with potentially explosive, sensitive issues. Surprisingly, the handling of labor relations seldom presented immediate, major problems to the American companies visited abroad.

The latent difficulties inherent in the U.S. companies' situations are apparent. The American subsidiary was an "intruder" in the foreign country to a certain extent, influenced by "absentee owners" and "foreign" managers. The U.S. company was spotlighted, its actions loaded with the overtones of international politics. Personnel policies and practices, working rules and conditions were viewed with magnified importance by both workers and management as establishing precedents for the years ahead.

Labor unions were often keen to gain an early foothold in the U.S. company, particularly when they saw it as a means of "whipsawing" local companies into improved wages and conditions. Once installed, the in-plant union leaders were usually untrained and inexperienced in union management and politics. National union leadership in many of the developing countries was often inexperienced and immature, and hence unpredictable to American executives.

The differences in culture and industrial experience between Americans and the local labor force impeded understanding. Language barriers blocked effective communication and forced the American company to depend on locally appointed managers to handle labor relations. Typically, these local men were not only inexperienced as managers and unfamiliar with the policies and principles of the American company, but they were also untrained in handling personnel practices and labor relations. For these reasons difficult labor relations and much conflict might have been expected during the early years of the operations of American manufacturing subsidiaries abroad.

This has not been the case. Although labor relations cannot be dismissed as an area of international management characterized by placid docility, there are few examples of serious labor dissension, unrest, and strikes in this study. On analysis, there appear to be some logical reasons for this history.

The explanation is rooted in the concept that discernible stages exist in the chronological development of labor relations. These stages are influenced in their timing and their intensity by the total labor relations environment and the management practices employed. Generally speaking, the early stages are marked by more cooperation and less conflict than the middle stages. The middle stages were those of maximum adjustment and change and hence are the least tranquil. Later, more mature relations are accompanied by somewhat less strident feelings.

Since most of the companies studied were in the early stages, the typically peaceful relations observed can be expected to be replaced in the future by periods with more problems.

THE CONCEPT OF STAGES OF LABOR RELATIONS

John T. Dunlop[1] proposes that an industrial relations system may be regarded as composed of "certain actors, certain contexts, and ideology which binds the industrial relations systems together, and a body of rules created to govern the actors at the work place and work community. . . . An industrial relations system may also be thought of as moving through time, or, more rigorously, as responding to changes which affect the constitution of the system. The web

[1]John T. Dunlop, *Industrial Relations Systems,* Henry Holt and Company, New York, 1958, pp. 7, 9, 16, 17.

of rules can be expected to change with variations in the three features of the context of the system" (i.e., technological characteristics, market or budgetary restraints, and the locus and distribution of power in the larger society).

Each of these environmental factors is subject to change with time. After the plant is producing and operations settle down, the company is apt to attract some attention from organized labor, and initial labor-management skirmishing over inevitable grievances is likely to begin. The passage of time begins to create precedents and a backlog of unsatisfying minor incidents. The very factors that tend to moderate industrial relations in the first years of a company's history such as an uninitiated, inexperienced labor force and an absence of precedent, or a web of rules often become the disturbing elements of the future. The end of the first stage is at hand.

As technology, economics, politics, and ideology change, the industrial relations so structured by these factors of environment also change. Selekman, Fuller, Kennedy, and Baitsell,[2] in the introduction to *Problems in Labor Relations*, give seven structures, or stages, of institutional relationships which tend to follow each other over time. These structures, they suggest, may be studied as "adaptive mechanisms" resulting from the combinations of corporate and union power at different times in their individual development. The seven[3] structures suggested are: (a) ideology; (b) conflict; (c) containment; (d) power-bargaining; (e) accommodation; (f) cooperation; (g) deal bargaining. The first three represent an early time period in which the relationships are often "on the verge of a showdown and recourse to the use of naked power." The fourth is an interim or adjusting period, and the fifth and sixth, a maturing stage in a "continuum of power relations." All six represent phases in the evolution of labor-management relationships.[4]

The existence of discernible stages in industrial relations began to emerge from this study after visits had been made to many plants in various national settings, founded at many different times. The sense of evolution and change in company-worker relationships was

[2]Selekman, Fuller, Kennedy, and Baitsell, *Problems in Labor Relations*, Third Edition, McGraw-Hill, New York, 1964.
[3]The authors add two other structures, "collusion" and "racketeering," which are beyond the pale of U.S. law and American values and hence in that sense, abnormal stages.
[4]The seventh structure is a specialized stage or period in which leaders at the top make deals and attempt to have them supported by their organizations.

heightened by visits to the subsidiaries of five companies in two or more countries.

The stages observed in this study may be described as: (a) a period in which managements and workers (in a collective sense) have strong concerns and aims, which they see as rights that are not fully respected by the other party; (b) a period in which power is brought to play, some rules to regulate the power struggle are worked out, and a struggle to achieve felt needs goes on; (c) a period in which adjustments are made, the conflicts are seen as less threatening to the "rights" of each party, and each side begins to accept the values of the other as "legitimate"; (d) a period in which relationships are more mature and conflicts are worked out with less reversion to power.

The stages in the relationships between foreign-owned subsidiaries and indigenous labor forces observed in this study appear quite similar to those noted by Selekman et al. with one exception—the early years, or the first stage.

This first stage, which we call the "honeymoon" stage, may be distinctive to the foreign subsidiary in a developing economy because the company arrives on the scene and overnight, so to speak, creates a plant. Hence its position is at once powerful relative to that of the workers, many of whom may have had little or no factory experience. They are apt to be utterly unorganized, whereas the company as an institution has had factory management experience in other nations. Yet both parties will generally be anxious to please and "get along."

The closest domestic parallel to this setting for industrial relations would be the new plant of a large U.S. corporation in a relatively underdeveloped, highly agriculturalized section of the United States. The same ingredients—new workers + experienced company + a new enterprise + mutually high expectations for the future— would generally be present. But the similarity ends with these parallels, for the U.S. workers are usually to be better educated, have a more realistic view of factory life, and have a different network of legal and political constraints than those found abroad in an underdeveloped country.

Most of the American plants studied overseas were set up less than six years ago. The period observed therefore is one that generally favors calm labor relations. In the early years of a new foreign subsidiary there is apt to be a kind of "family spirit" in which the company is welcome in the country and the new employees are typically eager for jobs, proud to have been hired, and expect their futures with a "modern and enlightened" American company to be happy and prosperous.

In Turkey, Pakistan, India, South Africa, and Nigeria this early period was accompanied by environmental conditions favoring management more than workers. Workers appeared reluctant to offend, perhaps because jobs were often hard to obtain and the pay represented an order of magnitude increase over that obtainable in agriculture. There was frequently a lack of support by government officials, to whom the unions constituted at best a disturbing element. This observation was confirmed by Walter Galenson.[5] He pointed out that the unions in the developing countries such as Indonesia, Pakistan, Brazil, Argentina, Chile, Israel, and Turkey are typically weak, particularly due to high levels of unemployment. He noted that to the governments' unions were "annoying pressure groups for higher real wages and more advanced social services than the economy can afford at a time when investment is a critical need." There was apt to be a relatively unfavorable legal and political environment for unionization in those countries where the economy was essentially agricultural and where the urbanized union worker represented only a small minority of the working population.

Another characteristic in the early years of a foreign subsidiary was that the plants were usually relatively small. These conditions influenced the management toward closer relations with employees and personal communication. It was reported, too, that new plant buildings and attractive physical conditions drew sufficient numbers of employees to allow more selectivity. This in turn added to a total atmosphere in which workers valued their jobs as especially desirable. Finally, the absence of a history of bad feelings and binding precedents apparently freed the workers, their leaders, and managers to work out an amicable relationship without the burden of ancient grievances.

Because labor relations in a foreign setting have been expected to be difficult, it has received top management concern in many companies investing abroad. Men sent overseas as general managers or production managers have generally had experience in dealing with labor in this country and, often seeing the situation as "potential dynamite," have devoted personal attention instead of delegating

[5]Walter Galenson, *Labor in Developing Economies*, University of California Press, Berkeley, Cal., 1962.

labor relations to lower, less experienced levels of management. All these factors in varying degrees in different situations appear to have contributed to more tranquility in labor relations than might have been expected.

To a management that has enjoyed such an interlude without anticipating that workers' dissatisfactions and pent-up feelings would cause it to end, the increasingly hostile atmosphere is disturbing. Managers begin to perceive workers as "ungrateful," "rebellious," "uncooperative," or "under the influence of outsiders." A sense of perspective therefore, both in terms of the different stages of a company's labor relations and in perceiving different phases of the area's labor relations environment, could allow managers to be less judgmental in coping with international labor problems.

Before moving on to describe the further stages detected, we expand this concept of change in industrial relations in underdeveloped, newly industrializing societies in order to assist the reader a step further in acquiring this sense of perspective as it relates to the ending of the "honeymoon stage." Kerr, Dunlop, Harbison, and Meyers[6] offer these observations on the evolution of industrial relations in underdeveloped economies:

> The actual course of the transition to an industrial society may be seen as an interaction between the imperatives of the industrialization process and the free existing culture. In every case of industrialization there are numerous points of conflict and of accommodation. In the language of Toynbee there is an "encounter between civilizations," there is a struggle for dominance between the new industrial order and the free existing order. The adjustment of institutions to changing economic circumstances may be a painful process. It is neither balanced nor complete. The new and the old are mixed illogically and in curious proportions, which differ widely from society to society . . . . The battleground is at a variety of points and levels: religious and ethical values, family system, class alignments, education system, government structures, and legal system. In this interaction the old society will be revamped to a greater or lesser extent, or in extreme cases it may be largely swept away. A combination between the old and the new may also create a distinctive industrialization society and the process and speed of industrialization may in turn be cause as well as effect in the accommodation of the old and new. An insistent question of the transition concerns which institutions

---

[6] *Op. cit.*, p. 28.

of the traditional society shall be preserved, transformed, and modified, and which shall be sacrificed.

Industrializing man sentences himself to hard work. Whether he be worker or manager, he is required to conform to an elaborate web of rules in the work place and in the community. His more highly developed potentialities struggle with leveling conformity.

Worker discontent is often voiced in the form of protest and disharmonious labor relations. As a society gradually industrializes, the political climate tends to change as the voters become increasingly urban and less agricultural. The increased political strength of the unions brings about laws which better protect labor. In this way the labor relations environment gradually changes and becomes less favorable to the management side.

The interplay of social and economic forces and management and employee practices and tactics make up a complex system. It is beyond the scope of this research to attempt to systematically relate causes and effects to be able to predict a certain pattern (e.g., in social system A and economic situation B and company C, if management chooses a set of practices E, the result will be a labor-management relationship of type F). Although precision is not possible, certain observations can be made about these forces and their interrelationships.

1.   The process of companies and employees evolving a mutually satisfactory relationship tends to pass through certain broadly definable stages.

2.   The stages are influenced by time, by the economic, political, and social environments, and by management practices.

3.   The environments in developing economies also evolve; certain patterns of evolution can be traced.

4.   The wise manager will attempt to identify what is going on in his company's labor relations. He will recognize the inevitability of change in relationships; he will analyze the pertinent environmental factors; he will realize that what he does today may help or hurt his labor relations tomorrow. He learns from history and he looks ahead. In short, he has a sense of perspective.

Our chief concern is that too few international managers, dealing as they are with a multitude of pressures and problems, have been able to see their own situations with objectivity. If labor relations has been no great problem to date, the common error is to assume that "Here in Pakistan (or South Africa, Turkey, Nigeria, etc.) we don't have many problems with labor. Unions are weak, the government is for business, and we take good care of our people." But all these factors are subject to change.

Changing labor relations environments

Accepting Professor Dunlop's[7] assertion that an industrial relations system is influenced by its actors, ideologies, and contexts, it is interesting to look back over the recent history of developing nations for general patterns or phases in the context. Since the changing context influences the stage in labor relations of any company, we shall examine some patterns of change in the environment before describing the stages in labor relations identified in this study.

The labor relations environment in the newly industrializing countries seems to pass through phases over time. (These phases are not equivalent to "the stages of industrial growth"[8] formulated by Rostow.) Each phase has its peculiar effects on company-worker relationships. The labor relations environment is affected by the economic milieu, cultural development, and the legal and political environment in which labor relations takes place.

Pakistan, Turkey, Nicaragua, and Nigeria are examples of agricultural societies in which the population move toward the cities and the establishment of industrial production are just beginning. At this phase of economic development unions are generally either new or nonexistent. The political environment is usually unfavorable to unions. The large proportion of the population is dependent upon agriculture and the unions represent a political pressure for higher wages at a time when the country's leaders are anxious to export in order to improve the balance of trade.

A factory law is passed at an early stage in nearly every country. It is written to protect the workers on a minimal basis, affecting the health and safety conditions in the factory. But even this minimum protection for the workers is seldom enforced in the early phase of development.

In *Personnel Management in India*[9] this early phase of economic development is described as one in which the workers are making the adjustment to industrial life from village and family society. The

---

[7]*Op. cit.*, p. 71.

[8]Walter Rostow, *Stages of Economic Growth,* Cambridge University Press, Cambridge (England), 1960.

[9]Indian Institute of Personnel Management, *Personnel Management in India,* Asian Publishing House, New Delhi, 1961.

workers do not accept the principle that industrial work should take precedence over their personal lives. In the very early stages of economic development the worker is apt to see his security as coming from the familiar village environment and consequently there is high turnover, with frequent changes, much absenteeism, migrant workers, and the tendency to return to the village at intermittent intervals.[10]

Over a period of time the attitudes change. When workers become more dependent on industrial jobs, their attitudes generally show more concern for security than at first, accentuated by the complexity and insecurity of the city life. The increasing emphasis on security, the introduction of provident funds,[11] the agitation of trade unions against layoffs, and the gradual increase in cohesion in the labor union mark a transition into the second environmental stage, that of the "mixed economy."

In a later phase the economic balance between managements and labor is shifted. Agriculture predominates, but the economy is experiencing a pronounced shift toward industry and a population move into urban centers, usually accompanied by a simultaneous increase in the number of companies competing in each industry. Unions begin to grow in strength. Costs become more important and profit margins narrow. Labor courts and protective measures for the workers are being established. Striving for power between management and unions is typical, but the political environment for the unions is still apt to be basically unfavorable.

Curiously, both India and South Africa appear to belong in this "mixed economy" category today in spite of the far greater degree of industrial advance in South Africa. Both these nations are in a mixed economy phase of labor relations environment because their industry is increasing while their economy is still predominantly agricultural and there is an essentially unfavorable political environment for labor unions and working men. In South Africa this is brought about by the fact that the large masses of workers in the factories are either *native* or *colored*[12] and the laws discourage their organization. There is somewhat more than minimum protection for

[10]These conclusions are largely substantiated in this study with the exception that the preservation of one's job is apt to be important to workers who have been living in cities for many years, even in the early stage of economic development.

[11]Forms of social security, medical care, and other social benefits established by law.

[12]"Coloreds" are defined in South Africa as a mixed race, a mixture of native and Europeans. In South Africa the population is about 28 percent white or European, 14 percent colored and 58 percent native (black-skinned).

workers in health and safety, but they enjoy relatively little political status. The European workers are given "job preference" and "job reservation," but their numbers are too small to create much political strength. European workers are often members of craft unions, but even they have relatively few rights of appeal to the government.

In India workers also receive a minimum type of protection through factory laws affecting their working conditions. But while labor laws and labor courts give workers rights of judicial appeal so that a certain degree of "justice" may be obtained by an aggrieved worker, nevertheless underemployment, the relative financial strength of employers, the lack of education, and the low social status of workers combine to give the factory manager the upper hand in most situations. The agricultural sector predominates in most provinces and unions are politically weak.

At a food-processing plant in India a union had represented the employees for a number of years. But after the union lost grievance after grievance in the labor courts, the employees voted the union out. The causes for the defeats in court could not be ascertained, but one conclusion appeared clear from discussions with company managers: the workers had to have a strong case to win in the labor tribunal, which appeared biased in favor of the stability promoted by company strength relative to the union.

A tire company in South Africa was typical of a company in a mixed economy labor relations environment. There had been several occasions when the company's incentive rates had raised objections, but no serious attempts at unionization had arisen. "They have all the benefits of the new Factories Act, and the Wage Determination[13] looks after the employees as well as any union could," one manager stated. In its wage policy, the company simply met the going market wage levels and made periodic surveys to make sure that they did not fall behind. The employees' interests were in the hands of the government and the employers through the use of "wage determinations" and "industrial wage agreements." These practices virtually eliminated bargaining between individual companies and the workers. Negotiations were carried on at a high level through company associations and the government and by the top representatives of unions.

An industrial products manufacturer in South Africa had five un-

[13]"Wage Determination" is the South African system for determing wage levels in many industries. In this system representatives of government, business, and labor negotiate industry-wide wage levels.

ions with industry-wide bargaining so the company officers seldom saw the union representatives. Strikes were illegal, but the workers could call "a dispute" and cause an "industrial council" to be established. Any unsettled dispute went to the government conciliators and if agreement was not reached there would be mandatory arbitration. Neither party wanted this, according to company managers, because they feared an arbitrary solution, In South Africa the natives were not allowed to join the union. They could have a workers' committee of their own. The European workers had a works council in which employees and management discussed local plant conditions. Many companies simply refused to recognize unions. There was no necessity to do so in this management-oriented environment, which is characteristic of a "mixed economy."

As a country industrializes and a larger percentage of the population works in factories, the unions typically become organized and stronger, although they are still not in political control. There are likely to be more stringent laws regulating health and working conditions, but, in addition, the total legal environment becomes more favorable to the unions. Often laws are passed to require union recognition. Bargaining is carried on with increasingly formalized arrangements, including those for handling disputes.

Spain is an example of a country in this phase. There the balance appears to be shifting toward the unions. "The unions are getting tougher here and they are increasing in strength all the time," was a frequent reaction of American managers. The government had begun to be aware of the political strength of the unions and recognized the importance of stability in their role in keeping industrial workers satisfied. The right to discharge employees is limited and employees have the right to petition the government to review their cases. Termination benefits are usually severe to the employer and strongly oriented against any arbitrary dismissals.

Employees at a pharmaceutical plant in Madrid belong to an industrial union, the Chemical and Pharmaceutical Workers Union; there is a worker committee which meets twice a year with a government representative attending the meetings. The personnel manager from the company also sits in, together with the industry union representative. A two-year collective agreement was established between the chemical pharmaceutical industry and the company. Internally there is an eight-man committee consisting of workers, administrative people, and technicians, and all groups have elections and appoint representatives. For example, an accounting clerk, the assistant to the chief accountant, was the representative of the administrative personnel. This committee meets with the head of the company (who delegates the duty to the personnel manager), and they bargain and discuss the problems of local working conditions. Company managers commented: "The committee cannot decide anything that is not already in the book. They cannot change the basic syndicate agreement except to improve the benefits or to pay more. If they change the personnel policy it must be approved by the government. The compendium or syndicate agreement is a set of minimums, so they can go higher and better but not worse. These are industry-wide agreements."

Here is an environment in which the balance is shifting from being heavily weighted in favor of the management to one that is more on the workers' side. There remains considerable interest on the part of the government to keep the workers under control. The government plays a major and continuing part in the bargaining process.

As an economy becomes more industrialized, powerful labor unions often exert a major political influence. Although in the U.S. unions have never been as politically oriented as in Europe, they have, of course, influenced legislation. The Wagner Labor Law gave formal recognition to the rights of workers to organize and bargain collectively in the United States. Union power was buttressed by law. Recognition of a duly chosen union became mandatory, making it very difficult for an employer to avoid bargaining. Later, a more even balance between labor, government, and employers has come about in the United States, West Germany, the United Kingdom, and Canada.

STAGES OF LABOR RELATIONS OBSERVED IN THIS STUDY

Chronological stages in labor relations are useful concepts but they must be understood and not misused. It would be a mistake to assume that the stages described are either inevitable or identical from one situation to another. The companies visited fell into one of the following five separable chronological stages of labor relations: (a) family style; (b) skirmishing; (c) battle; (d) postwar; and (e) industrial peace.

Family style

This first stage has already been partially described. It is the time when the company is new in the country and the employee is new to his job. Typically, employees have been selected from numerous applicants. They are proud and pleased to have been employed; they are eager for their jobs; they are looking forward to building a prosperous and satisfying career with the company. In many countries consistent unemployment renders workers especially grateful to have their jobs. They know that dozens, even hundreds of workers, are outside the factory gates waiting to take their place if they are found wanting.

In the newly developing countries this is a period in which many individuals are becoming accustomed to the disciplined life in a factory for the first time. The amount of physical labor is apt to be a good deal less than that required in an agricultural job. Managers and supervisors were generally eager to start their labor relations on a good footing, and there was an absence of ingrained ill will. Often the management showed feelings of paternal concern for the workers.

Individual rather than group-centered problems occurred at this early stage. For instance, in India a chronic problem of worker indebtedness tends to occupy the company in the "family-style" stage of labor relations. At one company, the management said that "the workers live like lords for one-half the month and then run into debt during the last half of the month. They are paying exorbitant rates of interest and often come to us for help." Problems with workers resulting in absenteeism, poor quality, and low productivity were handled by the managers by dealing with individual workers as one would with children: scolding, censoring, disciplining.

In many countries a probationary period ranging from one to six months was a normal practice. During this period the workers were reported as clearly anxious to be on their best behavior. In this period the workers appeared to value a direct relationship with supervisors, rather than dealing as a collective group with a union or committee as intermediary. In some instances the behavior suggested a feeling of concern lest the new boss be offended. The natives of South Africa, for example, tended to identify closely with their supervisor. If they liked the man, they made up happy songs praising him and took his name for their own.

At a pharmaceutical plant in South Africa, where economic development is quite advanced in contrast to Nigeria, Turkey, India, or Pakistan, labor-management relations showed the same characteristics of person-to-person relations. In this plant there was a close relationship between individual workers and the management.

In Turkey the same stage was evidenced in all the plants studied. A typical statement by Turk supervisors was: "We wish to take care of our workers; we treat them as we would children; we scold them when they misbehave but we take care of them in times when they need help."

The skirmishing stage

After a period of time[14] a gradual disillusionment with one's job and with the management, a feeling of tedium, reaction to the hard work and discipline in industry, and often a lack of mobility in advancement potential begins to find its expression in the industrial protest predicted by Karl Marx and observed by Dunlop et al.[15]

The discontent of workers is reflected in disruptive forms of protest, tends to be greatest in the early stages[16] of industrialization and tends to decline as workers become more accustomed to industrialization. The partially committed industrial workers with strong ties to the extended family and village, unaccustomed to urban life and to the discipline and mores of the factory is more likely to reflect open revolt against industrial life than the seasoned workers more familiar with the ways of the factory and more understanding of the reasons for the web of factory rules, more reconciled to factory life, more motivated by urban and monetary considerations and less attached to the traditional and rural society. The workers in process of the early stages of industrialization are more prone to absenteeism, prolonged and sporadic withdrawals from industrial work, wildcat stoppages, naked violence and destruction of machines and property. In later periods industrial workers can be more disciplined in their withdrawal of effort and in the use of the strike. . . . Protest tends to

[14]The length of these stages in relationships is influenced by many variables. Predicting the length of each stage would be a complex task and a useful topic for further research.

[15]*Op. cit.*, p. 28.

[16]These authors' use of "early stages" may not be consistent with the findings in this study. Evidence in this study suggests that worker protest and discontent does not typically emerge until after an earlier period of relative contentment and that the difficult adjustment of life in industry is generally accepted at first because the rewards (both actual and expected in the future) more than compensate for the penalties of industrial work. But, when expectations are not fully satisfied and the original benefits of factory jobs are no longer unique but commonplace, the protest presumably felt all along begins to emerge and predominate.

peak early. The initial generations of industrial workers tend to be critical from the perspective society.[17]

In the plants visited in this second stage the rise of protest against the web of factory rules and the discipline of the factory life took the form of skirmishing between workers and the management, grievances submitted to the foremen, complaints against the rules, demands for better working conditions, and requests for higher pay and bonuses. For example, this syndrome of rising complaints was developing in the pharmaceutical plants in Turkey in 1959. The two plants visited had been operating for five and six years, respectively. After the first few years of operation workers had gradually begun to be militant in their requests for annual bonuses.

At Wales[18] a major dispute occurred in the fall of 1959 in regard to an annual bonus.

Example 1

The labor representatives attempted to see the general manager to make their annual protest against the salaried workers receiving a bonus, while the hourly workers received none. When the production manager told them they were not to receive a bonus, they took their complaint to the local newspaper, which printed a sympathetic article.

At Abbott,[19] too, there had been a dispute over a bonus question.

Example 2

At the end of the fiscal year (November 30) a bonus of half a month's pay had always been paid to the hourly workers. In November, when the usual bonus was announced, one woman accompanied by six others protested to the superintendent that this bonus was too small, especially because the salaried employees were usually given a full month's pay. She and the other six returned their bonus checks to the company in protest over the amount.

The elected representative of the workers had told the seven women that they were in the wrong, but they did not accept his advice. He seldom brought worker complaints to the superintendent. The General Manager stated, "We act strictly in accordance with the law. If the law is wrong we're not responsible."

[17] *Op. cit.*, p. 28.
[18] The Wales Company, Harvard Business School case.
[19] Abbott Laboratories Turk Fabrikasi, Harvard Business School case.

At a pharmaceutical plant in India, after nearly six years of operation, a union was first formed when the company carried out a work-force reduction to cut operating losses. At once they began to have incidents with several troublemakers in the plant. Similarly, at a food processing plant in India, when a union was formed it began to take many minor complaints about the company to the local labor court. The fact that the union lost every one of these cases in court made them no less irritating to the management but it did weaken membership support. The union apparently felt it necessary to bring these cases to trial, even though they may have expected to lose after the first cases were decided against them.

It is in the skirmishing stage that leadership of a new union was observed to emerge in several of the factories studied. The leader was apt to be the able but discontented factory worker. He was inevitably untrained for his new role of responsibility.[20]

Example 3

At a plant in India the first signs of skirmishing were seen in agitation over objections to particular supervisors. "Labor relations were real good for the first year," a company official stated. There had been no real grievances or overt problems with the employees at first, but after the first year they began to emerge. There had been one short walkout over the use of "badli" (temporary workers) in one part of the plant. These were no more than skirmishes, however, because these disputes were settled in a few hours by company officials and worker representatives. Later, the workers claimed to be abused. A man was promoted from within and they began to make things hard for him. There was damage to machines. The company's response took the form of disciplinary discharges of about thirty men over a thirty-month period. The workers began to place complaints against the company with the labor court. Certain issues were taken to government conciliation. But by this time such skirmishing had developed open wounds and fixed positions and the future appeared ominous.

Battle

A stage of labor relations characterized by open, militant fighting follows the skirmishing stage when ideological principles are

[20]*Unions in Emerging Societies,* by Sidney C. Sufrin (Syracuse University Press, Syracuse, N.Y., 1963) discusses the emergence of new unions in Pakistan and contains examples of the erratic behavior of the new, untrained union leader.

threatened to the point that the naked use of power is preferable to compromise. The third stage becomes a battle for survival as perceived by the union and a battle for maintaining prerogatives and control in the view of the owners. Ideologies and "rights" are asserted by both sides and full use is made of power. Jurisdictional problems within the union may heighten the sense of insecurity of worker groups.

A later case from the same company in India illustrates this stage.

Example 4

After a year and a half of skirmishing, open warfare erupted between labor and management. Much of the problem appeared to stem from internal dissension in the union. There was a struggle for leadership between two different factions along with a jurisdictional conflict. Several months earlier managers had begun to hear about meetings for organizing a union. Outsiders were getting involved. The personnel director stated that "here in India management never knows who is in the union. It is so difficult to find out what is going on." There was no legal necessity for recognizing the union, but the company decided it would be best not to fight it and, further, they felt that recognition would help in dealing with the workers, the problem of communication with individuals being so difficult. In the negotiations the new union was utterly inexperienced. "We had to tell them what to ask of us." In spite of the fact that wages were higher than the community level there was continual agitation. In fact, the problem did not seem to center on wages as such. A "fancy union contract very much like one in the United States" was signed in December of 1962.

The contract specified that only company employees and no outsiders would be allowed in the union. (The contract used the word "indigenous" in qualifying men for membership. Later the union claimed that this meant that all members must be Indians, not employees.) The first contract stated that wages would increase ten percent, the company would put up a bulletin board for the union, paid holidays would increase from two to eight, the company would install a "provident fund."[21] They signed a three-

---

[21]A retirement pension plan.

year contract with a wage reopener after fifteen months. The company felt that it was unique in India.[22]

The company had attempted to introduce a concept of negotiating over differences, and a relationship in which two parties could come to an agreement and keep any third party out of it. This was a company philosophy applied on a worldwide basis. The management was fully aware of the newness of this approach in India and recognized that the workers could circumvent it.

The new contract worked out satisfactorily for several months and the company felt that it had a good relationship. The first formal notice of impending trouble came from the union in October, 1962, with a list of demands. The president of the union, age twenty-three, began to be undermined by a competitive group. Various groups then tried to gain control of the union. Outside people were brought in from the Congress Union in an effort to force the company union out. They tried numerous upsetting tactics, each group trying to show what it could do. These disruptions caused severe problems in production, particularly in team and crew operations.

The personnel director reported later, "we couldn't keep up with what was happening. They hit us at the wrong time. The supervisors were inexperienced and did not have the knowledge and understanding of how our company wants to run a factory. So we didn't cope too well."

Finally, the employees had an election and elected a nonemployee as president. The company then felt that it did not have to recognize the union, but it continued to deal with it on an informal basis for several months. The new president stated new demands: (a) A cooperative store. (b) A Provident Fund (this had not yet been established). (c) Ideas on how to increase productivity. (d) Opportunities for discussing how to get better management labor relationships. The personnel manager had informally invited him to come over and talk. The president wrote him and said, "you are not recognizing me as president so I won't come over and talk."

[22]A set of "standing orders" typically takes the place of Union contracts in India. The standing orders can be subject to government review and arbitration. Normally there is no contract and union demands go to a government industrial tribunal whose decision is binding. The contract and "standing orders" are interlocking and redundant in many respects. The net result is that when a company has a union contract it has a double system, in which both the union contract and standing orders form a legal base for company-union relationship.

"The situation could blow sky high," the Personnel Director said when interviewed. There were many "labor disturbances" and a certain amount of "milling around the plant." The former union president had resigned from the union, wanted to be a supervisor, and asked the company for "protection" against physical violence. The union claimed 400 members, but according to what information could be obtained only 50 were attending meetings. Company officers felt that it was most unorthodox that the union had nonemployees for its officers. They wanted the union to represent the whole plant. They were concerned that the union was so weak.

Late in the fall of 1963 the company finally signed a contract with the new union but then the new officers were not re-elected. The offices were filled with other men who had been affiliated with a third group.

A wildcat strike then took place. In the face of demands by the new leaders the company took the position that "we had a valid contract." The particular issues cited were: company clothing and housing, and a wage bonus for 1963 paid in 1964. The strike lasted for nine days. The local government labor tribunal declared the shutdown illegal and stated that the men must go back to work. The situation continued, seething with problems and discontent, as the company attempted to work out more satisfactory relationships with the workers while the workers attempted to develop a system of self-government. The government offered some stabilizing elements but it was not effective in smoothing daily labor relations.

The researcher later visited the company's U.S. headquarters. The Home Office personnel officers stated, "Our managers are angry because some of the strikers do not even work for us. I advised them to take another look at the whole situation. We may be winning the battle and losing the war. The company should be willing to compromise. It is difficult, though, for our men in India to depart from the 'company religion' and still hold onto some standards and principles."

At a pharmaceutical firm in India a serious period of battling was also in progress. The company had bought a smaller, indigenous company. The small company's union continued to represent the workers. Relations were satisfactory for several years until union management became more aggressive.

Example 5

"They were always requesting something." After a workman refused to work when he learned he was lower in grade than the work called for, he was suspended and dismissed. He had done the work for years until the union told him he shouldn't have to do that particular job without more pay. The grievance went through the normal legal proceedings to conciliation and was appealed to a higher court twice. The union lost the case but it took one and a half years and resulted in a great deal of acrimony. After the second appeal was settled, the company finally decided to withdraw recognition of this union although they had completed a new agreement with the union only three months before. For three years there were no formal union negotiations and much restlessness in the plant while the union attempted to regain strength and solidarity.

Then the union demanded new pay scales. The tribunal gave the award to the union but not all they asked for. The following year the company started a second shift in the department in question with 40 people. It was a five-day week at that time and they worked from 8 to 5:15 on the first shift, started the second shift at 9:30 and worked until 6:45. (They had to finish a shift before 12:00 midnight because of transportation problems at night so they started it later and ran all night.) The shift went on nearly a year. The company then suggested a six-day week starting at 7:00 A.M. and going until 10:00 P.M. with overlapping shifts. The union, however, did not want to work for six days and so the company did not push it. The union insisted on a night shift, but the company could not do this because female employees were not allowed by law to work at night. The union insisted on full rotation of hours even though they apparently knew it was impossible. The company gave the union two weeks' notice that they were going onto a six-day week at the hours of 7:20 to 3:20, 3:20 to 11:20, 11:20 to 7:20. The men said that they would not accept it. Instead of forcing this, the company went to the tribunal court and asked for a ruling. The court accepted the notice and set a hearing for later. While the company waited for the hearing it made no change.

Shortly afterwards, however, the night shifts sat down and refused to work. They asked to see the general manager. (The production manager was on leave.) The general manager came to the plant at midnight. The workers said that they wanted a shift allowance; this was the first time that this had ever been mentioned. They also wanted rotation. The general manager said he would wait until the production manager returned in one week. Five days later, the production manager returned and had a meeting with the second shift representatives, when they repeated the same demands. In five days nightly production had dropped from 85,000 to 60,000 units. The company said it would consider the demands, but first the union must restore production. The daily production went down to 40,000 units over the next two months. A month later when production had dropped to 24,000 the managers had put up a notice to the effect that if production was not restored they would have to take disciplinary action against those concerned. Production went down to 12,000 the next day. They "charge-sheeted" 23 employees, placing them on notice that they would be tried before company managers and if found guilty, dismissed.

The next day the entire plant went on strike for one day. The management made a decision to take stern action on the same day and in the evening they charge-sheeted the four union leaders for instigating this strike. The workers then returned to work and production went up to 35,000. Over the next three months they kept the charge-sheets pending and gave the men an opportunity for improving.

But the production did not increase. They then proceeded with the charge-sheets, held a company inquiry and dismissed 19 of the 23 and also asked permission of the court to fire the leaders. The court approved dismissal of the 19 as well as the union leaders. After the court approved this, the union asked to discuss the issues and negotiations were reopened. The company agreed to take back the people and cancel the dismissals if production was restored. The union agreed and signed an agreement to restore production to the old level and never to "go slow again." The company then took back all of the employees and production was restored to 85,000 the next day.

By this time the production manager stated that "I had changed my philosophy and I advised the management to recognize the union." The company then recognized the union. The production manager has since come to feel that he "couldn't really get along without a union." Since then there have been frequent union-management meetings and disputes have been settled through negotiations with the union.

During this process of skirmishing and then open battle both the tire and the pharmaceutical companies had changed their views on how to deal with labor. One production manager stated, "We now give more personal recognition to the leaders. We treat them more as equals in talking to them and not as outcasts." Both companies learned to move quickly against illegal threats and work stoppages. Employees of both companies began to learn to cooperate.

These are typical accounts of open battling between the unions and the companies and the struggles that go on as the union attempts to get itself organized and the company learns how to deal with individual workers, the union situation, and the local culture.

Postwar

Once a contract becomes the framework for working together and the union has become convinced that the company is not trying to destroy it, experience in negotiations is built up and more harmonious working together becomes the pattern. Even though there may be many differences, more responsible leadership emerges on both sides and a kind of "postwar period" is in effect.

Such a postwar period was seen at air lines in Pakistan and Vietnam. One ingredient in these situations was a well recognized means for handling grievances and working out differences, which had finally become established and routinized over the years. Remnants of bitterness and distrust flared up, but patterns and precedents for resolving conflicts were now available. At Atul Chemical in India, an indigenous company, the conflict-resolving process had been maturing to the extent that, while there continued to be differences of opinion and minor squabbles, there were legitimate outlets for the highly charged feelings of discontent and protest that carried over from the battle period of the not too distant past.

In this stage neither party wishes to go back to the period of open use of power with long strikes and bitter relationships. Lessons have been learned and mechanisms established for dealing with grievances and differences.

Industrial peace

The fifth stage is marked by mature and responsible industrial and union leaders who may be militant but recognize that they must live with both the employees and management. They are skilled in negotiating; they are wise enough to anticipate the outcome and implications of their actions. The managers are more en-lightened in their attitudes toward the workers and toward the unions. They recognize the necessity for dealing with individual union leaders on a personal basis; they accept the feelings of the workers and their needs for representation; they avoid creating unnecessary issues. Neither party is regularly motivated by fear of survival of their rights. Ideological conflict is at an end.

EASING THE TRANSITIONS IN LABOR RELATIONS

Study of labor relations in developing economies indicates that sub-stantial changes in labor-management relations take place more rap-idly than in more industrialized economies. In some countries changes that have required 40 years in industrialized nations have taken place in about 15 years. Rapid change appears inevitable.

But the evidence suggests that the characteristics of each stage may be either more or less extreme in their effects and that not all the stages just described are inevitable. Some companies have been able to make the transition far better than others. The battle stage, for example, has been avoided in many companies.

What factors reduce the painfulness of the process of moving from the family stage, step-by-step, to industrial peace? Based on re-search done for this book, we suggest that certain approaches and attitudes on the part of management can ease the transition through the various stages of labor relations.

Human relations on the factory floor

The development of supervisors who are able to meet the per-sonal needs of the workers can go a long way toward building sound labor relations. As pointed out earlier,[23] this is particularly difficult in the developing economies, where social differences be-tween the supervisor and the worker will probably result in a less than genuine consideration for the worker's welfare on the part of the supervisor. The tendency on the part of the management to del-egate little responsibility to the first-line supervision adversely af-fected the development of moderate labor relations and heightened

---

[23] See the Supervision section in Chapter 3 of this book.

the stresses inherent in the adjustment to industrial life, giving rise to strong protests by the workers against the company.

Management sensitivity for the workers' changing feelings and needs

Paternalism is difficult to avoid and, indeed, may be desirable in certain cultures and underdeveloped areas. The workers' lack of education and skills, their lack of union and political strength, their needs for company security to replace tribal, village, or family security all contribute to a genuine need for company protection.

In the beginning the workers appear to appreciate family style, security, and paternalism. But after the first few years of life in the city and in the factory, as seen in many plants in Turkey and India, their needs for company paternalism appeared to decrease. As their adjustment progressed they showed a desire for more independence and began to protest indirectly against paternalistic treatment. But many companies did not seem to be sensitive to the fact that the workers' feelings and needs had changed and that their accustomed methods, supervision, rules, and fringe benefits were no longer fully appropriate.

Richard D. Robinson notes:

I venture the thought that one of the fundamental problems related to accelerated development in the underdeveloped areas is that involved in the shift from paternalistic administration in industry and agriculture to a more equalitarian type of management. . . . Many of the more thoughtful industrialists in Turkey are aware of the transition that is upon them, but since it means a break with traditional relationships, they are at a loss to know how to proceed. . . . The substitution of state for private paternalism in industry, particularly in the absence of any deeply-rooted individualistic or liberal tradition, might well result in delaying any movement away from industrial paternalism.

The transitional step from paternalism to liberalism in Turkish industry, it seems to me, may be . . . founded on the best features of paternalistic administration, which recognizes the need for and provides the incentive and opportunity for labor to mature in terms of responsibility and independence. In the absence of such an intermediate stop, labor-management relations in Turkey may degenerate either into regimentation or near anarchy.[24]

[24]Richard D. Robinson, "The Problems of Paternalism in Turkish Industry," Harvard Business School case, p. 21.

Firm and consistent bargaining practices

At several companies managers were upset, bewildered, and resentful over workers' apparent "ungratefulness." "They've never been better off and they don't seem to appreciate it. They ask for more and don't turn out as much work as they used to." Companies which made it clear from the start that they would not give in to strikes or allow contract violators to go unpunished or allow workers to make management decisions on process, methods, or equipment developed a clear set of norms which prevented conflicts over power vacuums. Those companies that used power firmly and consistently but with a readiness to bargain and negotiate on wages, benefits, and working conditions experienced a smoother transition through the various stages of labor relations than those that did not. In the two examples cited from India both companies vacillated in their positions on what was open to negotiation and even tolerated wildcat strikes at times in order to achieve cooperation. The companies that used firm and consistent policies in bargaining were not only able to gain strong positions but developed fewer crises and appeared to be passing more easily through the skirmishing stage toward industrial peace.

A regular structure for handling grievances

Managers in several companies agreed with this statement by a local personnel manager who said, "By law, we have a worker committee. But in actuality this group means very little. We do not have to recognize it or deal with it in any way." This was usually a mistake. The inevitable worker complaints had to find an outlet or the workers felt helpless in the hands of the management and, eventually, the battle started. Those companies that accepted grievances as normal and inevitable and set up some administrative machinery to handle them allowed a legitimate outlet for workers' feelings of a need for a voice in their own lives.

Company recognition of inevitability of an individual group protest against factory life

Some companies allowed for the working out of complaints and protests in their supervisory process. They did not indulge in moralizing that the workers were "ungrateful" or fear that they were attempting to gain control.

This enlightened attitude is not easy to acquire. One major difficulty is that such a large portion of the daily industrial relations and personnel management must be delegated to local nationals. Many local nationals, extra sensitive to class differences, showed fear of a labor takeover. They were fighting the union and worker representatives over principles. Foreign nationals interviewed in many areas were 20 to 30 years behind the thinking in this country on industrial relations. Whereas most managers in industrialized economies have learned to accept unions as "here to stay" and use formalized negotiations and grievance procedures for the mutual advantage of the company and employees, many foreign managers still perceive the union in oversimplified, stylized terms. They are bitterly opposed to collective bargaining and see labor unions as threatening to take over management prerogatives; they often perceive union influence on the work force as interfering with a "healthy, close, family" relationship.

THE EXPORTABILITY OF THE AMERICAN SYSTEM OF INDUSTRIAL RELATIONS

Professor Charles Myers has pointed out that, although there is not a great deal of the American system of industrial relations that can be exported, the distinctive American contribution is in terms of managerial organization, personnel administration, and human relations. Our specific approaches in dealing with trade unions in this country are less applicable. The economic functions and objects of American unions are not necessarily relevant, although many features of American trade unions commend themselves to foreign trade unions. U.S. management has a potential contribution to make.

Our research confirms Professor Myers' conclusions. There is a great deal that can be exported in terms of the wisdom and know-how developed in this country in dealing with the workers both individually and collectively. This wisdom is in the form of attitudes and practices conducive to effective human relationships: supervisory practices and organized grievance procedures which promote healthy relationships because they provide outlets for feelings and the means for improving both working conditions and productivity.

It is surprising and intriguing that so few companies attempt to export their industrial know-how. In some companies the home office gets into the bargaining process at contract negotiation time. They attempt to advise the foreign subsidiary on what to insist on, what to give in on, when, and the approach to be used in bargaining. But these are exceptions and confined to bargaining. Generally very little influence or help from the home office was observed at any stage in the industrial relations process. When asked why this is so, the typical management answer at home and abroad is that "labor relations is a local problem and can only be handled locally."

In contrast, much could be exported by able and experienced personnel administration officers who could train supervisors and help the overseas management to develop a long-range point of view toward labor unions.

There have been a number of lessons learned in the labor relations area from the experience of companies abroad. The management which establishes good practices from the beginning creates a healthy labor relations environment. But differences in culture and dependence on foreign nationals tend to introduce difficulties in labor relations. The know-how acquired through stages of labor relations in this country is usually left unused. With a sense of perspective and a desire to be sensitive to workers' feelings it is possible to minimize difficulties and problems of adjustment as labor relations mature.

The managers involved in most of the plants abroad had a genuine problem in gaining a sense of perspective about labor relations. If managers recognized that both the environment and the labor relations process are changing and moving through different stages, they would take a longer-range point of view, find a broader perspective, and acquire a more moderate and enlightened outlook.

American production managers with more of a sense of history could not only be more effective themselves but could also help the foreign nationals understand the chronological development in labor relations. As one U.S. executive put it: "The condition of labor relations in Argentina, when I was down there six years ago, was strikingly similar to that in the United States back in the thirties. We have learned so much about labor relations since the thirties. Had I been able to see the parallels involved and to convince our men in Argentina of those similarities, we would have done a much better job of handling our labor relations in that country."

Daily issues are naturally absorbing to most managers. But daily events are often interpreted as threatening management prerogatives, control over the work force, and profits. Management attitudes toward industrial protest can affect ultimate productivity as well as alleviate strikes and conflict in labor relations. It requires a sense of perspective to know when to stand fast and when to give. Such vision could improve the labor relations in U.S. manufacturing subsidiaries abroad.

The conclusion that labor relations has not been as severe a problem as might have been anticipated must be modified by the recognition of the transitions and stages we have been discussing. The longer-range viewpoint can help a management to prepare during the family-style period for the inevitable skirmishes that are bound to come later. And during the skirmish period, a sense of stages can perhaps avoid the formation of battle lines.

The recognition of the time factors in these affairs can induce decisions that have the effect of a damping movement to moderate the inevitable stresses and strains as unions, managements, economies, and cultures mature.

5

THE CONTROL OF PRODUCTION

The foreign manufacturing operations of many American companies fail to reflect an awareness of the potential rewards of a purposefully organized set of controls of production. The typical pattern is one of relatively loose controls of costs, quality, and inventory, haphazardly derived. Weaknesses in this area of production management occur in the face of difficult and costly control problems overseas, which might have been expected to attract more management attention. The purpose of this chapter is to explore some of the more frequently observed control problems, to seek explanations for the phenomenon of inadequate attention, and to develop practical suggestions for improvements.

Controls of production answer the manager's question: "How are we doing compared to what we ought to be doing?" A standard must be determined and with this standard the controls take on meaning. A set of controls enables the manager to judge the performance of the plant against some predetermined value and to take corrective action when deviations indicate it may be necessary. Controls thus become the basis of a system that serves to guide and rate operations against a rational plan.

What needs to be controlled? In typical manufacturing systems the important ingredients are: quality, labor productivity, costs, inventories, and time. (Time refers to controls that aid the company make optimum use of its machinery and equipment and other resources, to provide good customer promise dates, and to meet those delivery dates.)

Vague or imprecise standards were more typical than not in the plants visited. In many plants abroad, the productivity of direct labor was judged by history: "The crew produced as much last month as the month before"; the control of cost was often measured by gross statements of profit or loss; quality was measured by the number of customer complaints and/or a cursory inspection at the shipping-room door; and inventories were measured by stock-outs or home office complaints about excessive investment. The effectiveness of scheduling was gauged by the number of idle machines, stock-outs of finished goods, and customers delayed. Corrective action on all these counts frequently took the form of management edicts to "tighten up," but there was little emphasis on systems analysis or development.

There were exceptions to these generalizations. Few companies were excessively casual in all these areas. Nevertheless, these observations suggest that the payoff in improved controls of production was potentially greater than was commonly realized.

Lack of effective control systems abroad is surprising in some respects, because the costs of poor control abroad were often substantial, and better controls would not have been costly in proportion. For example, in underdeveloped locations equipment is generally imported and hence is expensive, with resulting significant capacity limitations. Therefore scheduling and controls designed to get the most out of equipment would appear to be desirable.

Many overseas plants operated in economic environments that were unfavorable compared to domestic facilities. For example, working capital was often scarce and the rate of interest high by U.S. standards. We might have expected in such situations that inventory control would be given a high priority in order to obtain the maximum use of the firm's investment in inventory. Lead times for both imported and domestically purchased items were generally longer abroad. It would also have been reasonable to expect that production planning had been conceptualized to cut down lead-times and avoid internal stock-outs in every way possible, and that such practices were emphasized.

Often, too, the size of the production unit abroad is economically marginal. It might be anticipated that every possible cost control would be employed to insure maximum productivity from direct labor and equipment. The economic cycles in many countries tend to be more frequent and of greater amplitude than in the United States. Under these conditions forecasting and planning would be expected to require more care and analysis rather than less.

In the face of such environmentally derived problems and the high penalty costs of poor control, it was surprising to find controls of production in U.S. manufacturing subsidiaries abroad so casual and ineffective.

It is important to try to understand the reasons for this phenomenon, for identifying the causes may lead to solutions. In so doing we should be careful not to judge the overseas operations improperly by using the standards of more advanced industrial practice. To portray the problems encountered in the various areas where some degree of control is needed, each control area will be discussed separately.

DIRECT LABOR PRODUCTIVITY

Low productivity of direct labor was generally accepted. With a wry face and a shrug of the shoulders plant managers would state "we recognize that our productivity here is substantially lower than that in the United States. A technician from England working at a plant in Spain stated that "our plant efficiency here is very poor by almost any standards."

Observation of the pace of the workers revealed a generally slow tempo. At three of the plants visited, the work had gone at a slow pace for years until rising demand and limited capacity forced a higher output per person. Then by minor changes and general insistence the management was able to nearly double production per worker. This phenomenon of increasing the productivity when forced by necessity was observed in Pakistan, India, Nigeria, and Spain. The increase in production at these facilities was a fine achievement, but it revealed that the managers had not carefully analyzed how much production could be achieved per worker.

Lack of information about labor productivity was not confined to small plants in underdeveloped countries. At a major plant in South Africa, the management's only method of judging labor productivity was by comparing job cards from one lot to the next, the runs often being six to twelve months apart.

Much of the problem of poor control is due to the lack of standards. Any control system is based on a judgment of what is happening as compared to what ought to be happening. If there is no rational analysis to provide some standards, actual performance cannot be realistically evaluated.

The frequent answer to the question "do you have labor standards, and if so, how are they derived?" was "our standards are rather informal, but we get adequate control by comparisons with the past."

At a pharmaceutical plant in Pakistan, the plant manager said, "Our standards are based on the past, but we do get improvements. In packing we used to get an occasional maximum of 3500 units per day per employee and now we get up to 4500." When asked how this was accomplished, he replied, "By an occasional review of the worker's motions and methods and by suggestions to the operators about how to improve their methods of work. Productivity is strictly my worry and I continually push my superintendent for better results. But the superintendent does not spend time on analyzing productivity. He does not have the training."[1] In spite of the plant manager's optimism, productivity in this plant was patently low.

At another plant in Pakistan the manager stated that "We have no standards now, but after the assembly operation settles down, we will attempt to study it and balance it." He hoped that the foreman would be able to do this, but he said, "I doubt that he will; he doesn't have the right background; he has a government background." The parts this plant was producing had previously been made in Germany. The machinery, tools, and equipment had been transferred intact from Germany. The plant manager was asked whether they had obtained the production standards and records from the German plant. The answer was negative.

Some companies did attempt to transplant labor standards from one country to another. Generally this raised more questions than it solved. Although it gave some idea of what might be produced, there was generally much local resistance to the standards because they were not completely applicable and the conditions were so divergent. They were looked upon skeptically from top management on down. All concerned workers stated that the lengths of the prior runs were different, the tools were somewhat different, the equipment had been changed, the climate was different, the standard data did not include setups, or something similar.

These reasons are valid. Standards cannot be transplanted from one set of conditions to the next and then interpreted literally. But this misses the point. Because transplanted standards cannot be applied literally does not mean that the job definition, methods, and industrial engineering approaches used in their derivation are not

---

[1]The superintendent held a doctorate in engineering but had had little prior management experience.

useful as a starting point elsewhere. The standard can serve as a useful comparison. Several companies with large international operations compare standards from a variety of locations to provide insights in the foreign location to evaluate results. This gives the manager at least a starting place for deriving his own standards.

Few time study men or industrial engineering departments or functions were encountered in the researcher's sample. This was true even in some of the larger plants and in the more advanced countries. The notion of time study or industrial engineering is considered to be "advanced" and is generally postponed until "later."

A partial explanation is that direct labor is often viewed as cheap and fixed. In all of the plants visited in Turkey this was the contention. The management and the supervisors reasoned that it took a long time to train a worker and his skills should not be cast away in a layoff. In addition, there were often social and legal pressures emphasizing a company's obligation to its employees. For this reason layoffs were uncommon. At a plant in India the manager stated that "labor and overhead are fixed, so it is important that we increase our sales."

Low labor rates combined with the high cost of materials and a steeply graded salary schedule (which compensated the more educated and trained indirect labor force far more than the direct labor workers) generally resulted in a low percentage of direct labor to total cost. Direct labor costs of 2 to 7 percent of sales were typical in many industries. For this reason direct labor was seldom regarded as a key element of cost.

This conclusion is misleading even when direct labor itself is a small fraction of total cost. For direct labor productivity affects the production of the entire plant. With a given investment in inventory, facilities, and equipment, a production increase brought about by increased labor productivity with unchanged investment has a dynamic leverage.[2]

Often fringe benefits were as much as 50 to 60 percent of direct labor and this, too, meant heavier total costs, which were not reflected directly in direct labor cost. In the early years of a new plant's operations loose controls set precedents of acceptable productivity that were difficult to shake.

In many plants the low direct labor productivity could be attrib-

[2]This assumes the existence of an unsatisfied market, a condition prevalent for most of the plants visited.

uted to poor supervisors rather than the lack of standards or other factors such as old equipment or simple tooling. At a farm implement plant in Turkey the American production manager said, "Our biggest problem is in the supervision. They tend to stay in their offices and they are not out on the work floor. Whenever a worker is stopped for any reason whatsoever, he may lose an hour or two before the supervisor realizes it and cures the problem." At a large plant in South Africa (where white European workers had a large choice of jobs on the market), the production manager admitted that "Our productivity is off now and the only answer is better supervision."

Supervision is indeed a major element in achieving direct labor productivity in most operations. But in few plants was the supervisor given production standards to let him know what was expected and reasonable in the output of his crew. Occasionally management edicts were given to produce more, but in the absence of any systematic analysis the supervisor nearly always stated, "My people worked hard." And as long as the manager could not detect any flagrant loafing, it was difficult for him to apply pressure.

The interconnection between the efficiency of the total plant and direct labor productivity was seldom realized. One young, enterprising production manager in South Africa recognized this interrelationship; he made a systematic analysis of the lot sizes he was running and determined where they could be increased. But the concept of economic order quantity has, for the most part, remained within the United States. At a modern plant in Spain the researcher observed that some departments were virtually idle, whereas other departments were obviously overloaded. The guide stated: "This is a real problem. The work-load seems to move through the plant like a frog which has been swallowed by a snake." Workers learn the army term "hurry up and wait" in any language.

An effective system of cost control may help to obtain control over direct labor productivity. Professor G. G. Mueller states that the problems abroad are especially in financial accounting and not with "management accounting."[3] He makes the point that he generally finds relatively good systems of management accounting and control abroad. The author's findings contradict this conclusion. The system of management controls at the farm implement plant in Turkey, for example, was by no means unusual. In this plant the cost

[3]G. G. Mueller, "The Dimensions of the International Accounting Problem," *Accounting Review* (January 1963).

emphasis was almost entirely on "overabsorbed or underabsorbed overhead." The production manager stated that the accounting system was almost useless to him in determining what kind of a job was being done in the factory. And at a plant in India, the production manager stated "Oh yes, we have variances here. We revise them yearly in order to keep them less than 1 percent." In this case the standard costing system was better than its use. This was also true at a large and technically modern plant in South Africa. The accounting system was full of information, but it was being generated by accountants and ignored by managers.

Dudley E. Browne states that financial reporting differs between foreign firms and the U.S. in a number of respects, one of which is that the U.S. management prefers forecasted data to historical data for management planning and control.[4] This typical emphasis on the use of historical data is confirmed by our research. Often accounting data were based on accounting standards, reflecting only what had occurred in the past.

This story would not be complete without emphasing what some companies have accomplished in the area of direct labor productivity; for example, at a food processing plant in India, the managing director himself was extremely interested in direct labor productivity. His plant reflected this concern. He visited the plant every morning. The total workers in the plant had been cut back over a period of four years from 250 to 93 with production held at the same level. On one occasion when the managing director was dissatisfied about a production rate, he went out in the factory with his watch and timed a job and proved that it could be done much faster. Although this company relied on historical data for the most part, it also had a direct labor report which showed the output of each operation on a daily basis. This was an unusual device. In many plants there were no direct labor controls other than weekly or monthly outputs for a total department.

Some international firms, as previously mentioned, have an apparently effective system of worldwide reports and comparisons. Their systems do not imply that each of their plants should have an equally good productivity index, but home office personnel and the top management at each of the various overseas plants are made aware of how their performance compares to other worldwide plants. General Electric uses its standards carefully to compare plant productivity

[4]Dudley E. Browne, "Differences between U.S. and Foreign Reporting," *Financial Executive* (January 1963).

and then analyze the plant's operation to ascertain whether the reasons for the variance are justified. Some firms maintain these records in the home office but do not use them abroad. This is probably a mistake, based on the illusion that operations can be controlled from the home office.

The accomplishments of some plants in analyzing and improving direct labor productivity implies that other plants could do the same, and that there are in fact very few situations in which standards to measure by are neither possible nor practical.

THE CONTROL OF QUALITY

Although many plant managers freely admitted ignoring their dissatisfactions with direct labor productivity, such a fatalistic attitude toward quality was seldom encountered. Far more typical was the statement "We are an American plant. The reputation of our company is important. We are expected to produce consistently high quality products. Our products have much better quality than locally produced items." By and large, therefore, the management attempted to do a good job in quality control.

Most American companies operating abroad appeared to accomplish far more in managing quality control than their indigenous competitors. The products were engineered, designed, and specified rigidly to aim for high quality. Most companies had a system of final inspection which appeared to act as a reasonably tight sieve to catch substandard items before they could be shipped.

There were nevertheless a considerable number of problems in managing the quality control function. The intent was usually good, but loopholes in the quality control system often left much to be desired. Symptoms of this were noted not only in defective products but also in high cost of scrap and rework, and there was an erratic emphasis on quality throughout the factory.

Much of the problem lies in the execution of day to day quality control activities. Neither top management nor inspectors can themselves create good quality. It must be accomplished by the workers, by the vendors, by the product designers, by the toolmakers, and by the maintenance men. First-line supervision and middle managers are the only ones who can observe the hour-by-hour practices in the plant and correct them in time to prevent poor quality. Weaknesses in supervision and middle management caused quality problems for the top managements.

Quality controls were frequently informal and casual. For example, at a plant in Pakistan there was only casual inspection of the parts being made for the mechanical device being produced. Instead, formal inspection was performed at the final check of the completed assembly. At this point it was often found that parts would not fit together. Filing and handwork were sometimes necessary to avoid parts interferences and allow the machine to function.

At a vehicle assembly plant in Turkey the hood of a large truck would not close properly. A worker lifted a hammer and smashed down at the catch four or five times, paint chips scattering, until it finally closed. Then he turned to the researcher and said with a grin, "That's the Turkish way." The truck left the plant ten minutes later. At a pharmaceutical plant in Africa a worker was observed to spill several hundred tablets on the floor and then pick them up and put them back in the bottle. The industrial laboratories of many plants were dirty and the data sheets messy and poorly organized, a contributing factor to poor quality.

Part of the difficulty may be traced to improper product specifications. In some cases, specifications were unnecessarily rigid. Very often the specification was not changed from one country to another. The specification in the blueprint for the shape and size of an auto bumper, for example, would be transferred intact from Detroit. Seldom, if ever, were products redesigned to fit the local consumer or, even more important, to be more producible in terms of the tools, the workers, and the equipment in the country. William Edelberg points out that in many instances it would make more sense for a product to be extensively redesigned for foreign application.[5] This does not necessarily hold for products such as pharmaceuticals and cornmeal, but Goodyear has found it quite desirable to design tires for divergent conditions in various parts of the world. For many years it was felt that a single, high standard should be held throughout the world. More recently the company has set up industrial design facilities in Europe where tires are designed with specific qualities for different uses.

This is an area of management multinational corporations are only beginning to explore. Not only do markets and uses for a product vary considerably from one country to the next, but so do equipment, tools, and worker skills. There is much emphasis in the

[5]William Edelberg, "The Procurement Practices of the Mexican Affiliates of Selected U.S. Automobile Firms," unpublished doctoral thesis. Harvard Business School, March 1963.

United States on manufacturing engineering work aimed at making products more producible. But abroad there is typically less concern with producibility. The typical home office view is that the overseas plant is expected to meet "our product specifications."

Adjustment to environment is often important in product design and appearance. For example, colors have various connotations in different countries. Singer managers found that the decorations of their sewing machines were important; in Nigeria the company had an inventory of hundreds of machines with a decal that made them unsalable.

There were many problems in importing components of adequate quality. A truck firm in Turkey had four years of frustration and difficulty because the truck was not in production in the United States. The parts procured for use in Turkey would not fit. The vendors had changed designs slightly and there had been no home office effort to coordinate the design changes. A company in Pakistan importing parts from Germany found that sometimes these parts would not fit together. There was evidence in another situation that the Pakistani company had been sent "off-quality" parts, which could not be used in the European country and hence were sent to Asia.

Repeatedly the production managers of remote plants stated that they had trouble with the quality of shipments from home offices. Often, for example, CKD[6] vehicle kits were incomplete, had the wrong parts, or had excess quantities of some parts. Imports of items from Europe were frequently troublesome to an auto assembler in South Africa. The quality of mufflers and shock absorbers was not up to their usual standards. "The samples which they send us are fine, but the actual production items must be measured, checked, sorted, and then are often rejected." In many developing countries the government required that the company use local sources, although local plants were sometimes unable to produce the quality demanded.

These repeated examples of problems in importing and local procurement might have been detected by tight systems of receiving inspection. However, in many plants there was no receiving inspection department. The poor quality of purchased items often was not discovered until the items came out on the plant floor. Scrap and rework were the result.

Process control often proved difficult abroad. At a tire plant, the

[6]Completely Knocked Down.

production manager stated that "Trouble can hit very fast. We had a tremendous number of rejects which started to come back a number of months ago and we had to pull back the production of a month's work here because the tread cooling water had developed the wrong pH and tread separation was the result." Many of the process problems were the apparent result of an emphasis on inspection at the end of the line rather than inspection of individual parts or close enough control of individual processes.

Total quality control of an entire process seems to be a more advanced concept than is understood and emphasized at most plants in developing economies. Quality control as an entire interlocking system is not understood. Instead, "Quality Control" is much more apt to be seen as "good inspection." In many plants the quality control function was organized to report to the superintendent or sometimes to someone at a lower level. At a plant in South Africa quality control reported to the technical manager.

Lack of organizational emphasis on quality control reflected a certain smugness. Profit margins and product acceptance were typically great enough so that management felt no need to reduce rejects in an attempt to reduce the cost of obtaining quality. These factors diminished the organizational stature of quality control. But the increasing competition of industrial growth results in increasing pressure on sales and profits for almost every company. For this reason, increased middle management attention on achieving quality at lower cost and increased top management attention on total systems for quality control may be required in the future at many overseas plants.

PRODUCTION PLANNING, AND CONTROL

The controls of production involve the planning and scheduling of the plant operations in order to produce the right product at the right time, to promote a smooth flow of material throughout the plant, and to balance work loads. The use of inventory to obtain smooth flow and lower cost is counterbalanced by the cost of inventory. Effective inventory planning is important in its impact on the cost of operation.

Problems and accomplishments in production planning and control can be divided into five categories: (a) overall plant programming; (b) internal scheduling of machinery and equipment; (c) start-ups and handling of new products; (d) production control organization; (e) inventory control.

Overall plant programming

Over the long range a plant must have the necessary capacity to meet the demands of the market. Over the short range a plant must produce the correct amount of products in order to avoid finished goods stock-outs, distribution complaints, or excessive inventory.

Often the requisite sales forecasting is particularly difficult abroad. Company after company told of its difficulties in getting a good sales forecast. Forecasting was especially difficult for the Americans involved because of their limited understanding of the economy. Furthermore, in the developing economies economic swings seem to be more violent and less predictable (at least to nonspecialists) than they are in the United States. Government policies are sometimes less forecastable. Part of the problem is that customers seldom do much forecasting, so it is difficult for them to predict their needs. At a plant in South Africa, for instance, it was stated that one of the company's major customers, a vehicle manufacturer, had given the plant 48 changes in schedule over the last two weeks.

Marketing men frequently complained about their factories. One pharmaceutical manufacturer in Pakistan admitted that there was seldom a day when the factory was not out of stock on at least 5 percent of the items on the company's product list. At the same time, factory managers often made statements such as "Our marketing people are utterly inept at forecasting." At a number of different plants the production men stated that they were constantly forced to "second guess" the forecast supplied them.

Long-range planning is discussed in more detail in a later chapter, but it is appropriate to note here that four different plants among those visited had run into major problems of inadequate capacity due to the growth of the market, for which they had not prepared in time. The home office manager of one large plant complained sadly, "Our boys over there have really gotten caught shorthanded." Long-range planning was apt to be very casual and in many cases nonexistent. In some cases the market had been badly overrated in the beginning and, because the plants were oversized for many years, no organization had been established for looking ahead to measure capacity against the future market.

Internal scheduling

Uneven work flow, overloaded machines, and idle capacity were observed in plants in every country visited. A typical example was one large pharmaceutical manufacturer in Spain which had no system whatsoever for planning the work load for each department. Plants tended to be loaded (if any thought was given to the process) around certain pieces of bottleneck equipment. Idle time and overloads ricocheted from department to department. The concepts of setup time and downtime were foreign to many operations. In the pharmaceutical business, for example, batch sizes were usually determined by the home office. The overseas plant could choose which of a variety of batch recipes came closest to meeting its equipment and market needs. But relatively little thought was given to determing the batch sizes that were best from the standpoint of local setup costs versus local inventory carrying costs. In no case was an economic order quantity model used.

The inherent complexity of internal scheduling apparently caused many problems. Some plants had attempted to establish machine loading charts and rather complex boards. At one plant in South Africa they here humoring a rather new assistant foreman who was attempting to set up such a board. The foreman stated that they had tried that sort of thing before and it was not really necessary, but the assistant foreman was nevertheless working away at an elaborate board system.

At another plant in South Africa, however, the problem was becoming major, as the nature of the business gradually shifted from a completely industrial product to a mixture of industrial and consumer products. The planning of package sizes and the stocking of different brands was becoming difficult. No effective system had been evolved for this and, indeed, there was no one in the organization who seemed skilled or concerned with this type of thinking. Packaging machine setups were being torn down after a few hours in order to get out telegraphed rush orders from a variety of customers. There was no analysis of the cost of setup time or the establishment of minimum length of run. There was no good system for forecasting and pooling orders and setting up minimum inventory requirements. The nature of the business was changing, but the organization had not yet matched it.

Start-ups and new products

This was a difficult area of production control, perhaps because of its nonroutine nature. At a large new plant in Pakistan the sales department had planned on initial production for July. When the firm cut off importing completed devices, they had a two month safety stock. But by September the first units had not yet been turned out of the new plant. Initial production was expected, however, in the calendar week in which the researcher was visiting the plant. He went out to the final assembly department on a Thursday to check on the progress. It was difficult to determine when the first unit would be produced, for the parts were not fitting together well. It became clear after a short time that no production would be forthcoming until the following week. In the meantime the production control manager and the production manager were poring over various sheets of inventory records, unaware of the actual problem on the floor. They continued all day Thursday and most of Friday to expect to ship the first devices in that same week.

Problems in start-ups are much more likely to seen as "bugs" or difficulties in the parts and assemblies than as caused by inadequate paper work, records, or planning. In some start-ups obtaining the right amount of initial production volume was elusive. In many plants the production was much too low during the first year. The opposite was the case in a pharmaceutical plant in Pakistan which started our producing on the basis of a year's forecast. After six months they suddenly realized they had approximately one year's stock ahead of actual requirements.

At a farm implement plant in Turkey the management was attempting to introduce ten new products at the same time after having introduced only one product a year during the past five years. There was no organizational method for emphasizing the process of ironing out the difficulties attending new products. It was clear that no one person was following any one product. The new products floundered. Some were never completed and others were years late. At an industrial product manufacturer, however, where every new job is essentially a new product, the handling of this function was excellent. The company was organized around new products with a technical manager working out the details of each one and the production control system centered around each new job.

The production control organization

By and large production control was handled by the line organization without a specially focused group set up to handle it. At a plant in Turkey, for example, production control was handled by the sales manager, who also was in charge of procurement. Many plants had no production control manager or the equivalent, at any level. Some plants followed the conventional practice of considering production control as a department reporting to the production manager; but in many plants, particularly small ones, the production control function was simply an additional duty of an overloaded manager. He had the job of deciding what the plant should make and being sure that the necessary raw materials were on hand and that the plant produced what was required. Frequently his duties were merged with those of sales, procurement, and traffic. There were sometimes expeditors, but in most cases the line foreman was in charge of meeting his schedule, and the schedule was determined by the sales department in terms of end items. It was up to the foreman to produce in time the various parts he felt were necessary for the end items.

This lack of formal organization was evident in many of the small pharmaceutical plants visited, where the production manager himself sat down four or five times a year and established some ideas of the amount of production that would be needed and then determined the raw materials necessary. This was often adequate, but the same informal approach was not adequate in mechanical, metalworking, or vehicle manufacturing plants. In these instances problems of internal scheduling often occupied up to half of the production manager's time.

A growing need for production control was observed at a number of factories which had never emphasized it. For example, at one plant in Spain they had developed a new department, the "Coordination Department." This department was to be in charge of the overall schedules for the plant, the internal scheduling in each department, and the movement of materials between each department. A realization of the need for this function led to a four months' search of the country for a good man to handle it. The search was fruitless, and finally a middle-aged man who had been in charge of the company's warehouse was placed in charge of this function. The apparent nationwide lack of trained middle management able and equipped to handle this function seemed symptomatic of the fact that organization for handling production control was an uncommon procedure rather than an elementary, critical requirement.

The emphasis in one larger company on production, planning, inventory control, and procurement as a total function is rare and appeared commendable. They always separated the entire materials section from the plant. Their organization was something like the army G-3 in which the service of supply is a separate command. When a new plant is set up, the "General Merchandise and Material Control Division" (GM & MC) is staffed in strength sufficient to do an adequate job from the beginning. Usually Americans are sent abroad to man it until local people can be trained. An emphasis on smooth flow of materials and adequate internal scheduling is carried out by schedules on the work floor which are under the responsibility of the GM & MC manager.

Perhaps this organizational emphasis at this firm is derived from the heavy cost of its process equipment and the necessity for getting the most out of it. But at a large pharmaceutical plant in India where the equipment was vastly overloaded and the company was on three shifts and weekends, every ounce of production through bottlenecked equipment was important; yet this company did virtually no internal scheduling or analysis of setup time and downtime, and it had no production control organization as such. In contrast, a food processor in Spain, where equipment utilization was also the key to cost control, had reduced downtime over a two year period from 30 to 8 percent. This was done by careful planning, scheduling, and maintenance work and employee bonuses based on reduced downtime.

Three firms organized the entire area of materials as one department separate from the production organization as such. For instance, a pharmaceutical operation in India had the overall plant scheduling, raw material procurement, and warehousing-shipping-materials functions removed from the production plant and operated out of the Bombay office some 200 miles distant. The plant retained only the responsibility for its internal scheduling, which was a minor problem.

At a vehicle assembly plant in Turkey an American stated that "Paperwork has no place in a plant in an underdeveloped country. The men in the plant are not used to handling paperwork and inventory problems. It is much better to let this work be done at the office." The office was an adjunct of the sales and accounting department functions. An office manager was in charge of scheduling the plant and procuring the necessary parts, materials, tools, and so forth. The plant simply placed requisitions with the manager for items it needed, and the office manager was expected to keep the plant fully supplied. The purchasing functions were under his direction and, being closer to the sales and distribution centers, he was able to meet the needs of the plant better than a group located at the plant 30 miles away in the countryside.

There is much to say for this organization under certain conditions. An independent production control organization makes sense when several of the following factors are present:

1. The *internal* scheduling requirements of the plant are not complex and can be handled by the line organization.

2. The plant is physically remote from sales and sources of supply.

3. There is a heavy emphasis on purchased raw materials and parts.

4. The raw materials and parts can be relatively standardized.

5. The cultural and industrial background tends to produce a scarcity of trained and educated managers who are willing to work in the factory itself.

6. There are continuing problems involved in paperwork with the government for import permits, licenses, and the like.

7. The weight and flow of material is such that transportation costs are substantial.

The specialized attention that can be given to the material function under this type of organization is a substantial advantage. Experience has been that the production control function is often not given sufficient emphasis in the factory-based organizations. Under these conditions it is wise, as one American stated, to "Let the factory make the product and someone in a separate location keep track of it."

Inventory control

Inventories at the overseas plants generally had a ratchetlike effect: they kept inching up to provide additional safety and buffering action. Seldom was the cost of inventory given serious attention.

Inventories have an important function in factory operation. Raw material and parts inventories serve as safety stocks in the event of an uncertain supply. An inventory allows the company to buy in larger quantities. Similarly, at the end of the line, a finished goods inventory may allow the factory to stabilize its operations as sales demand fluctuates; it allows the factory to produce in advance of sales by providing for the uncertainties and difficulties of the market forecast. Work-in-process inventories between operations permit each operation to proceed on a larger order quantity, and they allow for less than perfect scheduling between operations, permitting a more continuous use of operator and machine time in spite of a variation in the flow of materials.

The necessity and advantages of inventory are perhaps obvious. Indeed, abroad, where there is often a high degree of uncertainty in sales forecasting in combination with growing sales, there is generally a tendency to produce well ahead of customer needs. Similarly, when there are difficulties in obtaining raw materials and purchased parts, there is pressure for providing a large safety stock in advance of actual needs. And where accurate scheduling is hampered by lack of personnel who are able to handle the intricacies of scheduling (and even a dearth of employees who can count inventories accurately), there is usually a tendency to produce in larger quantities and to have larger banks of parts between operations. Hence a larger work-in-process inventory is often considered necessary, relative to domestic operations.

But inventories have costs as well as advantages. The first cost is the capital necessary to pay for the inventory in advance of its actual use. Second, there may be a certain amount of scrap, obsolescence, and deterioration of those raw materials, parts, and finished goods produced or procured before they are actually needed. Parts rust, designs change, and items get lost. In addition, there is a storage materials handling problem and a need to keep track of the inventory, all of which result in both materials handling and clerical costs. The combination of these factors results in a total annual cost of inventory which usually runs anywhere from 10 to 50 percent of the value of the inventory.

These ABC's of the use of inventory and the cost of inventory are seldom articulated in developing economies and often do not seem to be understood. Inventory costs generally receive less attention than concern over too little inventory.

The reasons for this are not difficult to perceive. After each sour experience of running out of an item the tendency is for the general manager to say, "Let's carry an extra month's supply. It is cheap compared to the cost of running out." In four of the plants visited such a decision had been made within the past month on raw materials or finished goods inventories. The emphasis was on safety.

It is difficult to deny the validity of the need for larger safety stocks in many foreign operations. But in many instances the stocks were unnecessarily high because managers had been "burned" several times. There was a tendency to control the inventory by gross rules, that is, to establish a rule that the company would have five months' stock of *all* items, rather than focusing on those items which had caused difficulties and making specific rational decisions (on the basis of the cost and lead times of the different items involved). A wise young manager of a pharmaceutical plant in South Africa, with no help from the home office, made an analysis of all of his inventory items and determined (as is so often the case) that 80 percent of the cost of his inventories were in 10 percent of his 100 items and that if he devoted close attention to these 10 items he could cut his total inventory by nearly 50 percent. On the cheaper items it was not expensive to have a 12 months' supply and devote minor effort to their control.

Good inventory control takes this type of managing. It requires going into details and analyzing particular problems and taking specific steps to handle the particular categories, major parts, or raw materials groups separately. The tendency to lump all items into excessively broad classifications appeared to come from a lack of insight and attention on the inventory control function. In plant after plant the total inventory turnover was surprisingly low and few individuals seemed to be able to talk intelligently about particular items and particular causes of the low turnover.

It is surprising that the top management did not place additional attention on better use of capital. This is particularly so in the underdeveloped countries where the cost of interest sometimes ran between 1 and 2 percent a month. In nearly all of the multinational operations studied, capital tended to be in short supply; nevertheless, top management seemed to go along with the plant managers, who felt they needed large buffer stocks, and did not insist on analysis of the individual items that caused the problem.

CONTROL OF PRODUCTION: A LITTLE-RECOGNIZED AREA OF MANAGEMENT

It is important to try to understand why the control of production receives so little management emphasis and attention in many overseas plants. In the face of admitted low direct labor productivity and continual complaints of the sales department over stockouts, it is surprising indeed to find that the management placed so little emphasis on the various controls of production. The facts — long lead times, high cost of inventories, a long time to recover from work stoppages or stockouts, growing competition, shrinking profit margins — would indicate a payoff from better attention to details in the control of production.

Probably the most important reason for this lack of emphasis on control is that the production managers were not particularly trained or interested in production controls. Few foreign nationals in either middle or upper management have training in skills in quantitative methods of analysis.

Example 1

The production manager of a pharmaceutical plant in Pakistan is such an example. He had been told by the home office that production managers should keep track of production and he therefore attempted to keep track of his costs and inventories. But in response to the researcher's routine questions he had to look up figures to obtain answers. It became clear that he had no feel for numbers, in a cultural sense. When he guessed at certain data his guess was not even "in the ball park" by a proper decimal point. He had been required by his home office management to furnish certain figures for control purposes. He dutifully reported these to the home office, but in his own management of the plant he did not actually use this material. He was embarrassed with the researcher, recognizing that he should have known these figures better. A quantitative approach toward measuring direct labor productivity and the usefulness and reasonableness of his inventories was simply not a part of his ordinary, daily thinking.

Controls of production seem to require a certain degree of quantitative orientation in the middle management cadre. Costs cannot be "controlled" from top levels. A series of reports may be used at those levels, but only at the first level of supervision and middle management can actual changes be made which will ultimately result in lower costs and higher productivity. Similarly, in the control of quality only attention to those details affecting quality can result in achieving a proper level of quality of production. No top manager using even the finest statistical quality control system can actually improve the quality. Intelligent internal production scheduling must also be practiced by middle management personnel with an understanding of the various flows, measured in quantitative terms.

These skills are frequently lacking in overseas management, due to the fact that management as a profession is new abroad. Thus the thinking of managers in developing economies is more intuitive, with a paucity of abstract or conceptual understanding of the relationships between costs and the flows of material and factors affecting quality.

It is true, too, that often the men who have been sent abroad to manage plants have had to be relatively general in their background and in their abilities in order to handle the broader problems of overseas production. As pointed out in Chapter 1, the skills needed for successful operating in developing areas of the world tend to be more diverse than those needed on the domestic scene. The production manager abroad must deal with government, the problems of public relations, meeting sales requirements in a foreign economy, dealing with a foreign labor force, underdeveloped vendors, to mention only some of his responsibilities.

For this reason the more technically oriented production manager, firmly based in the quantitative analysis of cost control, quality control, and production control, is likely to be too narrow in his experience and competence to be selected for management at top levels abroad. Most companies abroad do not feel that they can afford American expertise in a production manager, quality manager, and cost control manager. These are generally considered middle-management jobs, which should be properly delegated to local foreign managers. But the local foreign managers usually do not have the background in industry or management education necessary for this work. Hence there is a management vacuum in many plants when it comes to the control of production.

Exceptions to these observations may point toward more fruitful approaches. Some pharmaceutical companies, paying critical attention to quality control, emphasize rigorous quantitative control throughout the entire business. Except for the example cited earlier of the pills on the floor, the evidence is that the pharmaceutical operations are quite rigorous in control of their quality. The same point of view is those companies—the emphasis on details, precision, and control—often tends to carry over into better systems of production control and cost control. However, the quality emphasis is often supplied from the home office and there is special training given for quality control. Thus this quality control skill does not necessarily help in cost control, production planning, and inventory control. Nevertheless, the quantitative point of view, the necessity for precise measuring, close inspection, and attention to a wide variety of details in running the production operation, tends to create an atmosphere conducive to better cost controls, better budgeting, better sales forecasting, and improved internal controls.

One firm's organizational emphasis on production and materials controls has been discussed earlier. Their focus on keeping expensive, scarce equipment continually producing and their organization for planning and inventory were evident in each of the plants visited. This firm has the philosophy that controls are important enough to export essentially the entire company system, along with an American to teach the system to foreign nationals. Little is left to chance; there are systems and procedures that are applied to each and every plant.

Part of this apparent applicability of common systems is due to the nature of tires and the fact that, by and large, tires are produced everywhere using the same general kind of equipment and processes. Therefore this firm's systems of controls and logistics are felt to be applicable regardless of location. They believe production controls have a major impact on the cost of making tires.

Finally, it was observed that in the more developed areas where there is a larger cadre of experienced, trained, and professional managers, there is usually an increased emphasis on production planning and control. This is partly due to the availability of men with the necessary interest and ability, but it also reflects the fact that there is great competition in these countries. Hence more careful quality control, cost control, and planning of the logistics function is required for short-run success than in the developing economies of the world.

The necessity for attending to details in operating a production plant becomes more obvious as an economy develops and competition increases. The trend in the developing areas toward increasing competition suggests that many companies must begin to place more emphasis on better controls.

Help from home office headquarters in the control of production will probably be rare, considering the value of this function and the absence of necessary skills on the part of overseas nationals. We saw one exception. The unified system of production used by the Otis Elevator Company is another example of the exported knowhow in this area of management. The use of a worldwide set of standards by General Electric is another instance of the beneficial results that can be obtained from exchanging information and control data.

Typically home office organizations offer too little help in this area. It is regarded as an area in which the local expertise must prevail; production control is typically seen as another "local problem which should be handled locally; the controls of production must be carried out by foreign nationals; it is too expensive to attempt to help them from the home office.

Most of these assumptions do not appear valid. Certainly, each country presents a somewhat unique problem in terms of forecasting the market, and each country may differ in terms of the licensing and bureaucracy which affect the importing of materials. But the point of view that operations can be measured, that a total systems concept of control and planning is necessary, and that it is important to measure and control the detail of flows and quantities and costs—this *point of view* can be exported and can be the basis for an intelligently worked-out local system of controls.

There is a further and often unrealized assumption that arises in discussing the controls of production with home office personnel. Home office executives frequently state that since overseas plants generally have a smaller and somewhat less complicated production process and fewer people, they are more manageable by one-man, intuitive control. Modern controls of production are thought to be unnecessarily and excessively sophisticated.

As one New York manager put it, "We certainly don't need the complicated paperwork system which we have in our stateside home plant out there in Bombay. The problem just isn't that complicated. And overhead costs are already too high. A good man out there can keep his finger on things without a lot of fancy numerical systems."

In fact, there is much evidence that conditions abroad often require expertise and management attention equivalent to domestic controls of production. When it takes six months to correct a mistake in an inventory count, when it is difficult to find people who can make a good count, when interest costs 1 to 2 percent a month, and it would require 2 years and an extremely expensive investment to increase limited production capacity—the conditions make it important to do a good job of controlling production costs and to schedule in order to make the maximum use of investment in inventory and equipment.

Sometimes the emphasis on controls is less than it might be because of the low cost of direct labor. The New York manager said, "We are only spending 5 percent of our cost on direct labor so we certainly don't need to get as fussy as we would when we are dealing with the CIO teamsters back in the States." This assumption seems to make good sense at first, but it, too, can be misleading. For lack of industrial engineering and good methods and time study may be creating precedents regarding "normal" productivity which are going to be difficult to break in the future. This is particularly true as union strength increases abroad. Moreover, when labor itself is not costly, often the use of materials and equipment is expensive. Efficient labor must achieve a high usage of equipment and minimize the loss of raw material. Hence the fact that direct labor is relatively cheap usually has little bearing on the advantages of controlling productivity, scheduling work, and improving the quality of production.

What should be done? Home office insistence on good budgeting, planning, and control is certainly one place to start. Home office help in the form of visiting experts and suggested systems and approaches is a second way to seek improvement. And third, management training focus on this area is needed in many plants.

An emphasis on better controls of production, development of middle management to effectively achieve better controls, and recognition that there is a fruitful payoff in doing a better job in this area will bring about improvements over a period of time. To take a suggestion from Adam Smith, competition will help force needed improvements. But the production system can become a more successful competitive weapon if initiative is taken in advance of the pressures of competition to run a more controlled operation and if the home office supplies needed help.

6

PROCUREMENT FOR INTERNATIONAL MANUFACTURING PLANTS IN DEVELOPING ECONOMIES*

Research into the experiences of 13 U.S. firms operating plants in six developing nations confirmed the expectation that procurement would be an immediate and major source of difficulty. But a second set of conclusions came as a surprise, namely, that a significant fraction of the companies studied were strangely unprepared in this management area, adapted slowly to new conditions and problems, and that procurement difficulties persisted as a result.

The purpose of this chapter is to report the findings of a research project dealing with managing international manufacturing, as they bear on procurement. This recently completed work was based on visits to forty-nine plants in India, Pakistan, South Africa, Spain, Turkey and Vietnam. Twenty-four of these plants were subsidiaries of U.S. international corporations, the balance being indigenous operations. Products manufactured included pharmaceuticals, autos, trucks, tires, construction equipment, and consumer durables. Interviews were also conducted in the U.S. home offices of the companies. The study, made possible through the cooperation of these companies, was financed by the Harvard Business School's Division of Research.

The purpose of this work was to identify problems in production management encountered by U.S. firms manufacturing in develop-

*This chapter first appeared as an article in the *Journal of Purchasing*, February 1967. It is reproduced by permission. Vol. 3, Feb. 1967, p. 5-19. Copyright Feb. 1967 by National Association of Purchasing Agents, Inc. and reproduced here by permission.

ing economies abroad, to isolate apparent causes of problems and to suggest guidelines to managers for improved results and to researchers for future research needs.

The scope of the problem may be grasped when one considers the spectacular increase in the number of U.S. manufacturing facilities established in foreign countries over the past fifteen years: close to 2000 plants in the relatively underdeveloped nations of Asia, Africa, South and Central America, and of Spain, Greece and Turkey in Europe. In the five and one-half years between July 1960 and December 1965, 908 new manufacturing facilities were established by U.S. firms in these locations.[1]

Obtaining parts, materials and supplies of adequate quality, reasonable cost, and with reliable deliveries has been a persistent problem for managers of international operations. Procurement at the plants studied has proved to be an annoying nuisance at best, and at the worst, it has caused shutdowns of entire factories.

Since none of the plants visited was operating in a highly industrialized economy, of course the problems came as no surprise. But the almost universally slow rate of progress in overcoming procurement problems was unexpected. Development of effective purchasing organizations and competent vendors proceeded at a pace which was considered disappointing and unsatisfactory by nearly all the companies.

This article begins by reporting the specific procurement problems encountered and evaluating their impact. Findings as to the principal sources of these problems will then be presented. But a further question puzzles the analyst probing into the many indications of poor state of company preparedness for handling procurement in the developing economies and a slow rate of progress in correcting basic problems. Why was this so?

Several common yet fundamental errors in management approaches to procurement in underdeveloped areas are suggested in the third section of the article as being at the root of the problem. At the risk of overgeneralizing to make the point clear, the basic cause appears to be that U.S. businessmen often made assumptions from their past experience which, while appearing entirely reasonable at home, proved erroneous in underdeveloped locations.

It is apparently incorrect to assume that

1.   The behavior of the overseas vendors can be predicted from U.S. vendors' behavior, or that

---

[1] *66 Months (1960-1965) of New Foreign Business Activity of U.S. Firms*, Booz Allen & Hamilton, Inc. Management Research Department, 1966, New York.

2. Men who know the market best, that is, local nationals will be effective buyers, or that

3. Policies should always be established at headquarters and the details of procurement should always be delegated abroad.

All three assumptions are based on normal American business customs and attitudes, but every indication is that they all may lead to trouble in locations where economic and cultural conditions differ from the United States. A set of more realistic guidelines derived from more successful experiences in procurement abroad is suggested in the final section of the report.

PROCUREMENT PROBLEMS AND THEIR EFFECTS

The problems in importing differed from those in local purchasing. Since importing was often considered more desirable by company managements because it avoided the use of inexperienced local vendors, let us consider it first.

Problems in importing

In the developing economies nearly every U.S. subsidiary has had problems in obtaining foreign exchange. In a farm implement plant in Turkey, for example, the original investment had been made on the assumption that tractor parts could be imported from the United States. Indeed, the Turkish government had guaranteed the foreign exchange necessary for importing, a condition upon which the company insisted before it went into Turkey. As it turned out, however, the government was unable to honor its foreign exchange commitments to the company and for four years the company suffered from its inability to import tractor parts. As a result the plant came close to a shutdown and was able to survive only through taking subcontracts and developing simple, indigenous products.

This story is familiar to plant managers in other developing economies. When an economy's balance of trade is in difficulty it must usually limit imports. There is very little that a U.S. firm can do to increase its ration of foreign exchange other than maintain a harmonious relationship with the government in order to try to get its share. The pharmaceutical companies were usually able to import critical raw materials but only because they were given priority by the government. Other manufacturers in developing economies have frequently been unable to obtain the necessary foreign exchange. One vehicle producer was shut down for several years after only a year of operation because the company was unable to obtain the necessary parts.

In an effort to increase local manufacturing content, governments of developing economies typically require import licenses and limit importing. In many companies this necessitated a procurement section set up to deal exclusively with red tape, import licenses, and the voluminous form-filling involved in meeting the requirements of the local government for importing. Import permits had to be applied for and, if the company made a mistake, there was often very little, if anything, that could be done to rectify the situation until the next import permit was granted. Failure to recognize the need for this expensive staffing was not unusual.

It was usually necessary to employ and train local nationals to deal with the government on these matters. One company sent abroad an American employee who was considered to be exceptionally diplomatic in dealing with foreign politicians and bureaucrats. Inquiring about his performance, the researcher was told by local nationals that he had been scorned within the government because he was seen as a "faker." Genuine skills in dealing with the government and handling red tape appear to be a requisite for effective procurement abroad.

Long lead times in overseas procurement were another source of difficulty. One or two months of paperwork time plus approximately three months in manufacturing and delivery was typically required in order to import standard items from the U.S. home plant. Companies had to reorder approximately six months in advance of needs in order to avoid stockouts. The problems of holding a half-year stock were considerable. Not only were inventories high, but it was difficult to recover quickly from errors. Errors required air shipments and/or special permits which involved delays as well as extra costs. Thus, overseas procurement made accurate forecasting of market and sales requirements a necessity, and it nearly always involved an extraordinary safety stock.

Difficulties were frequently encountered in planning requirements for maintenance supplies and expendable tools. Maintenance foremen and supervisors responsible for using spare parts and tools had to be especially trained in many locations to plan ahead so as to prevent running out of needed items. Even in South Africa, where items could be imported without major paperwork problems, the time requirements for purchasing overseas were lengthy and hence demanded skills in forecasting, scheduling, and requisitioning the right amount of the appropriate items.

Problems in the use and understanding of terms involved in specifications were legion. Specifications are subject to considerable interpretation under the best of conditions and, with the barriers of distance, language, and customs the possibility of receiving items which were not satisfactory was vastly increased.

In importing maintenance supplies, metal parts, and glass containers, for example, specifications difficulties were severe. A pharmaceutical company which bought inert glass vials from France spent several years in correspondence and in the shipment of vials back and forth before they were able to impress the French supplier that the dimensions on the bottle openings were important. Failure to hold these dimensions properly caused stoppages in assembly lines using mechanical closing equipment. Had the supplier been physically closer, it would presumably have been easier to communicate the nature of the problem to him.

The difficulty of buying at long distances was amply demonstrated by the fact that companies encountered many misunderstandings even in importing from their own home plants. The divisive effect of geographical separation between divisions, plants, or offices of the same company often badly offset the normal family cohesion of a corporation. The result was a good deal of wrangling, arguments centered around missing parts, wrong dimensions, credit and payment controversies, unforecast demands, long lead times, missed delivery promises and controversies over transfer prices.

Too often the home office desk was more sensitive to the complaints of the domestic plant than it was to the foreign one. As a result the foreign plant was short-changed when it was inconvenient to send parts or supplies needed. Such internal problems in interdivision procurement were minimized when the headquarters plant set up a coordinating or liaison section which was responsive to the problems of the overseas manufacturing subsidiaries.

Parts shortages and delays occurred when forms for imports, permits, tariffs, and payments were improperly filled out. Foreigners often felt that American "passive resistance" to paper work was a prime cause. British managers of one U.S. company located in India stated that "Americans are no good in meeting the paperwork requirements of foreign governments. Americans just don't take that sort of thing seriously. They are annoyed by paperwork, bureaucracy and red tape in any form, and, as a result, they feel that they can judge whether and how a form should be filled out. This is childish and immature. On the receiving end, we suffer delays and even more red tape because the Americans in New York won't do the job properly in the first place."

These examples are typical of the difficulties frequently experienced in importing across international boundaries. The delays and the consequent voluminous correspondence, often eventuated in stockouts, frustrations, mounting paperwork, errors in the items received, and excessive inventories.

Problems in local purchasing

It is usually not possible to be self-sufficient and avoid procurement problems, for the pressures of local government and nationalism require considerable local manufacturing, and the costs of investing in a complete and self-sufficient plant facility on a relatively small scale are generally prohibitive. The result is that the American company finds it necessary to buy locally.

Problems in local purchasing were even more frequent than in importing. In each plant visited, executives listed the management of local procurement as one of their major headaches.

A difficult task in an underdeveloped country is to find out "who makes what." Advertising, salesmen, catalogues, and directories swamp the purchasing department in the United States. The procurement manager and his buyers must often fight off vendors and salesmen, but this is usually not so abroad. Catalogues and listings by trade associations and governments could not be relied upon as complete. Even in South Africa or Spain it was difficult to acquire a reliable list of suppliers.

A useful and often necessary means of locating vendors was to travel, and follow up the clues obtained. Although this required time, in many countries it was the best way. One executive in a developing economy made a practice of spending a month or two at a time traveling about in the country and going into local manufacturing plants to see what they made. In this way he ran across a number of sources. These sources were not listed in any directory and there was no advertising which would have alerted him to their presence.

After a source of procurement for an item has been found, the U.S. manufacturer abroad has frequently learned to his sorrow that the vendor was not actually as qualified as first appeared. For example, a U.S. vehicle manufacturer in South Africa found that a common auto component could be obtained from the local plant of a large and well-known international company which supplied this component in many countries of the world. When the vendor's specifications for the part were studied, they appeared satisfactory enough. But for years, when the parts were delivered, a significant fraction were improperly made or assembled and otherwise faulty in their manufacture. Even though the U.S. company had found a company which apparently had the proper facilities, a consistent supply of the quality necessary was not insured.

It was found that the U.S. manufacturer typically insists on more consistent high quality and more rigorous standards than the foreign vendor is accustomed to deliver. Months of wrangling, rejections, and bickering over the costs of rejections or rework result. Sometimes the vendors have gradually improved their performance but often, where the items are in short supply, no improvement is apparent. In three different countries, for example, where the supply of glass bottles was limited to a government-backed monopoly, the U.S. company reluctantly found it necessary to accept all bottles delivered and then sort and throw away the unsatisfactory ones. They found that repeated visits to the vendor and insistence on higher quality accomplished little.

In South Africa where the economy was rapidly expanding and sellers' markets were prevalent, one company found that, although vendors stated that they would improve the quality "just now," the quality never did improve. The vendors, under pressure to increase deliveries to many customers, were running behind schedule. In other instances local manufacturers earnestly attempted to provide the quality which the U.S. company desired but were unable to do it, often due to inadequate equipment and/or lack of technological and management ability.

One difficulty in meeting specifications was that they were not understood. Often vendors were not familiar with blueprints and engineering specifications but preferred to work from actual models. One American company in Europe stated that it was clear that certain vendors never read the blueprints provided. A frequent attitude openly expressed by vendors was "We are doing the best we can. You will have to figure out how to use the item which we can provide you."

In nearly every company problems were experienced concerning lack of reliable delivery as well as quality. In some cases a different cultural emphasis on time seemed involved. For instance, in one developing economy, a U.S. company tracing delivery of an overdue part nearly always found that the part had bogged down in the vendor's plant. The vendor "showed no intention of pushing it along until we came looking for it, showing that now we really needed it. Dates mean nothing around here."

In many cases late delivery was apparently due to a lack of ability in scheduling and production control. In most American companies it was found necessary to expedite items being procured, for the foreign companies did not keep track of their delivery promises.

In India an American tire manufacturer found that the vendors' promises were "meaningless." The vendors will tell you anything, but they have no intention of meeting a promise. In Pakistan a pharmaceutical manufacturer stated that "our quantities are too small to be very interesting to the local vendors. We get the short end of the stick every time when it comes to delivery. They just don't make any attempt to give us what we want when we want it. As a result we are forced to pad our own delivery dates. We ask for earlier delivery because we know that there isn't a chance of getting things for a month after the date we show."

American managers often had to develop special procedures for handling purchasing relationships so as to avoid favoritism, relatives, and kickbacks. One company in Spain stated that while they had established a policy of obtaining three bids on every major item purchased, the men in their purchasing department always had many reasons why a bid basis was either unnecessary or impossible. "It is a continual problem to enforce this rule. We have found many instances of long-standing relationships with vendors which are hard to break into, and even find relatives hidden in the picture. While we could fire men for this sort of thing, it seems to be built into the way of the people."

In the Far East and in Europe, U.S. companies encountered the problems of kickbacks. Purchasing agents were occasionally found to be receiving compensation from the vendor in one form or another. This was usually an ancient pattern of doing business in these countries and only gradually is it being discouraged.

The net effect of difficulties in local purchasing was a low degree of assurance of receiving on-time deliveries of adequate quality. The high cost of this uncertainty was a common management complaint. It represented a considerable source of frustration and difficulty, in addition to the actual costs of intermittent production, extra inspection, rejects and rework, and extra inventories.

SOURCES OF PROCUREMENT PROBLEMS

American businessmen are usually exasperated and frustrated by overseas vendors but, in fact, their expectations are often unrealistic. Foreign economies differ from the U.S. economy as to the stage of development, the level of competition, and the customs and methods of marketing. Factors built into the culture and the economy make good vendor performance by U.S. standards very difficult. Disappointment and expensive falldowns result. Even in countries where American plants have been located for ten years or more, vendors have been slow to develop, again judging by U.S. standards. For example, an American company in South Africa pointed out that vendors were frankly reluctant to invest in facilities and a management organization which could provide the quality and delivery which the U.S. company considered necessary. Their business outlook centered on shorter term return of capital. In countries where the cultural emphasis on time was entirely different from that of the United States vendors still failed to pay adequate attention to delivery dates after many years. They regularly failed to meet due dates and only delivered after the item had been expedited.

In developing economies, vendors cannot be expected to perform as relied upon in Chicago or Los Angeles. In underdeveloped locations the economies have usually been growing rapidly, and, hence the better vendors are often overloaded. Even in Europe, vendors with customer oriented managements are not commonplace. A U.S. plastics manufacturer which established a plant in Scotland found that it was necessary to provide far closer surveillance of vendors' quality and delivery than necessary domestically. Outside of Europe the situation is, quite naturally, even more difficult.

To comprehend overseas procurement it helps to recall our own experiences after the war, when, in times of shortages, the performance of vendors deteriorated. Those years remind us that in any location most vendors do not spend money and management time on improving customer service until forced by competition.

In some situations studied the vendor did not appear to have the technical and management background in manufacturing requisite to comprehend the necessity for the tight U.S. specifications. They tended to view these specifications as somewhat arbitrary and unnecessary. And in many vendors' plants the skill of management had not developed to the point where adequate production and quality controls were functioning.

Many vendors abroad had a different point of view toward business from that of the American companies to which they were selling. The uncertainties of political and economic situations, the frequency in which wars or revolutions had unsettled businesses, and different values and beliefs often resulted in a high-profit, short-range point of view. Vendors were not usually willing to build up an organization, the facilities, the systems and procedures which would require an investment and a short-range reduction in profit just to satisfy the American company. This basic difference in philosophy plagued relationships between the American companies and their vendors.

The serious impact of inadequate procurement, however, cannot be attributed solely to weak vendors. The high cost of problems resulting from procurement has partly been the result of unrealistic expectations of U.S. manufacturing managers who were ill-prepared to deal with an underdeveloped vendor structure.

Only three of the companies visited had provided in advance for an adequately staffed procurement organization with which to deal with these nearly inevitable problems. It was rare, indeed, for the American company to send an American procurement expert abroad. The typical pattern was to find a foreign national who appeared to know the market and to give him responsibility for procurement. Most Americans abroad felt that they did not know anything about the local markets and it was necessary to hire local men to do the buying. But most of the local people employed did not know enough about company products, specifications, and delivery requirements. Sometimes a high status executive would handle the procurement of two or three major commodities and delegate the balance of purchasing to a clerk. In fact, it was normal to find that a clerical employee would handle the procurement of most items purchased, even those of major value and usage.

Inadequate systems and procedures in the procurement area were also behind some of the difficulties. Since the assumption was usually made that procurement had to be an autonomous local function, there was relatively little investment at the home office in developing systems and procedures for handling purchasing better; instead, these procedures were left in the hands of the overseas management to be developed as necessary.

In spite of the fact that the companies ran into major problems in procurement and faced these problems over a period of years, many failed to develop the organization and management emphasis at home or abroad to supply the necessary work and expertise. Many complained about the inadequacy of the vendors, but argued that "this is an inevitable problem of doing business abroad which will not be overcome until the entire economy and culture become modern industrially." The much more successful results of a few companies suggest that some positive steps can be taken. These are outlined in the final section of this article.

SLOW ADAPTATION AND IMPROVEMENT:
SOME FUNDAMENTAL ERRORS

Detailed study of the history of each company's operations reveals that few of the firms made immediate or decisive changes in their procurement organization or operations even though they encountered costly problems. There was seldom an early organizational reappraisal and shift in management strength or policies to try to improve spotty deliveries and marginal quality. Problems were usually either lived with or worked at slowly by asking vendors to try to do better. An understanding of the possible reasons for these apparently slow reactions would begin to provide insight into the process of improving overseas procurement management.

Analysis of interviews and case studies collected in this research bring to light four factors which may have contributed to the typically slow adaptations and improvements observed abroad.

1. *Managers did not expect to encounter these problems.* They appeared to assume that vendors would be motivated to improve their performance for their own advantage. They assumed that the vendors would act in their own self-interest, would accept the standards of the U.S. companies and adjust their operations to those requirements. This assumption was based on experience with vendors in the U.S. and in developed economies such as in Canada and Europe. It was not realistic in underdeveloped locations. The lack of competition, the variance in cultures and business methods, and the scarcity of trained technical and management personnel meant that many vendors did not behave as anticipated.

2. *Procurement was an underemphasized area of management for some of the U.S. companies both at home and abroad.* In such instances procurement was delegated to a low organizational level without recognition that "procurement" involves more than simply buying. Procurement personnel can improve results by playing a part in the engineering of the product and product specifications, but the realization of the potentially broad functions of procurement was too little appreciated in the U.S. offices of some firms. It was natural then that in the foreign operations there was little emphasis on more comprehensive and dynamic management in the procurement function. The companies which were doing more sophisticated work in procurement management in the U.S. generally had the better procurement operations abroad. They adapted more quickly and imaginatively; they were staffed to offer competent technical and managerial assistance for helping vendors to develop.

3. *Procurement was not recognized as a management function in which foreign nationals at middle management levels must make most of the decisions.* There is a significant amount of important detail in procurement; a large number of parts or items are apt to be procured, and the procurement managers require local knowledge and information for each particular item or class of items. These decisions involved are too numerous and detailed to be handled at top levels. This makes it necessary to delegate procurement to the local foreign nationals who staff middle management.

But the foreign nationals handling procurement operate under severe handicaps: they must bridge a cultural, communications gap between the American company and the foreign subsidiary; they must understand the parent company and its products well enough to recognize which specifications are critical and which can be adapted to local conditions, and they must understand the local market and the economics of each item well enough so that they are able to select the better vendors and bargain for good prices. Before foreign nationals were sufficiently developed in one American company, the management found it was better for U.S. managers abroad to handle procurement. This was because only the Americans knew the product and the company well enough to know where they could compromise and substitute. The foreign nationals did not have this "feel" for years. The company observed that it was better to sacrifice local knowledge for better product and company knowledge.

Most companies concluded that the massive detail work in procurement had to be delegated for economic and political reasons; foreign nationals who could handle these challenges and the responsibility adequately were rare. The mercantile outlook prevalent in many countries perceives the function of procurement as hunting for items in bazaars and then haggling over the price. This is too limited a view to suffice for most modern industrial firms.

Men who have the ability to handle problems in procurement — ranging from suggesting changes in engineering designs and specifications down to the driving of the hard bargain over price and terms of the purchase — are difficult enough to find in the United States and virtually impossible in the developing economies. The slow process of developing competent middle management was a key reason for the slow resolution of overseas procurement problems.

4. *In conventional management wisdom, procurement is usually considered as one of the local problems which the headquarters must delegate to managers abroad.* Recognition of the need for lo-

cal market knowledge is realistic, of course. But the assumption that the headquarters could not assist in the development of vendors and of managers, systems, and procedures appears generally incorrect. For instance, Sears made quite the opposite assumption when they sent a dozen men experienced in vendor development to Mexico. They were instructed to go out in the countryside and find and develop local vendors. This effort and skill in developing vendors by assisting them in management practices, production planning, technical processes, and quality control would have been valuable in many of the companies visited. Such assistance was generally either not seriously considered or seen as too expensive.

The companies which saw procurement in underdeveloped economies as "a new ball game"—with a new set of rules and attacked it with a situationally oriented point of view rather than previously conceived assumptions, performed far better than their counterparts.

EXPERIENCES IN EFFECTIVE PROCUREMENT MANAGEMENT

Analysis of the experiences of several American companies which were able to purchase with relative success suggests several recommendations which could aid many corporations with plants in developing economies in their management of the procurement function. The companies with the best results in procurement incorporated these assumptions and approaches:

1.   The assumption that procurement would be a function critical to success abroad.

2.   The assumption that procurement would be a difficult function to manage successfully.

3.   An organizational and staffing emphasis was placed on procurement, both in terms of assigning experienced company personnel and delegating considerable authority to them and assigning sufficient numbers of indigenous personnel, and in terms of mounting immediate training efforts for the indigenous employees.

4.   An aggressive effort was made to develop vendors, rather than assuming it would come about in the normal course of events.

5.   Specifications and designs were analyzed and changed where possible to adapt the product to minimize manufacturing problems, conforming to available processes, skills and techniques.

6.   The home office played a major role in assisting in establishing effective systems and procedures, training indigenous personnel, vendor development, and specification and design review.

Let me briefly elaborate on several of these lessons from experience.

Realistic expectations

Several of the companies which properly anticipated a difficult procurement environment were forewarned by a thorough pre-investment analysis. Purchasing officers visited available vendors and examined their technical and managerial skills even before the firm made the decision to invest in the country. Indeed, in these firms such a survey was a vital part of the analysis leading to the go-ahead decision and, equally important, the plans for the operation. The resulting make or buy decisions determined the size of the plant, the processes and equipment needed, and essentially influenced the entire economics of the manufacturing operation.

Advance analysis of the procurement potential not only saved future headaches but in some cases helped to solve the common problem of working out an economic manufacturing system in spite of a small market and reduced scale of U.S. standards. It pinpointed the dependence on purchasing and allowed the company to take the necessary steps in internal staffing and training and externally in vendor development to prevent later discontinuities in production.

Developing procurement management

A procurement department in an underdeveloped economy requires special attention on management development. Effective management development in procurement offered training pertaining to the functioning of the product emphasizing critical specifications. Educational efforts often included courses in cost data. In addition procurement officers were frequently given both technical and management training so as to be able to go into vendors' plants and help them improve their operating practices.

Special programs to speed the development of knowledge and "feel" of the mores of the American company and its attitudes and corporate policies were seldom offered. But this kind of training would appear to be vital to the personal adjustment of a foreigner as he attempts to function in the island of American culture in which he is making his living.

Vendor development

Companies which have been successful in overseas procurement have often seen payoff opportunity in company programs for vendor development. Such programs typically require a staff able to go out to individual vendors and work with them tactfully and persuasively, training their people, helping them to improve their facilities, and introducing production management techniques in quality control, production control, and cost control. A sewing machine company, to cite one case, has a full-time expert in cabinet manufacturing who goes from country to country assisting cabinet manufacturers in making products which can meet their standards.

When vendor performance is marginal there are many steps which can be taken to promote their development. Firms with large operations can better afford a full-time local staff for this purpose. Vendor development involves constant surveillance and expediting within the vendors' plant and, frequently, it may involve financing as well. Some companies have made long-term loans to vendors to assist them in providing the necessary facilities and techniques. In the absence of a planned effort of assistance, experience indicates that vendors' skills and results generally improve too slowly to satisfy the U.S. company.

Specification and design review

The possibility of design changes to ease procurement problems has barely been scratched. A few international manufacturing firms have seen the potential of contribution specification and design reviews to make products and processes appropriate to the needs and skills of each country. Many American companies assumed that their product must meet the same specification in the foreign country as in the United States, and hence rigidly adhered to domestic specifications. This made it unnecessarily difficult in some instances for the vendors abroad to meet specifications. Research on U.S. companies in Mexico points up the advantages of special product designs for the Mexican market.[2] And one auto firm in South Africa made a major change in the design of its bumpers in order to adapt them to local manufacturing presses smaller than those in Detroit.

Make-or-buy criteria unique to each country would often be useful. Decision rules should be tailored to local costs, skills and available processes as well as the worldwide procurement possibilities. For example, several companies have successfully established multinational procurement functions on a regional or a worldwide basis.

[2] *Op. cit.*, p. 106.

A central buying office has been established in a central country such as Switzerland or Holland or the United States. Here are pooled the various requirements of branch plants all over the world. The results have been: (a) a better selection of vendors; (b) larger and more economic order quantities; (c) application of expertise and coordination on a regional or worldwide scale.

Headquarters assistance in procurement management

Up to this point we have not mentioned the cost of the proposed organizational emphasis on procurement. Costs of extra staff, Americans or third-country nationals, vendor development, design and specification review all must be justified and supported.

In small plants in the less developed nations this is more of a problem than in facilities serving larger markets such as South Africa or Spain. In the latter the scale of savings from reduced stock-outs, reliable quality, and lower unit costs of items procured can usually justify expenditures on the procurement function. This is especially clear when the flow of future savings is taken into account in accepting start-up, training, or vendor development costs, which represent an investment.

But in the cases of small, marginal operations where the firm is counting on gradual growth in the market and subsequent expansion of manufacturing, the investing corporation faces the dilemma of uneconomic scale of production and hence the need for procurement, the typical trade imbalance which forces local procurement and prohibits or, at the least, discourages importation, in combination with a dearth of competent vendors and small aggregate profits from which to invest funds in developing procurement skills and vendor abilities.

One answer to this dilemma is in the use of headquarters assistance to the branch plant in procurement management. There are a number of ways in which a headquarters staff organization can be of substantial assistance, either on a temporary or on a continuing intermittent basis. Probably the area of vendor development provides the best examples of headquarters contributions.

Vendor development from the headquarters office can be handled by a visiting staff which services a geographic area, visiting and working with the vendors to improve their manufacturing systems and management organization. This staff can be especially useful in helping a new branch plant to get started; providing the extensive man-hours necessary in order to find possible sources, and then assisting the vendors to get set up to meet company specifications.

A visiting staff can also play a useful role in make-or-buy studies made in a foreign country when planning the overseas plant. A full and careful make-or-buy analysis can be a critical determinant of the overseas plant's chances of success. The difficulties implied by the decision to make instead of buy are often underestimated, even as the problems in procurement abroad are similarly underestimated. A trained and experienced home office procurement staff can provide a degree of objectivity and expertise which is hard to acquire abroad.

CONCLUSION

United States companies are playing a substantial and important role in U.S. foreign policy by assisting in the economic and social development of small or underdeveloped countries. Faster improvement in standard of living is desirable not only for humanitarian reasons but for the political effects of narrowing the gap between the rich and the poor nations. And investment in the early stages of a country's development has already proven wise and profitable to hundreds of companies.

In undeveloped locations manufacturing poses unique and difficult problems, not the least of which are encountered in procurement. Experiences of U.S. firms to date point to the conclusion that procurement is a function of critical importance and that it represents a management area at which a careful and flexible adaptation of exported "know-how" can mitigate or avoid many problems which arise when it is considered as a purely local function.

7

TECHNOLOGICAL STRATEGY

In the manufacture of most products the producer has a series of process choices to make. The costs and implications of each choice affect the equipment needed and the entire production system. Choices of equipment and processes are the result of a firm's technological strategy, its objectives, and policies relating to the use of technology. This chapter is concerned with technological strategy in the management of international manufacturing.

A production system centers around the process used for transforming materials into the finished products. A process may be carried out with one or more alternatives of equipment. The particular equipment selected places its set of demands on labor skills and attitudes, supervision, industrial engineering for tools and manufacturing techniques, materials and supplies, maintenance, production scheduling and inventory controls, quality control procedures, and so forth.

Each of these ingredients in a production system is affected by the environment. The economic environment affects costs and availability of labor, equipment, and materials. The cultural environment affects attitudes, values, and motivation of workers. The political environment is sensitive to nationalistic pressures, which may influence what the plant makes and how it makes it.

For these reasons a firm's technological strategy is both an independent and a dependent variable, independent in that it is the starting point for the whole production system and dependent because the production system itself is affected by the environment. To be effective and viable the demands and ingredients of a production system must be congruent with those of the environment. It follows therefore that a successful technological strategy should be derived in part from a realistic assessment of the total environment in which it is to operate.

Analysis of the technological strategy of the U.S. firms in this study indicates that in practice the choice of process and equipment is seldom influenced by a systematic study of alternatives and their congruence with the total environment. Processes and equipment are seldom developed or selected expressly for a particular set of circumstances in an overseas location. Instead, the technology is more often exported unchanged from the domestic operation.

This approach is not without its advantages. It requires less engineering time, and it is a low-risk strategy because it exports tested technological methods with which the company has had experience. But its disadvantages are that it is a gross or crude fitting of technology to circumstances and its fit may be random. It is safe but often expensive. The price is paid chiefly in cost and low productivity of the production system as a whole, including costs not only of direct labor and equipment but of inventories, overheads, and customer service. When operating margins are ample and competition is minor, it may be a good strategy. But as competition grows and margins narrow, technological strategy needs to be more precisely tailored to maximize the fit of the production system to the critical environment factors.

Technological strategy—domestic and international

In domestic production the choice of equipment and process is a highly developed area of management decision making. Manufacturing process alternatives grow out of product designs. Industrial and manufacturing engineers choose the most economic and feasible process and develop or select the equipment and plan the plant layout for the entire manufacturing sequence. The facility may be engineered as a system composed of various interlocking elements. The entire system and each of the elements are worked out considering possible choices of process and equipment so as to produce the product at the proper quality level at the lowest cost.

Various technical elements enter into the choice of equipment: the technology of materials, tools and processes, time and motion study, cost of the equipment and its operations, skill and safety requirements, setup time requirements, probabilities regarding maintenance and repairs. These technical aspects are combined with the management decisions pertaining to the appropriate meld of labor and supervisory skills and controls of production and quality, with judgment and analysis of uncertainties always taken into account. It becomes clear that this is a complex area of decision making. An extensive body of theory and practical knowledge has grown up around this area of plant management, for it is susceptible to tangible measurements and quantitative analysis.

In addition to technical elements in the choice of equipment and process there are also engineering economics ingredients dealing with costs. In developing an understanding of the economy as it is affected by businessmen's decisions, economists analyze the rationale of the typical choice of equipment or process. Labor-intensive and capital-intensive alternative processes are compared by the economist, using various criteria, before he recommends the final process in terms of its impact on the business and, on a macroscale, the nation's economy. In the economist's model, the businessman calculates the amount of capital and the amount of labor required at different rates of production, and, depending on the cost of capital, the cost of labor, and other less tangible factors, he makes a rational decision on the process to employ in his plant.

Exporting a given process for use abroad requires careful reappraisal. The scale of production and the total market size are likely to be lower than (or at least different from) that of the domestic plant; the costs of money, capital, and labor are different both absolutely and in relative proportions; the skills of operating, supervising, and maintaining an operation are probably less developed; sometimes the product quality required may be different from that in the United States. Technical changes in the process may therefore be indicated, with subsequent changes in the surrounding production system.

Since a different mix of ingredients abroad might be expected to result in a unique choice of process and equipment, it seemed odd that most of the companies appeared to have invested less careful analysis and study in their choice of equipment and process overseas than at home. This was in spite of the fact that the same analytical approaches[1] to the problem which are used domestically could, essentially, be applied abroad. If this had been done, the decisions resulting would presumably have been different. For example, the relative advantages of labor-intensive versus capital-intensive pro-

---

[1] Engineering process analysis in combination with engineering economics and industrial engineering principles.

cesses as pointed out by many economists would have been apparent in developing economies with labor surpluses. Analyses of this kind were largely ignored by practitioners in the companies visited.

Overseas decisions pertaining to choices of equipment were typically simplified by international managements who allowed these decisions to be largely dictated by one or more of these factors: (a) what the product called for in a technical sense; (b) what the engineers making the process and equipment decisions were accustomed to using domestically; (c) what equipment could be most easily obtained. Limiting the factors in this way vastly reduced the number of alternatives considered. The relative simplicity of this method of making decisions is in sharp contrast to economic theory and conventional domestic practice.

Contributions of economic theory to technological strategy

Economists studying industrial development devote considerable time and publication space to the issue of capital-intensive versus labor-intensive processes. For example, in an article entitled "Capital Intensity in Industry in Undeveloped Countries,"[2] the authors point out that the determination of the appropriate choice of production process is a key issue in any program of industrialization. For individual plants it involves a choice between different manufacturing alternatives. At an overall national planning level it may involve choices between establishing different industries. The authors develop a case for labor-intensive policies in developing economies based on their bringing about (a) increased employment; (b) decreased capital requirements; (c) wider distribution of purchasing power; (d) lower skill requirements in maintenance, equipment operation, and management; (e) reduced setup and breakdown time due to use of less complex labor-intensive equipment.

Economists are often divided over which of the two directions it is better for industry in a country to follow. In contrast to the U.N. Bulletin cited, some economists recommend capital-intensive policies for developing economies because they result in high efficiency and therefore a larger amount of production, higher national income, increased savings and investment, and hence a greater surplus for capital formation.

[2]U.N. Bureau of Economic Affairs, "Capital Intensity in Industry in Underdeveloped Countries," Industrialization and Productivity Bulletin Number 1 (April 1958).

Such diversity of opinion sometimes produces pressure on managers in a developing economy toward one type of process or the other, depending on the school of economists in power. For instance, in India some of the new steel mills have the latest equipment and processes, partly because the national government wants "modern" steel plants and partly because capital-intensive theorists feel that this is the most efficient approach to steelmaking. They argue in effect that "Just because India has a labor surplus, they should not have an old-fashioned plant." But at province or town levels, pressure is often placed on companies to use processes that involve large numbers of people rather than a capital-intensive alternative.

Business researchers as well as managers are also frequently divided on this question and attempt to influence businessmen to their own school of thought. Richard D. Robinson, in his *International Business Policy*[3], recommends that the American businessman give much more attention to the possible imaginative development of labor-intensive equipment in plants in developing economies.

The author's survey likewise demonstrated that there was a singular inflexibility on the part of a substantial number of American companies in their *productive processes*. A member of the export division of an electrical appliance company observed that he had designed a plant for Chile which the company's engineering department had estimated at $190,000. He added "I had it down to about $40,000." He then went on to explain that, of course, his experience in manufacturing was about 30 years behind him, but perhaps that was why he could think in terms other than the most modern manufacturing innovations.

A tractor company executive spelled out another difficulty: "We know how to make 10,000 tractors a year, but not 500. In Mexico we are doing things by hand that we'd never do here." In planning the Mexican assembly layout, the vice president had asked the company engineering group for a "low-cost assembly line." The engineers evolved a line costing $175,000 — to build 16 tractors a day. The engineers planned on a paint room, a drying room, and other elaborate installations which were taken more or less for granted as part of any American assembly line. Besides other changes, the vice president ordered the use of a tent for a

[3]Richard D. Robinson, *International Business Policy*, Holt Rinehart and Winston, New York, 1964, p. 180.

paint room and a hand sprayer. The result was that $50,000 investment in paint facilities was reduced to $750, and the overall cost for the assembly line from $175,000 to $29,000. The vice president added, "Our people simply can't think in these terms."

Analysts of manufacturing policy abroad draw on the thinking of anthropologists, economists, and engineers in recommending more flexible thinking on equipment decisions to take into account the economic needs of the country, the skills and attitudes of employees, and short- and long-run cost ingredients. Professor Jan Tinbergen[4] points out that often both the industrial planning authorities and the engineering experts have seemed to be unaware that there is a choice of technology in planning for industrial activities. He states that undue emphasis is often given to purely technical aspects of equipment and manufacturing selection process and that consideration of national prestige has frequently led to unnecessarily ambitious facilities. A high degree of mechanization is often employed to avoid dealing with larger numbers of workers and their families, housing, and utilities needs.

In making the same point, the authors of "Capital Intensity in Industry in Undeveloped Countries"[5] suggest that managers and engineers are often so convinced of the superiority of familiar, mechanized techniques that they do not seek labor-intensive ones, although alternatives may be available. They admit that there are certain industries for which Western blueprints can and should be used almost without change. For example, in chemical process industries, equipment choices are typically determined by technical requirements for certain reactions and processes which cannot be operated efficiently on a small scale. Units now operating in highly industrialized countries can be copied with relatively few changes, with the qualification, however, that highly trained engineers are generally required to erect and operate such plants.

But in most other types of industry the authors assert that equipment designs can often be adapted. It may be desirable to decrease the size of the equipment and demechanize it to make possible a reduction in both the capital expenditure and the length of the training required to obtain operators, maintenance men, and foremen. Many of the mechanical industries fall in this category as well as some of the chemical processes.

[4]Jan Tinbergen, "Choice of Technology and Industrial Planning," U.N. Department of Economic and Social Affairs, Industrialization and Productivity Bulletin Number 1 (April 1958).
[5]Op. cit., p. 142.

These authors feel that fresh thinking should be devoted to the specific requirements of industry in the underdeveloped countries. They point out that recommendations of engineers proceed largely from technical considerations and that there is evidence that in many cases there is a ready, almost indiscriminate, resort to mechanization.

R. F. Eckaus[6] states that among equipment and process proposals by engineers

"There are few, if any, which entail alternative factor (labor and capital) combinations. Government policies, however, seldom recommend or are explicit enough to guide technicians in the field and there are major gaps between government policies and industry practice. In many cases the choice may be nonexistent or at least severely limited, but there are a large number of industries where alternative factors and combinations are applicable in major processing operations. Much research is needed in order to determine the proper mix. It is necessary in order to reveal the possible technical combinations to achieve a much higher degree of disaggregation than is currently practiced or appears feasible.

Much of the discussion of this subject by economists may seem irrelevant to industrial managers because it refers to the choice of planners of a developing country as to whether to seek labor-intensive or capital-intensive industry. But the part of the discussion that deals with process alternatives at the theoretical level could be effective in influencing industry.

Theoretical economics are in fact more important to industrial managers than is usually realized. Company managers should pay attention to the policies and the thinking of economists and government officers concerned with national industrial development policy. It is wise for a company to give every possible assistance in the achievement of national objectives if their stay in a country is to be satisfactory. Several companies studied benefited both politically and in better technological strategy from a purposeful sensitivity to recommendations of top government planning people.

Instead of fighting against "hopelessly academic and unrealistic government planners," as some managers considered most foreign government economists, a few companies took a more positive attitude by inviting them into their plants to explain the necessity for company decisions that had been made and to listen to their points

[6] R. F. Eckaus, "The Factor Proportion Problem in Under-developed Areas," *The American Economic Review* (September 1955).

of view. Experiences like these indicate that effective efforts can be made to win government officials to a company's point of view. Such communications may also help in making sounder government policy recommendations.

A second and probably more important reason for considering theorists' views of equipment decisions is that they offer a point of view that often has merit and should not be dismissed as merely "theoretical." Choices of equipment and process available in most industries are less limited than industrialists usually infer. Economists who suggest more company research and innovation in seeking alternative industrial processes tailored to fit each particular environment are realistic more often than not. Industrial nations export familiar processes and techniques (many of which require engineering and maintenance skills not available abroad), but the evidence indicates that they seldom export a most vital industrial tool—the attitude and frame of mind which constantly seeks improvement. Economists who criticize U.S. industry for sending ill-adapted processes abroad have little difficulty in marshalling evidence to support their position.

Inadequacies in the economics-oriented position

In fairness, now, to the international firm, we must also criticize some of the economists and theoreticians who complain that international companies envision only a fraction of the alternatives possible in establishing processes. Using the capital-intensive, labor-intensive dichotomy they cite that there is more than one way to make a radio, to assemble vehicles, to package food, or to compound pharmaceuticals. Companies are criticized for "playing it safe."

But economists who conceptualize the choices as labor-intensive versus capital-intensive tend to overlook or minimize some less measurable or quantifiable factors, which can be very important. There is a wide gap between the theory of tailoring a production process to the environment and the actual, detailed plant design. Someone must tailor the process, and it is a problem to get the right people in the right place. Equally important is the fact that for some products or processes alternative choices are not readily available. For any new process the start-up and "debugging" problems are usually considerable, especially abroad. Special equipment may cause problems which are not readily solved by recourse to past experience. And judging from maintenance problems experienced

abroad, maintenance of specially designed processes would often
be a nightmare. Although the conservative practices of U.S. firms
overseas may run counter to economists' theories, they take into
account some practical realities which could prove critical if overlooked.

The notion of designing processes to fit the environment is sound
in a conceptual sense, but it is in fact too gross a generalization to
be very useful. The experience of U.S. firms overseas dramatizes
the necessity of anticipating problems and reinforces the wisdom of
using tested processes while suggesting fruitful approaches for moving (as economists suggest) toward better adapted choices of equipment and processes.

Observations on equipment and process decisions

Companies tend to use basically the same processes and equipment abroad as currently or previously employed in the United
States. Often the equipment abroad will be of a type used in the
domestic plant two to fifteen years before and now outmoded by its
scale or the labor-saving features of new models. This research discovered that the primary reason for not innovating abroad appears
to be that these decisions are usually made by technical people
employed to use their knowledge and experience to recommend
processes that work and will consistently produce proper quality.
Companies are often under time pressure to meet tight schedules.
They lack the time and pressures to develop new processes tailored
to the specific economics and practical realities in each different
industrial location.

The general tendency observed is toward too much mechanization rather than too little. The following factors help to explain this
orientation:

1.   The engineering orientation involved in equipment decisions.
2.   The prestige factor, from both the company and the national
standpoint.
3.   The trend toward increasing mechanization in the United
States.
4.   The tendency toward copying processes known and proven in
the United States.
5.   The lack of time and impetus toward fresh study of the problem abroad. Often those responsible for equipping the new overseas plant have not been able to visit or observe conditions in the
foreign location.

6.   The argument, sometimes specious, that cheap labor is not really cheap, and that high quality and production are most easily assured by more mechanization rather than less.

By and large the decisions on equipment and process abroad appeared to be made on practical bases rather than on economic considerations of cost of labor and cost of capital. Noneconomic factors such as availability of equipment in different countries, the problems of repair, maintenance, quality, vendors, supervision, labor skills, setup, and production planning and cycle time factors received most of the emphasis. Companies interviewed on this question tended to explain their equipment decisions primarily on the basis of technological considerations, the need for achieving quality and keeping maintenance to a minimum, with relatively little consideration of the economics of a wide variety of alternatives and the industrial engineering aspects of different manufacturing approaches.

The technological ingredient tends to dominate U.S. equipment and process decisions, whereas the economic and industrial engineering elements are more often neglected. Equipment decisions encompass more than the major process decision. A "right" equipment choice may be "wrong" if the equipment is not subsequently operated properly. There are choices of how to operate the equipment or assembly line,[7] decisions on maintenance, and the effect on quality — which are apt to be just as important as the major process decision typically made at the U.S. home office. The former decisions must usually be made abroad, and they, too, need intelligent industrial engineering analysis.

In these decisions on how to use the equipment and to carry out the process, more basic industrial engineering work is needed abroad. American industrial engineers have been carrying on such analysis for at least 60 years. The trade-offs between labor and capital, which are a large part of the question, are seldom looked at in detail abroad. There are additional and equally important problems of improving the balance of assembly lines and the related items of equipment in materials handling, scheduling, and quality effects.

Most American companies abroad have taken a practical and safe approach to these problems by delegating plant design to the home office engineers. As a result their process and equipment decisions have been worked out with less emphasis on maximizing total pro-

[7]For instance, in machining a part on a turret lathe there is frequently considerable choice in the order of different steps, the tools to use, the frequency and methods of checking results. The skill level of the operator is also open to analysis and choice.

ductivity and more on achieving adequate quality and continuous production. Instead of devoting time and attention to developing more economical approaches with an equal assurance of quality and continuous production, they tend to try to accomplish it with equipment alone.

Bounded by the major equipment decisions of home office engineers, overseas plant managements tend to delegate the important detail of designing specific operations and processes to foreign middle managers. But they, in turn, tend to delegate these "technical decisions" to the home office.

The use of industrial engineering abroad

Why is the time-proven process of industrial engineering innovation not usually applied well abroad? The basic process of industrial engineering, as pioneered by Frederick Taylor in the early 1900's, takes apart an industrial process, examines all of its ingredients (practical, human,[8] economic, technical), and works out a combination that will result in lower costs for achieving the necessary quality. This type of research and development has been a key to the achievement of productivity for which American industry is famous. Nevertheless, we tend to set up overseas facilities with relatively little emphasis on the achievement of productivity. Time and again new plants were established abroad by more or less directly lifting processes from the United States.

New equipment was often ordered with virtually no economic analysis, frequently justified by hope for some future labor savings and buttressed by the fact that U.S. plants had proven the technical feasibility of the equipment. However, the analysis of savings and improvements from projected new equipment and the planned payback of the investment, analysis rigidly demanded in most U.S. plants as part of the appropriation process, was often omitted abroad.

The remark of a plant manager in India was typical. He said in reference to a new machine that was being ordered, "It will be economical, I am sure." The order for this equipment had already gone in; it had been approved without any economic analysis of its payback. A quick calculation by the researcher indicated that the payback time on this particular equipment would be at least five years and probably closer to ten.

[8]Modern industrial engineering typically encompasses the social and human factors as well as those of the old-fashioned "efficiency expert."

A number of reasons help to explain this phenomenon. First, the American companies rarely send industrial engineers abroad. They do send engineers with a technical emphasis, but relatively few companies have a home office industrial engineering staff which does on-the-scene work to improve the productivity of overseas plants. Citing a problem in improving the productivity of a certain operation, a plant manager in the Far East stated, "We will not get help on this problem from the home office because they are a *technical* staff and this is a plant *operating*[9] problem." He perceived that the *technical* staff was involved in engineering decisions affecting quality and producibility but not in improving productivity.

Second, the lack of "disaggregated" analysis of equipment and process abroad appears to be due to the shortage of middle management experienced and competent in this sort of detailed analysis. In general, middle management men were observed to consider decisions in this area as "technological" and therefore to leave them to someone else. In fact, the achievement of productivity involves a much broader area than the technological. It requires a thorough on-site analysis of the problems in the process and the equipment as they affect and are affected by such factors as labor skills, setup, supervision, worker attitudes, quality specifications, maintenance and production control.

Finally, an absence of American top management attention and effort was observed in this area of managing the business. "Technical" problems are delegated to "experts." To a large extent this inattention may be because labor costs have been generally low and operating margins substantial in comparison to U.S. plants. Therefore, in contrast to U.S. operations, top management has not emphasized "squeezing the fat out" of the overseas process in order to gain a few more cents on the dollar.

This type of reasoning seems essentially faulty and shortsighted. Competition is increasing abroad; as a country industrializes, there is typically more competition rather than less; there is a tendency for profit margins to narrow over the years; labor costs generally increase as labor organizes. Unfortunate precedents are being established in permitting low productivity.

A typical example of low productivity seen in plant after plant in both undeveloped and developed countries was an unbalanced assembly line. Foreign managers often appeared to believe that the best way to organize work was on an assembly line, apparently a

[9]Author's italics.

symbol of modern industry. Workers were positioned in an assembly line with virtually no time and motion study analysis of the actual operations at each station.

The assembly line in a packaging operation in South Africa was typical.

Example 1

Twenty-four operators were on the line. Most of them seemed to be working at a rather leisurely pace. Toward the end of the line one operator was operating a mechanical closing device. He was working at fever pitch, limited by the location of his supplies and a fumbling step in fitting two parts together. The entire line was paced by his work. Yet his job could have been readily facilitated by a simple, inexpensive fixture and some rearrangement of his work-place layout.

Overseas plants are generally less productive in terms of the output per hour than plants in the United States with the same equipment. Apparently such inefficiency is permitted because management has not considered it vital to work at improving productivity in labor-intensive operations. The labor costs involved are usually relatively small by U.S. standards. Since management expertise is limited and the U.S. home office typically offers little or no advice, it is almost inevitable that production operations will be sloppy.

An additional problem is that of learning to set up and operate small-scale plants. Many manufacturing investment propositions have been turned down because too large a capital cost was foreseen in the face of possible market uncertainties and unfavorable political conditions. Some of these decisions might have been affirmative if more imaginative effort had been invested in planning the operation.

Richard D. Robinson noted in his research that "Virtually every management, other than those already heavily involved in foreign manufacturing, commented about the difficulty of going abroad because of the small national markets. It seems, however, that the real difficulty in many cases did not lie in the small national market, but rather in the inflexibility of the company itself in terms of product, manufacturing processes, and organization."[10]

Willys Jeep Company furnishes an example of a more flexible approach. The U.S. company owned a 25 percent interest in their plant in Turkey and the capital invested was Turkish.

[10] *International Business Policy, op. cit.,* p. 143.

Example 2

The Turk owners and operators were extremely resourceful in setting up the overseas operations. They were assisted in this by an imaginative American, Mr. Robert DeBoer, who went to Turkey in late 1955. He helped to establish a plant along the shore of the Sea of Marmara 30 miles from the nearest industrial resources.

In setting up this plant, Mr. DeBoer established simple processes tailored to the situation which had never been used before. For instance, in the paint spray operation, he completed a satisfactory paint spray tunnel at a cost of only $2000. American engineers interviewed stated that this was fantastic, that it is impossible to do a decent auto paint spraying job for a capital cost of anything less than $25,000. If $25,000 had been projected originally, this type of plant would never have been built.

PRACTICAL PROBLEMS IN FACILITIES MANAGEMENT

The start-up phase

The production manager of a pharmaceutical company in Pakistan stated, "We had problems on every piece of equipment. It was necessary for me and the American to spend several months working with the supervisors and the operators on this equipment, using dummy material at first, to work out the processes and to get the 'bugs' cured. It was not that the equipment was new or different, but simply learning its operation, its maintenance, and training the workers took us a long time." This experience was not unusual, in spite of the relative simplicity of the equipment and the fact that an American process engineer was present to help the operation start up.

Time must be allowed for the start-up phase in scheduling initial production from overseas operations. In typical instances considerably more time is necessary than in most domestic start-ups even when using well-known and tested equipment. In another U.S. company in Pakistan the start-up problems were underestimated. Delays in the construction of the building forced the production group to go through the inevitable break-in problems under severe time pressure. When the plant itself was ready and workers could finally be hired and placed at work on machine tools, many problems developed in achieving good quality machine work. Production techniques and processes had to be worked out so that the parts actually fitted together. Scheduling and coordination skills were also underdeveloped and the entire organization had much to learn about working together as a cooperative unit.

Many of these difficulties had not been anticipated because the same machines and tools had been used for identical operations in Germany. At the time of the researcher's visit after four months of operation the stockrooms of finished products were virtually empty and the first units were just beginning to trickle out of the new plant. Top management foresaw at least three or four more months of reduced sales and operating losses in order to get through the start-up period.

Building and construction problems were legion in every underdeveloped country visited. Industrialists in the United States have grown accustomed to knowledgeable and experienced contractors who can work with little supervision. When men who had been involved in the establishment of new plants abroad were asked "What would you do differently?" the first answer was often "We would have given the contractor much closer supervision."

A tire plant in India is a good example.

Example 3

In spite of the fact that the U.S. company sent over experienced construction engineers to work with the contractor, there were numerous problems and many delays. The company managers complained that the contractors simply could not read blueprints, and that the quality of the concrete, the electrical work, and the mechanical and plumbing work was consistently poor. In many instances work had to be taken out and done over. There were difficulties in concrete forms; the electrical subcontracting dragged on months late; there were problems with licenses, documentation and other government clearances. The production manager had to spend a large portion of his time on the building and the construction process instead of on the hiring and training of workers and supervision. There were still many sections of the building uncompleted when the company finally had to move in and start production. This sequence of problems came about, in spite of the fact that they had used a group of contractors which had the best reputation in Pakistan, due to the problems of communication and variations in standards of adequate and acceptable construction.

Other examples from Turkey, Nigeria, Spain, South Africa, and India are numerous. For instance, an American company experienced months of delay in building a new plant near Bombay. Achieving the quality they required in their electrical and concrete work was particularly time-consuming. A large part of this particular problem was due to difficulties in procuring materials. The Americans praised the architect, but the building was delayed by a three-month strike of the roofers. Delays in importing equipment due to problems in import licensing further postponed the eventual start-up of production.

Problems with secondhand equipment

In many cases the companies studied made use of secondhand equipment in locations where labor costs are low. This decision was sometimes made because secondhand equipment could be obtained in the foreign country without importing. When used equipment was available, the foreign government was generally reluctant to grant licenses to import new machinery. In other cases secondhand equipment was sent overseas by the parent company on the assumption that the economic environment of the new overseas plant called for an earlier stage of mechanization relative to U.S. plants. The assumption made was that older equipment was generally more simple, required a higher input of labor, and was easier to operate and keep repaired.

These assumptions were not always reliable. Although the authors of the article in "Industrialization and Productivity"[11] point out that simpler equipment requires "relatively simple skills, less maintenance, less management and organization, will result in fewer breakdowns and waste, an increased use of machinery and decreased downtime," this is not true in all circumstances, especially when the simple equipment is secondhand. And even when new, an ordinary lathe, for example, requires more skill on the part of the operator for certain jobs than does a more mechanized turret lathe or an automatic screw machine. The more advanced machines require considerable skill on the part of a setup man, but once set up the machinery does the work and relatively less skill is required on the part of the operator.

Nor can it be assumed that second-hand equipment will require less maintenance. Maintenance requirements may vary both in re-

[11] *Op. cit.*, p. 142.

spect to the frequency and the complexity of maintenance. New, complex machinery may take less maintenance but involve work at a more sophisticated level. Older, simpler equipment may take more frequent maintenance even though it would be considered elementary work to the skilled tradesman. But abroad, trained maintenance workers, as we shall discuss, were often a rare commodity.

Several companies that had used considerable secondhand or specially designed or developed equipment abroad felt that in the final analysis it had been unwise, and they would not do it again. A pharmaceutical plant in India, for example, employed mostly secondhand equipment in combination with locally designed processes, largely because they had been able to obtain it cheaply and would not have been allowed to import new equipment. Because of shortages, several supervisors had developed ingenious rigs and processes, but there were repeated difficulties because this equipment proved marginal in its ability to maintain the necessary quality.

The plant manager several times referred to his marginal equipment as his major problem. He said, "These problems affect us seriously; each machine has its own defect. We are able to overcome these difficulties by taking extreme precautions. We know our machines and process equipment so it doesn't actually hurt us very often. But, for instance, our ampule filling machine does not necessarily provide uniform quality and accuracy. And the ampule sealing machine does not give uniform quality in its sealing. Our solution preparation filtration methods and our vacuum set-up are both poor. Many of these things could result in problems, and we are always on edge that our quality may suffer because of the marginality of this poor equipment."

At a tire plant in India a 41-year-old bias unit suffered repeated breakdowns. The maintenance manager felt that the use of secondhand equipment had not been wise because there were so many breakdowns, some of which tied up the whole plant.

Labor-intensive equipment at this plant placed additional reliance on the workers and on the supervisor. Where the machine itself performs a smaller portion of the job, the lower degree of mechanization typically requires more skill of the operator. This is turn demands more competence and reliability on the part of the supervisor. In developing economies, trained and reliable supervisors are relatively nonexistent, and, in this particular plant, this placed a relentless load on the U.S. expatriates. They had to be everywhere at once because the labor-intensive equipment would not hold specifications and automatically pace production without their watchful attention.

Maintenance problems

The frequency of maintenance problems overseas suggests that tested and trouble-free equipment should normally be a higher-priority objective than that of employing more labor and reducing initial capital outlays.

The maintenance function was often at a relatively low organizational level in the plants visited. It was frequently a second or third duty of an operating executive and, overall, given less attention than it deserved and required.

Typical problems in managing a maintenance operation in undeveloped locations were recounted by a chief maintenance engineer who had been sent to India from England.

Example 4

The English engineer found that equipment serviceability was badly affecting productivity. His predecessor had had to spend the bulk of his time handling breakdowns in the factory. Even the quality of repairs was shocking. He found his men brazing instead of welding; they were inept at welding; they were even using mismatched nuts and bolts.

He felt that the men's attitude toward tools was "nonsensical." They took poor care of tools and seemed to have no feel for which ones were correct to use. They sometimes used a pipe wrench on nuts instead of a proper spanner wrench. The maintenance and repair people had no concept or feel for the strength of materials and safety factors. There was "a sloppy attitude in regard to engineering problems. They tend to accept half-baked jobs. The maintenance organization was poorly organized."

He also pointed out a shortage of materials for proper repairs. There was no stainless steel, no high carbon steel, no bronze for bearings, and they often had difficulty in obtaining the necessary perishable tools and supply items. (They had recently discovered, however, by an aggressive search effort that there were actually many items available locally that they had struggled along without for years.)

They did not have an adequate supply of spare parts for the machines. Bearings, for instance, had to be imported; they were able to find some equivalents after extensive searching. They lacked nuts, springs, lock washers, and they found that no other companies seemed to stock them or use them. In addition, the Indian master mechanic was not up to his job. "I had to fire him," he said, "He worked hard but he had a grasshopper mind. He did not organize the operation, and in spite of the fact that he had been a sea-going engineer he was extremely sloppy about everything."

The quality of replacement parts which were fabricated locally were "terrible" in terms of tolerances, dimensions, finishes, and materials. But after many rejections from vendors, the company was able to increase the quality it received. Some vendors even refused to quote, but, finally, the company was able to develop better suppliers, although deliveries of spare parts continued to be a severe problem. The maintenance engineer went out to see these vendors, for he considered purchasing a very significant part of the maintenance job.

This manager had been able to achieve considerable improvement during the year he had been in the plant. He said that his men had learned to do a good job on routine tasks but that new jobs still created snags.

One approach he had used in improving the operation was to be much more selective in the hiring of maintenance men. He personally interviewed all candidates, asked them semipractical questions through an interpreter, e.g., to identify metal, to set a micrometer at 0.487. He also had them do a few operations, such as filing parts to make them fit. He was able to discover which of those interviewed were "relatively practical." He found, too, that by "placing pressure" on his men he was able to increase the amount of work that was accomplished. He could then weed out the many men who could not take the pressure. There had been a 30% turnover during the past year.

The plant engineer advised that, when he returned to England in a year or two, his successor should have "good practical engineering and design experience but he should particularly be a good organizer. A man needs 20 years of experience in order to set up in a place like this because there are so many problems." He would advise his successor to contact the expatriate engineers of other companies to get opinions of the competence of the local talent, and to hire and train their own maintenance men and foremen rather than relying on their prior experience. "There is a real problem here in that the local tradesmen don't like to get their hands dirty. In addition, we've had problems because our maintenance men make their helpers do much of the work. Their refusal to do many simple operations themselves slows down the work."

Culturally based problems further affected the maintenance organization. For example, because the operators of machines refused to clean them in India, the sweepers performed this work. Thus, in effect, the sweepers ended up doing whatever maintenance was done on a daily basis, which amounted to very little.

Because of the large number of maintenance problems over the years this company had worked out some administrative improvements, such as learning the causes of breakdowns on different pieces of equipment through better record-keeping. By training, pressure on supervision, and gradual weeding out of employees they had cut down time from 16 hours for making a mold change-over to typically two hours (a record of 50 minutes had been set by one maintenance man).

The Chief Maintenance Engineer said in parting, "Don't let American management send second-class people to a place like India. They have got to be first-class people and unusually competent at home if they are going to succeed here. The people at home have no idea what it is like to run a plant out here."

Nevertheless, these same types of maintenance problems were met in many parts of the world in a variety of forms. To the responsible manager these problems were troublesome and annoying, and in several instances machine breakdowns due to inadequate maintenance significantly affected production output. Modern and enlightened practices were rare. Better record keeping, more systematic lubrication, and preventive maintenance often would have paid off in fewer breakdowns and longer equipment life.

One cannot avoid the sense that some of the chief maintenance engineer's complaints were due to the violation of his vocational norms. His standards of the "right way" to do maintenance work, developed throughout a disciplined career, were flagrantly desecrated in India; his reaction was one of near revulsion at the inept, casual, apparently careless procedures he observed.

The seriousness of maintenance failures depends on the process, and this can determine the priority given to this function. Over the short run the effect of shoddy practices is not as costly in light industry (where the process depends less on continuous flow or linked mechanized steps) as it may first appear. Disrespect for tools and a temporary patch instead of a permanent fix is more important in heavy, equipment-centered industry.

Lack of replacement parts and skilled first-class mechanics, coupled with the typical firm's reliance on the functioning of its own equipment (since there are generally fewer standby sources) add up to an enlarged dependence upon the maintenance function in the environments of developing economies. Equipment requiring a high degree of maintenance skill and attention should generally be avoided.

CONCLUSION: DECISION-MAKING APPROACHES IN TECHNOLOGICAL STRATEGY

Technological strategy decisions culminating in choices of original processes and facilities abroad are frequently dominated by the home office technical staff. Men in such positions are naturally concerned with their reputations and aware that it is easy to criticize equipment if it produces only marginal product quality or is inadequate in its output. They also know that they will not be involved in the operation of the equipment. There is a built-in tendency for them, therefore, to overspecify, overdesign, overinsure quality and capacity, and often overmechanize.

It is curious, however, that once the plant has been set up, replacement and expanded capacity decisions in the companies studied were seldom initiated or analyzed by home office engineers. Instead, after the plant is operating the facilities are turned over to the local plant managers and when more equipment is necessary, the plant managers usually make the decision. Typically these plant managers had relatively little knowledge of possible alternatives and virtually no training in engineering economics. Relatively little "know-how" in industrial engineering was made available. Like maintenance, industrial engineering is usually on a "do-it-yourself" basis abroad.

American managements are sometimes prone to dismiss the writings of economists as academic and to feel that technological factors limit the process alternatives far more than they do, in fact. Too few alternatives are recognized and studied. To a large extent a lack of organizational emphasis and the apparatus for making effective equipment and process decisions is responsible for this state of affairs. Increasing pressure for lower costs and higher quality may tend to change this in time, but already the opportunities for developing more economic processes and equipment are considerable. An increased emphasis on industrial engineering and improved maintenance management could be fruitful in many of the plants visited.

The experience of a U.S. food-processing plant in Spain furnishes a good example of the contribution of the industrial engineering point of view. Faced with inadequate capacity due to increasing sales, the managers tentatively decided a major expansion was necessary. However, before going ahead they learned, through an extensive industrial engineering analysis of their entire system, that by breaking three bottlenecks they could increase production by approximately 15 percent using the same facilities. An incentive plan was established to reward continuous production and penalize downtime. This placed further emphasis on total equipment productivity, allowing the company to meet growing market demands and delay an expensive expansion program.

In this chapter we have offered three conclusions from research abroad:

1. Technological strategy decisions by international manufacturing firms often appear to be conservative and limited in their vision of possible alternatives, dominated by a technical point of view.

2. Economic theorists could help broaden the typical industrialist's point of view with their notions of adapting technological strategy to the environment, but economists' contributions are frequently too gross and aggregated. They tend to leave out such practical considerations as start-ups, problems with labor intensive processes, and maintenance.

3. The industrial engineering point of view is too infrequently employed abroad since its approach is situational and pragmatic, disaggregated and detailed. Broad in its notions of a production system and total productivity of the system, it offers both an outlook and the mechanics for an improved handling of technological strategy decisions.

The industrial engineering function, available domestically, is typically weak or absent overseas. The gap between economic theoreticians and practical industrial decision makers could be filled by an able industrial engineering staff encompassing both the broader alternatives seen by the economists and the practical, conservative requirements emphasized by industry. Industrial engineers are trained to develop processes and methods to fit the environment. This is precisely the gap that must be filled overseas.

The culprit in the technological strategy area is the decision-making process itself. Decisions on both original and replacement equipment and equipment maintenance are too often considered "technical." But wise decisions go far beyond this dimension into marketing, finance, human and political factors which may be just as important. Equipment and process choice is more a matter of technological strategy than a mere technical calculation. A longer-range, multidimensional outlook is needed; however, it cannot be provided by only specialized engineers and technicians, able as they may be. Industrial engineering is management-oriented rather than technically oriented.

Too often managers act as spectators and never get involved. Facilities planning is a proper and vital arena for managers' responsible participation through the use of industrial engineers, who speak their language and bridge the gap between technological and economic theory and daily practice.

8

ORGANIZATIONAL PROBLEMS ABROAD

Improper organizations have been a prime source of overseas manufacturing problems. Many of the problems discussed thus far have been compounded—if not actually caused—by poor organizational practices at the overseas plant. In discussing the control of production, the management of the work force, and procurement, for example, a common conclusion was that increased organizational emphasis was needed in order to improve the handling of these functional areas.

In the preceding chapters we have been discussing some of the problems frequently encountered in operating overseas plants. This chapter will examine these areas from a different point of view, identifying a chronic contributor to the existence and persistence of problems, focusing on the managerial organization of the overseas plant. The international organization of the multinational corporation will be discussed in Chapter 9.

The most serious organizational fault observed in the manufacturing subsidiaries visited was that organization structures and approaches were not tailored to fit the circumstances. All production plants need not be organized alike, and, clearly, each organization requires thoughtful planning. Nevertheless, numerous alternatives in organizing each manufacturing facility were frequently overlooked. In most companies there tended to be a kind of corporate pattern, described as "here at the KYZ Corporation we organize our plants (in such and such a manner). . . ."

Although many variations in organizational patterns were found, by and large the variations did not appear to optimize an organization for the particular demands it faced. Instead, organizational variations appeared to have evolved around one or more of such factors as a copy of the U.S. basic organization, a mirror-image of other overseas plants, the philosophy of one key top-level individual in the company, or a strong individual. It was typical to give little or no management attention to planning the organization.

The results of organizations mismatched to the circumstances were frequently serious. In Turkey, for example, during the days of inventory shortages and foreign exchange restrictions, inventory control received very little organizational emphasis. In India, where problems of procurement were frequently serious because of industrially inexperienced vendors, procurement seldom was staffed to overcome these problems. In a large plant in Pakistan critical long-range planning decisions were not being made because there was no organizational mechanism for making them. In South Africa several plants had inadequate capacity because no system had been established for analyzing the capacity of equipment compared to the work load and making timely provisions for expansion and growth, both in organization and in facilities.

Five explanations are suggested for the organizations abroad that were not fitted to their circumstances.

1. There was a tendency to rely on the Americans for organizational know-how and to wait for changes to be initiated by the American management. As one Spanish executive put it, "We look to Americans for organizational ability. After all, your industrial society is far ahead of ours and you have learned a great deal about organizations. We therefore expect you to advise us and to make changes here. We are not always aware of the problems." While foreigners often relied on the Americans for organizational analysis, American home offices were inclined to set up relatively conventional organizations abroad and failed to differentiate between the specific circumstances and problems of each country.

2. Organizations sometimes failed to adapt due to a tendency for the headquarters' managers to perceive overseas plants as small, simple, elementary facilities, with the resultant necessity to keep management staff overhead low. By comparison with domestic plants, overseas branches are in fact small, and the customary headquarters role is to discourage the luxury of executive manpower. In seeing the problem as "how can we set up a minimum organization for a small plant?" the emphasis was almost entirely on organization

charts, highlighting the absolute number of key executives. Seldom was an organization perceived as consisting of an allocation of functions and as a system of procedures, policies, and mechanisms involving not only executives but the clerical, paperwork, and lower echelons as well. Even when there are only a few executives in a small plant, there can be a well-organized management system.

Reliance on orderly and carefully established policies and procedures can substitute for executive personnel to a large extent. Many Americans tended, however, to view the establishment of proper procedures for handling problems as a local duty that should be handled by the overseas personnel, whereas the overseas personnel were often too engrossed in daily problems to clearly appraise their organization.

3.   The fact that many foreign nationals were in the learning stage also contributed to organizational problems. Hierarchical systems with restrictive attitudes toward delegation of management authority were under pressure for change by the parent company. But only a certain rate of change could be tolerated. It was observed at several plants that foreign managers were too preoccupied with personal adaptation to the expectations of headquarters to be able to analyze their own organizational structures.

4.   A vicious cycle may develop in which poor organizations and mediocre organizational planning result in less planning, infrequent analysis and reappraisal of the organization. This in turn results in organizational structures continuing by their own momentum with relative inflexibility. This causes less planning, less flexibility, less reappraisal and analysis, and so on. A poor organization tends to perpetuate itself through the lack of a mechanism for appraisal, because key individuals are so busy that they are unable to recognize problems and make the necessary changes.

5.   It was noted that American managers sent abroad on a long-term basis could not often be classified as "organizers." Typically they were line type executives, competent in getting things done and improvising but often not accustomed to thinking conceptually. Methodical and analytical assistance might have been brought in to carefully appraise an entire situation and develop organizational structures necessary to handle it.

Organizational planning is further complicated by cultural variations, and by rapid change in the concept of the nature of management, and the source and nature of authority and responsibility differ from culture to culture. The beliefs and values of a culture influence the type of organization and management behavior which is effective.

Culture compels much of the behavior of both the governors and those governed.

Cultural analysis is beyond the scope of this study, but this example noted by several U.S. businessmen illustrates the point: many Indian managers and supervisors tended to act scornfully toward their inferiors, to be stubborn, proud of their own accomplishments, and to delegate little authority. One interpretation is that Hindus feel responsible only to their gods for their behavior and ignore their resonsibility to their fellow men. Their criteria of proper conduct seemed to include relatively little emphasis on respect or kindness to others.

In Turkey, where a degree of fatalism seems to arise from the Muslim concept that tomorrow is in the hands of Allah, there is a tendency to do very little forward planning. What happens tomorrow is decided by God, "Insallah."[1] In Nigeria the limited industrial experience of native supervisors results in their frequently appearing relatively immature or childlike to Westerners. They seem to give little thought to the future. As a result of tribal and village customs their behavior toward employees is likely to be paternalistic while they are simultaneously acting childlike toward their own superiors. Such factors as these exert considerable influence on management behavior and the organizational patterns in a company.

Environments are apt to be changing more rapidly abroad than in the United States where industrial society has been established for many years. For instance, changes in the value of the currency may cause drastic changes in wage rates, which in turn influence the behavior of unions and call for careful management approaches to wages and industrial relations. Another example is the major revisions in the tax laws which occurred suddenly in India after the Chinese crisis in 1962, changing the capital markets and national cash flow overnight. In all the developing countries movement to the city and rapid urbanization have changed patterns of living and the needs and composition of the work force in surprisingly short periods. Rapid environmental changes tend to keep the industrial situation so fluid that many companies have found it difficult to make the corresponding adjustments called for in labor relations, work-force management, procurement, and production control.

The rest of the chapter covers four topics relating to organizational problems abroad: (a) An analysis—with specific examples—of a number of organizational problems observed abroad. (b) The

[1]A Turkish expression meaning "With the help of God."

common misunderstandings that contribute to overseas organizational problems. (c) Alternatives in planning organizations. (d) Some conclusions suggested for ways of improving this area of management.

ORGANIZATIONAL PROBLEMS ABROAD

The central conclusion from visits to overseas plants is that the typical organization is not specifically tailored to its conditions and situation. Some results of failure to develop an organization for a specific task were serious; other problems were less serious than they might at first appear.

Ten problem areas stemming from improper organization are presented in the following examples.

Inadequate emphasis on certain key functions

Often relatively little organizational emphasis was placed on the procurement function in spite of the facts that the plant was dependent on both domestic and overseas procurement and that local vendors were often marginal in quality and delivery; for example, in the Winston truck plant in Turkey procurement was the responsibility of an individual who was also responsible for sales, credit, production control, relations with the government, and the plant's efforts to subcontract for other companies.

In a pharmaceutical plant in South Africa employing approximately 100 persons the production manager himself attempted to manage the quality control function. In actuality, because he was also in charge of nearly every other responsibility except accounting, he was unable to do more than occasionally look into the quality control laboratory.

In a 300-man mechanical operation in a relatively underdeveloped country a company was attempting to produce ten new products within a four-month period in a desperate effort to bring in needed sales volume. There was no means of internal scheduling of parts and assemblies in order to coordinate and control the development of the new products. Instead, the managing director of the plant attempted to keep up with all these projects himself because the manager in charge of production control was also in charge of sales, purchasing, and customer service and, in addition, had no experience in the field of production control. The total effect was that no one in the plant knew where each new product stood; no one had a list of tasks and priorities. Confusion reigned supreme.

A lack of planning

Managers in both home offices and overseas plants frequently stated that volatile swings in the economic cycle plus the instability and unpredictability of politics and international economics made it difficult, if not virtually impossible, to do any long- or short-range planning. A typical statement was "with the roller coaster that we are on in the underdeveloped countries, we can't plan ahead at all. The best we can attempt is a strictly play-it-by-ear approach and try to be just as flexible as possible." This attitude is an understandable response to dramatic, overnight changes in economic and political conditions. Not only do conditions change suddenly, but Americans find them difficult to predict and to understand.

Herein lies an enigma: conditions in underdeveloped countries require careful planning, yet forward planning is difficult. It is complicated to reverse direction, difficult and time-consuming to remedy errors or to make adjustments for changes in the market, government action, or economic environment. Companies employing careful planning can anticipate problems and set up the organization and procedures necessary to meet them and thus avoid costly and time-consuming changes of direction.

Neglected policy decisions

In a number of instances a vacuum in decision making developed between the overseas plant and home office so that neither made needed policy decisions. For example, the home office of a farm implement plant in Turkey passively resisted expanding the product line beyond tractors. The Americans abroad recognized the necessity for developing other products because they were unable to import American parts. Nevertheless, they were unwilling to make the decision alone or continue trying to persuade the home office to do so. Consequently, three years passed during which the company produced virtually nothing. The tug of war over the locus of manufacturing policy[2] determination is discussed in Chapter 9.

This example illustrates the fact that a company must provide an

---

[2]Decisions as to what products to manufacture, the plant size, capacity, basic investment, and correlated decisions relating to the fraction of the product that will be purchased and subcontracted.

organization and system for handling basic policy decisions as well as daily operating decisions. When the home office insists on having the final word on policy decisions, overseas personnel tend to conclude that the major decisions are always made at home and that policy is not their job. At a large plant in India, the foreign nationals had repeatedly urged a change in a major manufacturing policy which they felt would create a stronger competitive position. The Indians told this researcher that the home office had turned the request down so often that it was clear they would never accept the recommendation because there were always more attractive investments elsewhere in the world. These nationals felt that since they were not allowed to move in the direction they were convinced was necessary, the initiative for major changes, recommendations, and policy directions would henceforth have to come from the New York office.

This state of mind is not conducive to inspiring recommendations for changes from the managers in the foreign plants, who often understand the overseas situation as well as or better than home office executives.

The organization frequently did not feed back the information necessary for adequate controls

It was not unusual to observe that an excessive amount of authority held closely at top levels discouraged the feedback of control information. The shortage of trained middle management at many plants made for a relatively autocratic organization.[3] Limiting decision-making to the top generally weakened middle management, which, in turn, created an information gap.

The common gap between the higher and the lower management levels was difficult for the top man to bridge. He did not have the time (or inclination) to get out to the workplace. He relied instead on reports and limited contacts with low-level subordinates who could not be depended upon for objective and perceptive reporting.

Foreign nationals who were given little authority to make decisions and expected only to obey and do what was asked of them were seldom communicative with their superiors. They did what they were told, and they passed on information they felt would be

---

[3]It is interesting to note that European managers have been cited as criticizing American plants for being "overmanaged," using an unnecessary amount of staff department help, paperwork, and controls. Abroad, many American plants have been forced into a more European pattern by a shortage of middle managers.

viewed favorably. This, too, added to the problem of the men at the top in learning what was going on.

This syndrome was observed at a pharmaceutical plant in South Africa, where major authority was vested in the managing director and the production manager was a relatively low-level supervisor. The managing director had a busy schedule and "as long as production seemed to be coming along all right" he had little to do with it. He was uninformed about potentially serious problems in inventory control, scheduling, and quality control.

A noteworthy exception was the general manager of an operation in India. Instead of abandoning control, he drove to the plant each day to spend at least two hours reviewing results with his plant manager. He toured the assembly lines and seemed to observe and be interested in every facet. He may have delegated too little responsibility, but he knew what was going on. This Indian manager recognized the lack of information coming to him in reports and discussions with middle managers; he felt he had to get out and see for himself and he did so. In this case he adapted himself and his organization to the environment.

One plant suffered badly from lack of control information primarily because the plant manager did not understand the potential of control reports. He had competent middle managers and a competent possible source of control information, but he had never been trained in developing and using reports. He had worked his way up through shop operations and he was unable to get accounts, reports, figures, and controls organized. He obtained little help from the home office in this task. Indeed, it appeared that no one in the home office recognized his problem.

Excessively informal organizations

Of course there is no clear definition of the "proper" degree of formality or informality in organizational behavior. It depends on many circumstances, including the nature of the personalities, abilities, and relationships of key men in the organization, as well as on the type of job that must be done. An auto-assembly plant, a railroad, a jam and jelly factory may be expected to be relatively formal in organization with the duties laid out clearly and with little or no variation from this pattern. On the other hand, an electronics plant, a research development outfit, and a rapidly expanding chemical firm may require more informality and a less restricting structure in order to handle more frequent variations and changes in the product and markets. For this reason companies should not be criticized for being excessively informal merely because they are not rigidly organized. The test is a pragmatic one: How well is the particular pattern working?

Certain organizations studied seemed to be less effective because they were excessively informal. Lines of authority and communication were so scrambled that individuals were confused about who was doing what. Duties overlapped or were overlooked. Sometimes overseas firms found that although rather informal organization had been effective in the past, it was no longer so because of growth and enlarged complexity.

This problem was encountered in Southern Europe, where an American company had bought control of a European company that had previously been family managed. Family members required little formal organization in order to keep things running smoothly. After the acquisition the American managers needed a set of controlled communications mechanisms, which had not been necessary before.

Some companies had been dominated by two or three strong men who had worked together for years. The idea of dividing the duties in a formal way, or of delegating responsibilities or allocating authority, was a foreign notion to such men. A good example of this was at the same plant in Southern Europe.

Example 1

The new owners sent over a few men to appraise the operation. They found what appeared to be a sea of confusion, with three different men running the sales department, the production functions divided among several other men, no one handling the personnel management function on an organized basis, one old woman handling the large purchasing sector of the business, and no apparent system for cost controls or other organized information for feedback. All this was appalling to the American managers who asked for help from the home office. Eventually they found that the problems were not as bad as they seemed, but there was a clear indication that if the company was going to grow and problems were to be met in a more systematic fashion with less "back of the envelope" figuring, a more formal organization would be required.

When raw materials and purchased parts made up most of the production cost, direct labor costs were low, the process was relatively simple, quality was relatively easy to achieve, there were few problems in scheduling or meeting customer delivery requirements, and the production manager was usually a relatively low-paid individual, perhaps with a technical background but with little training in administration. This was often the case in the compounding of pharmaceuticals, the simple processing of foods (such as bottled beverages), or the assembly of vehicles in plants where the parts were not manufactured.

Such a low status production manager and manufacturing organization often became inadequate when manufacturing conditions became more difficult. For example, during periods of foreign exchange shortages in Turkey the production manager suddenly became a key individual in the company success. Production performance had not been critical to company success. In such situations the production operating margin had been substantial and there was little pressure on the production manager to cut his costs. Now it was not possible to import the foreign parts on which the operation depended. New products had to be developed, the existing labor force had to be utilized rather than laid off, and expanded local procurement became necessary. Under such circumstances the low-paid, perfunctory production manager became obsolete.

Example 2

A producer of a mechanical/electrical items in Nigeria unexpectedly faced drastic price competition from Japanese products. In the degenerating competitive situation it became necessary to increase the local manufacturing and procurement fraction of the product and to place ever-increasing emphasis on cutting costs. The production operation had received so little organizational emphasis that it was managed by one individual with no educated subordinates.

Another example illustrates the frequent need to upgrade production management abroad.

Example 3

An American corporation with four plants located in environments with a wide range of economic and political circumstances had production managers who were strictly technical men with little prior administrative experience or expertise. They were given such limited authority that even the plant schedules were not under their control. Facility and equipment expansions were originated by the managing directors. Production managers did not direct the warehousing and shipping operations nor the procurement of material and supplies.

In the less developed countries the operating margins were high enough so that the excessive decentralization of production responsibility made little difference. But in more developed South Africa, margins were tighter. Pressures for quality reliability and on-time deliveries were substantially greater than in the other three plants. A recently appointed young but able production manager had to fight the whole organizational tradition of the company to acquire the authority and responsibility which he needed to properly meet the local demands for better performance of his function.

In rapidly changing environments the nature of requirements for the production manager's function is continually changing. A manufacturing organization must be modified to fit the circumstances.

Organizational conflicts of interest

Some overseas manufacturing organizations were set up without the internal logic, or balance of power, which is often considered a characteristic of a good organization. In a large industrial organization in Turkey, the time study department reported directly to the superintendent of the operating group in the factory, who used the time studies for rating plant efficiency. As one might expect, the standards developed were relatively loose and the use of time and motion studies for the purpose of operating control was sloppy. It would probably have made more sense to place the time study operation under the supervision of the plant manager rather than the superintendent.

In a large plant in South Africa the industrial engineering and the personnel jobs were combined. It might be expected under these circumstances that the personnel manager would either tend to apply relatively mechanistic[4] approaches to his personnel job or, conversely, might attempt to apply relatively humanistic values to his industrial engineering work. Here the personnel department was run with a mechanistic point of view with the implicit objective of

[4]For a definition of "conventional mechanistic procedures" as contrasted to different assumptions about human behavior see Robert L. Katz, "Toward a More Effective Enterprise," *Harvard Business Review* (September-October 1960).

bringing rationalization and order into the plant. The emphasis was on precise job descriptions, job evaluation, pay grades and ranges, and the use of carefully engineered incentive wage payments. The price paid for combining these operations was poor morale, apparently due to the fact that the working group was not respected individually and was subjected to rigid rules, standards, and collective treatment.

It makes sense in most circumstances to recognize the conflicting interests between different departments and achieve a balance of power by separating the organizations that have different interests.

Missing: A mechanism for bringing about organizational changes and improvements

Within a conventional manufacturing organization, the director of manufacturing, the vice president of manufacturing, or the plant manager normally has the responsibility for making necessary organizational changes. But at the overseas plant the executive responsible for the manufacturing operation was frequently at too low a level in the international hierarchy or was too inexperienced to be able to recommend needed changes. Sometimes this was because the plant manager was given only perfunctory responsibility.

An alternate mechanism for bringing about organizational change in domestic operations is sometimes found in the use of home office staff at a relatively high level to appraise production operations, study problems, and recommend changes. But such an approach was rarely used in international operations, because manufacturing operations were seldom reviewed from headquarters by other than technically oriented staff. Overseas plant managers appeared to be too close to their tasks to perceive the need for changes. In many instances this problem occurred when the overseas plants were so small that there was no one with the time or capacity to objectively appraise the operation and bring about organizational changes.

In a comparable domestic firm of 15 to 20 relatively small branch plants it is probable that all the individual plants would not have managers with the experience and background necessary to do their own organizational analysis. Frequently under these circumstances in the United States a vice president would visit each plant regularly to see that the necessary changes were made.

Three reasons help explain why this is infrequent in overseas operations. In the first place, international companies rarely have a manufacturing vice president. It is more typical to have a regional or area vice president who is more apt to have a sales or financial than a manufacturing background. He tends, therefore, to leave the manufacturing problems to the local managers. Second, manufacturing problems are considered to be so different from one country to another that they are best left to local personnel. Third, the manufacturing staff assistance available from the home office is usually in the form of technical rather than administrative aid.

Lacking: A mechanism for self-appraisal

When a mechanism for self-appraisal was lacking, the cause was typically an overload on the local plant manager or his inability to analyze results and problems in his organization and to survey the allocation of responsibilities and authority and the flow of information.

The situation of a manager of a new plant in Pakistan furnishes an example. He was under pressure from sales because start-up delays had caused a total stockout. There were manufacturing problems in every direction: production control had failed to move parts through the shop in matching sets; there were breakdowns of equipment and tooling; the building was incomplete; the supervisory group was inexperienced. At this time the manager was being asked by the home office to develop plans for a major diversification, which called for producing four products (rather than one) within a year. Only one other English-speaking manager was present. It is no wonder that there was no time to stand back and make a critical self-appraisal.

This problem, primarily one of overload at the top, could be alleviated by home-office staff aid for the top manufacturing executive or by counsel from the managing director at the overseas plant. But it was rare to find a managing director who had sufficient production experience or even enough interest in the plant to help. Managing directors, typically sales-or finance-oriented, were not able to offer much assistance. Neither were home office engineers, who were not interested in manufacturing administration. The overloaded overseas production manager was usually left on his own to develop the organization by trial and error in the midst of other demanding tasks.

Restrictive domination by foreign nationals

Several failures to adapt organizations to the current situation were caused by the domination of a high-status foreign national.

The typical situation involved a man who withhheld information and decision-making authority. The relatively low level of education coupled with the lack of adequate middle management and a traditional concentration of power and education in the hands of a few led to the tendency of one or two individuals to dominate. When this occurred it tended to prevent the natural adaptation of an organization to its environment as the plant operations expanded, grew more complex, and faced greater competitive pressure. Some family-oriented companies that merged with U.S. corporations were forced by the parent company to delegate more, to more clearly designate authority and responsibilities, to divide duties, and to develop more systematic procedures.

This pattern is, of course, not unusual in American and European industry. It was common in the early days of American industrial management and it still exists in many small companies. It is becoming less common as the group of professional managers grows, the general level of education rises, and competitive pressures challenge it. American industry has moved toward more systematic organization, increased delegation of responsibility, and less domination by a few individuals, whether they be family owners or top corporate officials. This process will probably gradually take place abroad, but in the meantime many organizations have developed a power focus which will probably have to change.

COMMON MISUNDERSTANDINGS CONTRIBUTING TO ORGANIZATIONAL PROBLEMS

It is seldom recognized that organizational patterns which have evolved in the United States involve adaptations to unique features of American culture. When organizations are transplanted to another culture, it becomes necessary to understand the rationale underlying American practices so that the essence, rather than only the external appearance, may be preserved. A description of some common misunderstandings follows.

A small foreign operation is elementary and simple and therefore cannot afford a manager for each key function

When this assumption was used, key functions were often left unidentified and organizations were set up more on the sole basis of what could be afforded rather than the basis of a total production system designed to meet specific demands, including cost restrictions. Stated in another way, when a foreign operation is small, it may require even more careful organization and system planning than larger ones in which full-time managers are appointed for each function.

Lack of competent middle managers forces duties and responsibilities onto the top management

Frequently there was a dearth of trained or experienced candidates for middle management jobs and the plant manager attempted to personally handle many responsibilities, sometimes including conflicting functions.

In contrast, the shortage of middle management was partially mitigated in several companies where many tasks were systematized and spelled out procedurally. When a plant manager can develop systematic procedures and systems for handling repetitive duties and thus reduce the variety of decisions which come to his attention, these functions can be delegated to lower positions in the organization. With such guides, men who are not fully trained can perform better, thus giving the proper organizational emphasis to their function. In other words, organizational emphasis can be created through effective development of systems and policies even when it cannot be accomplished by assignment of authority and responsibility to competent middle managers.

The "cult of flexibility"

A great deal of the lack of planning and organizing abroad is due to what can be labeled the "cult of flexibility." Conventional wisdom often asserts that "the overseas plant is apt to be in such constant turmoil due to rapid changes in the economic and political environments that it is impossible to plan ahead." This "cult of flexibility" is based on the belief that under unpredictable conditions "we must play by ear, be entirely flexible, roll with the punch, and always be ready to make changes."

This ignores the possibility of achieving flexibility through better long- and short-range planning. The critical need is to develop plans to deal with fluctuating eventualities rather than making plans that assume certain eventualities. For instance, plans were needed in Turkey for the eventuality of shortages of foreign exchange. But because the foreign exchange picture was so unpredictable, several plant managers said, "We can't plan ahead in this business; we will just have to take what comes and adapt as we can." When foreign exchange shortages virtually shut down their plants, they had no plans for using the available labor force or for using new products or local procurement sources. Flexibility is a "must," but it can come through good planning and is not obtained by failure to plan.

The nature of control

The lack of adequate information systems and feedback mechanisms for the achievement of control by the top executives could frequently be traced to a misconception of the basic nature of control. Both Americans and foreign nationals tended to assume that effective control by the home office could be obtained by a system of written and personal reports, submitting budgets through an organizational hierarchy, and random personal visits.

Although a good deal of information can be obtained this way, this is not "control," for control does not result from information. One executive does not control the performance and behavior of another if he receives reports from him, even if the reports are well designed. Some aspects of a subordinate's performance may be modified through reporting and budgets, but executive control is not in fact exercised through such mechanics.

A more realistic point of view is that an executive actually has relatively little real control over a subordinate. This is particularly true in functions whose quality of performance is difficult to judge from a distance, such as labor relations, salary administration, development of vendors, and installing effective time standards. Many such managerial functions are virtually impossible to control secondhand; they are controlled by the quality of decisions of the manager in charge and not by the executive over him. The superior executive can advise and help, but only the personal operation of the subordinate manager on the scene can actually result in good work.

When this distinction is understood, it suggests a different concept of the nature of control in a foreign plant where distance separates the top executive from the operation. The implication is that managing an effective foreign operation requires competent men of considerable independence and integrity. Until this quality of professional, able management is on the scene, no amount of "control" or information feedback, budgets, or reports, will improve the operation. The emphasis must be on the development of able men at the foreign plant rather than on the development of controls.

The initiative for policy and planning rests with the home office

Some of the organizational problems abroad were rooted in home office domination of policy and planning. When the home office determined basic manufacturing policy and controlled both long- and short-range planning (often through the budgetary process), it was no wonder that executives located abroad tended to shrug their shoulders and say, "Well, actually it is the function and privilege of the home office to make the big decisions and to plan ahead. We are pretty much limited to operating decisions here."

But this approach has the obvious weakness that it is difficult for home office managers to initiate plans and policies which are fully appropriate to local situations. They can do little more than respond to policies and plans initiated at the overseas plants. If the overseas managers shrug the responsibility off to the headquarters, carefully worked out and sensitive plans based on local situations will not be initiated abroad. Under these circumstances the evidence shows that plans were developed overseas on a rather perfunctory basis for budgeting purposes, not initiated as the plans of an executive group which felt itself responsible for the future of the overseas operation.

When organizational changes are needed it will be obvious

Many companies used this rationale for not establishing mechanisms for regular review, analysis, and possible changing of their organization. Instead they relied on the top managers to know when to stand back and make an appraisal. But, as stated earlier, top managers were overloaded, too involved, or sales- or finance-oriented and usually did not perform this function. Unfortunately, the potential benefit of an organizational change is not always obvious and sometimes is, in fact, quite subtle.

ALTERNATIVES IN PLANNING ORGANIZATIONS

What are the choices involved in planning an organization? Conceptually the choices involve decisions on the number of managers in the organization, the allocation of responsibilities to the different managers, and the policies and procedures by which the chief executive and his manager handle the functions of planning and control.

Functions basic to most industrial organizations are (a) manufacturing supervision, including supervision of the work force, (b) production planning and inventory control, (c) purchasing, (d) methods of manufacturing and process engineering, (e) quality control, (f) personnel management, (g) financial and cost control, and (h) plant and equipment maintenance.

In organizing a plant, needless to say, not all of these functions need be managed by department heads reporting directly to a plant manager. Indeed, functions such as procurement, personnel, and frequently accounting were not a part of the plant management in some of the companies studied. In some plants the quality control function reported separately to the top executive, in theory to gain independence. In addition to variations in the level at which each key function reports there are often subdivisions of plant management which concentrate on particular areas of the plant, special products, or certain operations; for example, in a large auto facility in South Africa, battery manufacturing had a line and staff operation that was virtually autonomous from the rest of the plant.

Size introduces another factor. A small operation does not need and cannot afford the staff organization in production planning, control, personnel management, cost control, and so forth, of a larger and more complex operation.

The organization should fit the requirements of the products it is to manufacture. For instance, in a pharmaceutical operation the manufacturer must exercise precise quality control. In contrast, the type of quality control necessary in automobile assembly is quite different. Both plants need what may be called "high quality and reliability," but the quality is determined and influenced by different factors. For this reason the quality control organizations of these two plants would be expected to vary.

The organization should also be modified to fit circumstances determined by its particular location. For example, Turkey's shortage of foreign exchange demanded special accuracy in ordering imported parts since this called for scarce foreign exchange. Under that set of circumstances a production control department was needed to play a major role in the operation of the plant. It should be well-staffed, report close to the top of the organization, and probably be the full time function of an able individual. There should be as much flexibility as possible built into the equipment, process, product, labor force, inventory policy, and the organization to cut down the time required for making changes. The equipment should be general purpose; the company should have standby products ready to go when imports necessary for regular products cannot be obtained; trained and dependable vendors and subcontractors should be developed in order to provide substitute capacity. This would help materially in meeting crises which cannot be forecast, and in being able to move quickly to adjust products, processes, and organization as the economy, the market, and the government situation require it. There is a substantial difference between such built-in flexibility and an unplanned, rigid factory operation with a management that avoids plans in order to "keep loose and flexible."

There are at least five steps in developing an organizational structure:

1.   Divide the functions to decide who is supposed to do what.

2.   Each individual who is given responsibilities is delegated some degree of authority. Some decisions must be referred to a higher executive; some can be delegated to subordinates; some the individual can make himself.

3.   Establish a system of acquiring, transmitting and evaluating information about what is going on.

4.   There must be mechanisms for handling both operating decisions and major policy decisions which establish a pattern or a basic approach.

5.   Finally, to achieve better performance, an organization needs to have a means of self-appraisal and an apparatus for planning.

In questions for evaluating manufacturing organizations to appraise organizational effectiveness, the analyst can ask whether and how well these primary requirements are being met. Specific questions probe further:

1.   Are the overseas plants well-organized in terms of results? (Are decisions being made instead of deferred? What is the quality of decisions made in the different areas of operations? Is effective planning done throughout the organization? Is there an adequate information system with "feedback" to analyze the day-to-day results and the policies of the organization?)

2.   Are problems found in the overseas plant traceable to ineffective organizational approaches?

3.   What are the mechanisms for planning?

4.   What is the mechanism for making organizational changes and improvements?

5.   What functions are strengthened or weakened by the organization structure, manning, and executive appointments in the plant?

This kind of analysis could aid the overseas manager to develop an objective point of view for scrutinizing his own organization. It can bring out for appraisal the emphasis given to different manufacturing functions through allocation of responsibilities, organizational level, the planning apparatus, and control systems.

The goal of this kind of appraisal is to tailor the organization to the needs of the situation by changing the assignment of responsibilities, the degree and methods of delegation, the mechanisms for control and appraisal of effectiveness, the mechanism for making policy decisions and planning.

Three companies studied suffered less from organization problems than the others. It is interesting to look at their experience to see what lessons can be learned.

Companies A and B were alike in that the organizations tended to be strong where they needed to be; there was an organizational emphasis on the key functions; and there was a strong system of clear organizational delegation of authority. Both of these companies manufactured a few products, which were virtually indentical whether they were made in New Jersey or Johannesburg. Thus the manufacturing process could be the same everywhere, permitting standardization which in turn resulted in structuring of similar organizations. They were similar in the division of responsibilities and in the emphasis given to functions that were important for their respective products.

In addition to the influence of the product on these organizations, they both had strong home office headquarters organizations which handed down elaborate systems of organizational approaches, policies, and procedures in a rather authoritative, directive fashion. Although this somewhat heavy-handed approach resulted in a variety of problems (discussed in the next chapter), these companies were well organized.

These companies' apparent freedom from organizational problems abroad has been supported by home offices applying the benefits of experience in many countries because of the uniformity of their product rather than by reappraisal of the organization. One may question whether, in the future, they may tend to suffer from inflexibility and fail to adjust the organization to changes in competitive and economic conditions in each country. Indeed, it appears that the companies have such strong headquarters influence that each tends to have a "company way" of looking at problems.

A food products company's overseas plants also showed few organizational problems. There is very limited product similarity from one country to another, and as a result the organization in Asia, keyed originally to production of soft drink concentrates, is entirely different from that in Africa where the concentration has been on packaging processed foods. This in turn differs considerably from Southern Europe, where the product line is much broader and the emphasis has been more on processing vegetable oil.

This firm's approach is quite different from most of the other companies studied. Their organizational adaptability appears to lie in their philosophy of decentralizing the authority and policy initiative in every way possible. Because of this, the tendency has been to develop quite flexibly in each location. Local manufacturing organizations clearly are the responsibility of each local management. They are expected to call on the services of headquarters and regional staff groups and frequently do so. This company's organization showed a capability toward self-appraisal and natural adaptation in each of the four locations studied.

The conclusion illustrated by the successful experiences of these three companies is that organization problems can be avoided by a clear assignment of the responsibility for appropriate organization to the overseas plant, buttressed by an able headquarters staff group operating with a strong service orientation. Overseas plants should be expected to use headquarters and regional office assistance. This staff group can supply help in the formulation of systems, procedures, and policies and can exert considerable influence through the reappraisal of overseas organizations on an invitation basis. This approach has been quite successful.

CONCLUSION

Organization is a key factor in the success of any production operation. Authorities, responsibilities and systems, prodedures and policies need to be carefully derived and explicitly stated with certain key functions emphasized. The production organization must be changed as the circumstances change.

None of this happens automatically. With the prevalence of lags in organizational adaptation abroad it is necessary that organization receive more attention as a key ingredient in operating overseas plants. It can seldom be handled without assistance by overseas personnel. Organizations need planning and reappraisal just as much as the performance of executives needs surveillance and judgment. The supervision of the organization and its operating procedures need to be considered a prime area for analysis, appraisal, and review by the home office personnel.

9

THE HEADQUARTERS

Managing geographically decentralized organizations is an ancient task. As the Roman Empire spread out around the Mediterranean and into the wilds of Europe, the Emperors attempted to cope with the political, commercial, and military affairs of the far-flung domain from their seat of operations in Rome.

Managing a remote enterprise requires that the geographically decentralized operating units—whether they be nations, armies, or commercial enterprises—be led at a distance to conduct their affairs in a way that will bring success and profit to the entire organization. In this chapter we are concerned with the headquarters functions of organizations in which the owners[1] are physically remote from outlying operating units.

Earlier in business history this same task of remote ownership was faced by such firms as the East India Company, the Hudson Bay Trading Company, and the Balfour-Guthrie corporation. Headquartered in London, Balfour-Guthrie began its operations on the California West Coast in 1823. They experienced the same kind of problems as the modern international enterprises studied in this research: problems of achieving effective control and sufficient direction in policy.

It is inevitable that the role will be difficult. The local units must be planned, organized, instructed, and controlled not only to do a good job locally but to coordinate their efforts for the benefit of the

[1]Ownership may be 100 percent as in the case of a wholly owned subsidiary of a U.S. corporation or partial, as in a joint enterprise.

organization as a whole. Daily operating decisions must be made at the decentralized units to lead to ultimate profit there, yet these decisions must also be in accord with the total strategy of the international firm.

This book, thus far, has been written chiefly from the standpoint of the overseas operating units. In this chapter we look at the problems of the headquarters, which has the responsibility to the owners for the performance of the multinational organization.

CONTROL IN A MULTINATIONAL CORPORATION[2]

Many international firms convey an impression of containing a "cold war" in which the headquarters is seen as the enemy by the overseas unit. And to the headquarters, the overseas units are often a somewhat rebellious, unnecessarily independent, and strongly nationalistic neutralist power.

The human problems involved are many. Managers at the home office feel a heavy measure of ultimate responsibility and yet have a genuine problem in keeping track of what is going on in the field. They are hungry for information and often feel the need of some personal sense of control and influence toward men in the field. But the men in the field usually feel that they have a closer and more intimate knowledge of their problems than the headquarters. They naturally tend to resist and resent the attempts of the home office to establish control through reporting, visits, or withholding authorities from the field. They accept the fact of remote ownership, but they resent the apparent lack of confidence shown by efforts to control.

It was no surprise to find at home and abroad a ready response to the writer's invitation to discuss mutual relationships. So eager were both parties to vent their feelings and their personal philosophies on this issue that often the discussion was initiated before the subject was raised by the writer. Every international executive interviewed regardless of his base—either at headquarters or overseas—had a strongly stated set of beliefs on this subject. The men in the field tend to feel that they should be given more authority and more responsibility, allowed to spend less time writing reports and that they should be judged on their ultimate performance. Headquarters managers frequently feel that the men in the field have little or no understanding of the complicated and difficult nature of running an

[2]The rest of this chapter is reprinted by permission from the author's article in *Worldwide Projects and Installations Planning* (May/June 1967).

international division. They assert that the need for headquarters coordination to control and manage finances, products, pricing, and multinational sourcing is not understood in the field.

The different schools of thought on the subject of managing geographically decentralized companies are polarized around the decentralization-centralization issue which in turn is discussed in terms of the allocation of responsibility and authority. Managers tend to take a position on the issue consistent with their personal "lessons from experience."

Key issues in headquarters management

Disagreements over manufacturing policy are natural. Disagreement between home office and overseas plant personnel is not necessarily harmful or even avoidable. Resentment and stress are often only surface manifestations of the existence of more fundamental problems. But beneath external complaints and protests there are issues which are not always seen clearly.

The locus of international manufacturing policy is a battleground. Headquarters holds the purse strings and has a strategic concept for the corporation. The branch plants abroad have local knowledge and often a sense of trends and perspective for the particular area which is impossible to acquire at the home office. Key issues are:

1. *The issue of home office control:* the amount of control, the type of control and the areas in which control is used, ranging from the areas of basic policy through financial and equipment decisions down to the operating decisions at the local plants.

2. *The issue of home office support:* the type, amount and nature of the support and contribution offered by the home office staff.

3. *The nature and type of the communications between the home office and the overseas plant.*

Little common agreement was found on answers to these issues. There was no common agreement even on what factors should be considered. Managers need some rationale or framework for deciding these three issues. Let us examine the issue of control, as the issues of home office contribution and communications are largely dependent on the home office control considered needed.

Headquarters control

The issue of control is usually argued in the dichotomy of which is better: "centralization or decentralization?"

Perceiving headquarters problems as revolving around "authority," "responsibility" and "decentralization" is, in the writer's opinion, oversimplified. The controversy over which is better: "centralization" or "decentralization" is meaningless and bound to be fruitless. In their proccupation in trying to find an "answer" to the ancient dilemma the protagonists fail to understand the problem. They see it as a struggle for home office control over the overseas plant. But this is the wrong problem.

It is the wrong problem partly because it has no answer. The problem of operating a plant in Spain might be expected to be quite different from one in India. And the problems involved in India might be expected to be quite different today than five years ago, not only because of changes in India, but also because of changes in the executive personnel involved. Different degrees or kinds of control, service, and reporting would be most suitable in each situation.

There is no one answer because organizations, communications, and control systems must be built around the particular products, markets, technology, individuals, and political and social environments involved. A situational point of view and a flexible, tailor-made approach is needed to each individual plant, country, company, executive group and product. If it is true, as asserted earlier, that it is fruitless to ask whether one favors centralization or decentralization, the problem needs to be broken down into more detail in order to decide what is "right" and makes sense in any given situation.

It is a fallacy to think of headquarters organizations as control centers rather than as service and coordination centers. The headquarters office can provide vital services for the operating units abroad, in terms of supplies, procurement, executives, technical aid and managerial systems. They may also perform service functions in providing financing and coordination throughout the international organization for pricing, quality, interchange of parts, engineering design and overall marketing efforts. But because they have an ultimate responsibility to the top management and stockholders for profits, they are lured into the delusion that by "controlling" the operations abroad and by exercising their authority by this "control" that they can actually change the behavior of overseas managers and hence increase profits.

This researcher's observation is that the changing of behavior of men located abroad is only slightly influenced by the directives, and controls of the home office. Only the individual can change his own behavior. Reports, policies, and controls do not affect it as much as many home office executives assume. Often the only real change which comes about in behavior overseas as a result of home office directives is the reluctant submission due to heavy-handed orders with a recognition of the ultimate need to please those in final authority at home. A reluctant submission does not usually accomplish the effect desired.

The difference of opinion between home office and overseas managers over how home office managers ought to do their job causes tensions. But it is probably inevitable that there will never be a consistently pacific, mutually satisfying relationship between branch plants and headquarters. In fact, this might be unfortunate if it reflected a dull, passive equilibrium of relaxed contentment. What seems more important is the lack of a pinpointed approach to the particular problems of each different plant. Most companies do not adopt their headquarters operations, systems, procedures, and policies to the unique problems and circumstances at each location.

If a company operated in an industry which involved heavy materials moving and expensive logistics and inventory, a close control from headquarters over materials handling methods and supply procedures might play a key role in influencing its success. And in a chemical industry, where the big dollars go into fixed investment and equipment, and work force costs are a small percentage of costs, it would be expected that the home office might play a strong role and make greater contributions in the equipment decisions than in work force management.

Different local situations might require considerably different home office emphasis. For example, in an underdeveloped situation where there are relatively few competent or experienced local managers, especially in middle management, it would be normal to feel that the home office could help more than in a country such as Western Germany where the managerial resources are considerably more developed. And in a location where able vendors are few and far between, such as in Turkey, the home office would aid substantially in procurement management, such as in establishing the organization for purchasing, assisting in formulating purchasing procedures, and sending over staff to aid in the development of local vendors. In Western Europe where the vendors are more plentiful and competition is keener the procurement function might properly require no control by the headquarters group. This would depend, too, on the skills of the U.S. managers abroad. Thus, it can be expected that differences in the product, the industry, the managers, and the situation in a particular country might each be expected to influence the effectiveness of a given approach toward corporate control from the home office.

From what has been said thus far the reader may pluck one broad suggestion, namely, to "be sure to vary your approach to fit the needs." But this is at best rather general advice. To be more specific we need to examine more closely just what control is. The word "control" suggests a high element of *involvement* and a sense of *command* as well. These two components of control may be separated and each can be applied in different orders of magnitude by a headquarters. These two components of control should be seen as two distinct ingredients in the headquarters-branch relationship. For example, a headquarters may be deeply involved in the affairs of an overseas plant on a consultive basis and exert little direct command. Five different degrees of command and involvement can be defined to provide a more precise way of measuring control.

Degrees of involvement

Degree one. No headquarters control or involvement. Complete decentralization of independent subsidiaries.

Degree two. Headquarters is only involved in general policy. It helps to establish guides, objectives, and strategic directions. Its involvement is in long-term planning. It receives information on overall results.

Degree three. Headquarters is involved in not only long-range plans, broad policy, and setting objectives but in shorter-range planning as well. It plays a major role in reaching general policy and decisions on particular approaches for achieving aims and carrying out policy. Its planning functions would ordinarily include participation in the establishment of regular, annual or semiannual plans and the financial and personnel requirements for meeting these plans.

Degree four. Headquarters are involved in the functions described in degrees 1, 2, and 3 and additionally in the design of the total production system of the subsidiary, including the management organization, management selection, systems and procedures, and specific procedures for accomplishing general policy and the long- and short-range plans of degrees 2 and 3.

Degree five. The fifth degree occurs when the home office is deeply and consistently concerned with specific operating decisions in addition to all functions in degree 4. They are required to be involved in short-range operating decisions regarding schedules, manpower, expenses, labor and personnel practices in addition to general policy, long- and short-range planning and changes in the organizational structure.

We now have a rough measure for appraising the amount and type of headquarters involvement. But the way that this involvement is carried out is another important dimension of the problem. Headquarters may be consulted about policy or they may unilaterally decide policy. The degree of *command* measures the "how" of involvement.

The degree of command is a definition for measuring or describing the extent of control which the home office attempts to exert. These degrees might be described as follows:

Degrees of command

Degree 1 — to observe the situation abroad, but to give no advice.

Degree 2 — to observe and render assistance or give advice if requested.

Degree 3 — to observe and to suggest changes on a unilateral basis and to insist on being kept informed in detail.

Degree 4 — to observe and to be kept informed in detail and to require plans to be submitted in advance for approval before action is taken.

Degree 5 — to have specific detail knowledge through observation, reports, and frequent plant visits, to give specific orders on decisions other than the most minor.

Exhibit I shows a matrix in which the degree of headquarters involvement in the management of the local plant is represented by the vertical axis and the degree of command over the local plant is shown by the horizontal axis. This matrix is a method of describing a profile of the control and influence exerted by the headquarters operation for each overseas plant. Five degrees are in each axis. Point A (5.5) would indicate a very high degree of headquarters involvement and a high degree of headquarters command. Point B (2.4) would show a low degree of headquarters command with a relatively high headquarters involvement. Such an approach to headquarters management was used by one large company which has an unusually well-trained and experienced headquarters staff organization which did considerable visiting and was highly involved in many facets of overseas plant operation. But in terms of authority, or command, the organization is very decentralized.

EXHIBIT 1.   Headquarters involvement and command

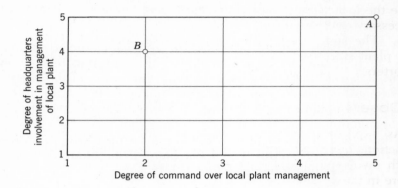

In the writer's research, the functions of 12 company's headquarters relative to each overseas plant were observed and studied within the framework described. Headquarters involvement and command were also appraised regarding various functional areas such as labor relations, procurement, etc. using the same framework. Naturally, certain expectations were held in advance. These were as follows:

1.   Different companies will handle the headquarters or home office management quite differently, due to differences in the nature of the product, the number of products, technology requirements, cost of equipment, etc.

2.   The profiles within one company should differ markedly between countries: As the skill and experience of local foreign national managers increase, the profile rating should decrease; as shortages and scarcities in foreign exchange, the profile ratings should increase; as adequate vendors and supplies become more readily available, the ratings in procurement would be expected to decrease.

3.   Where there are many products and/or the investment is relatively small and/or the company image is not so clearly identifiable or susceptible to damage in a given country, then it might be expected that the profile ratings would decrease.

4.   The degree of involvement will be independent of the degree of command because the involvement appropriate should depend on products, technological factors, investment, and what functions are most critical to company success, whereas the desirable amount

of command should vary more with the judgment and executive ability of the plant management at each overseas plant. The more able the local plant management the lower the degree of command necessary or desirable.

5. The larger the number of Americans abroad in proportion to the plant size, the lower degree of command necessary from headquarters.

Observations contrasted to expectations

As expected, different companies handled their headquarters functions quite differently. Several companies had high degrees of both involvement and command, several were quite low, and two were in the middle ranges.

But contrary to expectations, the companies' headquarters did not handle the different countries very differently. Each company tended toward the same degrees of command and involvement worldwide. Most companies follow the same approach regardless of the countries, the number of Americans abroad, the political and economical situations in the countries, and the competence of the foreign national managers on the scene.

Generally, where the different products were many and/or investment was relatively small, the degree of command and involvement decreased as expected. For example, companies making tires, elevators, or automobiles were apt to exert high headquarters command and involvement. Companies with a large variety of different products as in the food industry had lower ratings.

High involvement and a high degree of command went hand in hand rather than being independent. This finding contradicted the *a priori* expectations. If a headquarters was involved in many functions and much detail, it tended to give detailed orders rather than suggestions, and this was regardless of the competence of the local management as judged by the writer. Judging from observations of companies visited high involvement and low command is most unusual.

Apparently each company develops its own approach in headquarters operations and uses it fairly consistently. The number of Americans abroad did not appear to have a direct relationship to the degree of command and involvement. The most consistent relationships observed were those relating the number of products and the degree of technology with the degree of control exerted (both involvement and command). As the number of diverse products increases control decreases. When technology required for meeting production specifications and quality control is greatest, headquarters controls are apt to be more pervasive. As diversification increases, the ability of the headquarters to control effectively the branch plants with a heavy degree of involvement in many facets of the business is reduced. Long-range policy may be influenced but detailed decisions of operations affecting each of the diverse products are close to impossible.

One conclusion which this analysis infers is that headquarters exercises a good deal of control when they can, but when they cannot practically acquire and exercise this control, they give up the effort and decentralize. If this conclusion is true, it is quite revealing. For it suggests that the function and role of headquarters is established more on the amount of control which is possible than on the more logical basis of what kind of control is most appropriate.

It indicates, too, that particular companies tend to establish a certain pattern of handling their manufacturing subsidiaries and to use this approach regardless of whether the plant is in Europe, or Asia, or Africa and regardless of the particular managers or problems involved at the different plants. It indicates that when a company holds a basic philosophy of "centralized" headquarters management, for example, they are apt to centralize regardless of the circumstances and, to some extent, to give less attention than might be expected to the functional, operating areas of production management. For example, most companies seem to regard work force management, procurement, labor relations and production control as within the jurisdiction of local plants and in nearly every case exert less influence on these areas of management as compared to the areas of manufacturing policy and make major facilities or buy decisions.

Headquarters exercises greater control over manufacturing policy decisions (choice of products manufactured, product designs, make or buy, and choice of equipment and processes, plant expansions, etc.) than over short-term operating decisions affecting the functions of work force management, procurement, production control, maintenance, etc., because it is assumed that the former elements have the greater effect on the company's investment, the headquarters company's image, the possibilities of multinational coordination and the longer range future.

It is easier and it seems much more important to control a few big decisions over what the company makes, and how many plants it has, how much should be invested in each plant, and what parts should be bought instead of made, than it is to be involved in a production control system and a myriad of problems in the area of work force management, or the operation of a procurement department all from a remote headquarters. As long as the problem is conceived in terms of "control," there will be a tendency to centralize policy-making and decentralize operations.

But this conventional "operating" vs. "policy" dichotomy is not a very useful way of conceptualizing the decisions in international manufacturing. For in operating across international boundaries the environmental factor becomes very critical. The unique environment in the overseas plant made it far more difficult for the headquarters to make good policy decisions from New York. And the environmental factors of typically a relatively inexperienced and untrained foreign management group repeatedly created situations where home office expertise in the operating aspects of manufacturing became critical in its effect on profits.

For example, in the pharmaceutical companies in developing countries, it was observed that the difficulty of forecasting in the face of variable foreign exchange made it critical to do an expert job in production control, scheduling and inventories. These factors affected the company's results more than the selection of compounding and packing equipment, but invariably, the home office had little or nothing to do with the production control functions and yet exercised a tight rein over the relatively simple, inexpensive and not very important choice of equipment and process. The popular notion of having the headquarters handle manufacturing policy and delegate operating decisions to the local plant missed the mark.

A midwest tire company's policy of strong headquarters influence in the important area of production control, inventory control, and procurement makes sense. These are areas which are quite important to the operating margins and the success of the local subsidiaries in the tire business. It would appear that it would be wiser to divide the decision into the degree of involvement and degree of command for each particular function in a particular location and its effect on the operating margin and *not* on the basis of whether the problems are "policy" or "operating."

Instead of leaving "local functions" to local plants it would be better to look more precisely at the effect of the different production management areas on operating margins and to ascertain where the home office can help the most. The degree of involvement should, therefore, be related to the functions which rank highest in their effects on operating margins.

The degree of command should be selected separately from the degree of involvement. The headquarters confidence in the ability of the overseas management should influence the degree of command. If, for example, many able, experienced Americans were abroad, the command degree might properly be relatively low; similarly, with sufficient competent foreign nationals in the particular area, the headquarters might be able to keep a low degree of command, and yet a high degree of involvement could take place in terms of offering services and advice in an area where the operating margins effect warranted it. The headquarters coordinating function could often be more effective through headquarters assistance in the operating areas of production control, procurement, work force management, maintenance, industrial engineering, and labor relations. These management areas now, in fact, are usually the least affected by the home office.

In conclusion, analysis of operations abroad suggests that companies tend to exercise more command and involvement in the manufacturing policy and less in the operating areas. Most companies have basically the same profile in functional departments regardless of the location. One direct inference is that many firms do not analyze the home office contribution in terms of the particular local situation, but instead tend to take a philosophical stand based largely on what they can control and influence. They decentralize where they must (or in some instances, on the basis of a broad management philosophy).

When international companies are decentralized there may be a resulting tendency toward more harmonious headquarters-branch relationships and less overseas protest. But the profit results may not be as good as they should be. Decentralization of authority may result in less smoke and fire, but it does not necessarily mean that therefore the company is being properly managed. In some countries, where some of the companies studied were highly decentralized, for example, there did seem to be a general feeling of peace and harmony. But it was clear that some functions which needed more scientific or experienced management were not getting it primarily because of the company's philosophy: "We let the local managers stand on their own feet."

Because high involvement is expensive and high command may retard management development and hurt morale, and because some of the factors listed above will usually be in transition, the selection of the proper degree of involvement and command of the headquarters for each plant and function should be reviewed annually in order to decrease involvement and/or command when possible. It may be argued that a home office cannot be as flexible as we are recommending. But the response to this concern is simply that several firms in this study were intuitively flexible for the same reasons as suggested below and show in their results that this practice can be practical and successful.

RECOMMENDATIONS

Several recommendations are suggested for international management's wrestling with the issue of how to achieve effective headquarters contribution and control. These are as follows:

1.   Treat neither all plants nor all functions at each plant alike in delegating authority and providing assistance.
2.   Tailor headquarters operations according to the needs of each plant and function.
3.   In tailoring headquarters operations differentiate between involvement and command and decide on the best degree or level for each.
4.   Factors affecting the proper amount of involvement:
    (a)   importance of the function to the success of the plant
    (b)   abilities of overseas managers of the particular function
    (c)   potential contribution of the headquarters staff to the function
    (d)   the investment, corporate image, quality standards at stake.
5.   Factors affecting the proper amount of command would include:
    (a)   interrelationship of plant and function with the total corporate
    (b)   financial implications of mistakes
    (c)   abilities of overseas managers at top levels
    (d)   nonfinancial risks involved
    (e)   effects of the degree of command on management development overseas
    (f)   the expertise and familiarity of headquarters executives with the functions and issues at question.

10

THE FOREIGN NATIONAL MANAGER

American production men were typically disappointed over the performance of their counterparts and subordinates in overseas plants. They criticized the foreign national production manager as "impractical," showing no "follow-through or sense of responsibility," or as "a fairly good technician but no manager." An American production man who said, "My managers are pretty weak but they are showing signs of improvement," voiced unusually high praise.

These criticisms are open to various interpretations. Many represent the complaints of frustrated expatriates who have been unable to communicate with their foreign subordinates, do not understand their behavior, and therefore condemn their performance. Many reflect the genuine difficulties with which the managers of international manufacturing operations must grapple.

The objectives of this chapter are (a) to deal with the fact that foreign managers, no matter what their nationality, typically are different in their approaches from their American counterparts, and (b) to discuss how various managers and American companies have coped with the resulting problem. We explore the criticisms of the foreign national managers encountered in this study, the effects of problems with foreign national managers on results of the plants visited, and ways the U.S. managers perceived and dealt with this facet of their work. A framework is suggested for the U.S. manager's thinking about dealing with the foreign national manager and his development.

We believe that the central problem of the foreign national manager is inexperience—inexperience in manufacturing in general, in a particular industry, with a specific company, and often as a manager. The foreign manager must make many adjustments and adaptations. The task of the expatriate manager is twofold. First, to understand the nature and extent of the adjustment each foreign manager is undergoing, and, second, to help facilitate that process.

REACTIONS OF AMERICAN MANAGERS

Businessmen interviewed abroad tended to be shocked, surprised, irritated, or dismayed over their foreign national managers. This observation can be made without regard to the country, the area of the world, the type of plant or industry. Typical reactions of American managers abroad may convey some of their feelings to the reader, who should be cautioned to distinguish the responses of the American managers from the researcher's evaluation of the performance of the foreign managers which follows later in the chapter.

Expatriates' criticisms of foreign managers may be grouped in seven areas.

Theoretical and impractical

In Turkey, many American managers felt that the Turk manager tends to do everything "by the book. He lacks practical judgment." For example, Mr. deSalle of CFIT felt that jobs tended to be either undertooled or overtooled.

Example 1

The shop was asked to manufacture six parts missing from 50 plows. Mr. deSalle discovered that they were preparing tooling which would have doubled the cost and tripled the time before the plows would be completed. "The Turks love to work out elaborate tooling, always going by the book. They don't seem to have the practical judgment necessary to make good tooling decisions."[1]

In India a large American company was particularly critical of its Indian managers. "Of the whole lot," the production manager said, "there is not one really practical, realistic manager, and there are no good ones coming along." The American production control manager stated that his progress in developing Indians was "very, very

[1]California Farm Implement Turk, Harvard Business School case.

slow," although he admitted that "this is my job." The top management, echoed by the home office, felt that the Indians were not able to fit into the daily management meetings, and that none of them "really knows how to run the business yet."

An American manager who had established a large mechanical factory in the Middle East stated, "You can tell people to do things, but you must go back over it again and again. They assume they understand, and they say they understand, but then you nearly always find out differently. The most dangerous ones of all are the ones who speak a little English but don't understand it very well. And beware of poor translators; they can really confuse things."

This tendency to "go by the book" was often observed when foreign nationals set up job evaluation, merit rating, and incentive plans. Plans or outlines from manuals or textbooks were followed almost verbatim without checking into their specific workability. One American manager stated:

> The foreign manager has learned limited ways of doing things. He tends to feel that a writeup in some textbook or an engineering principle is the only way to approach a problem. He fails to think through to fundamentals and work out practical solutions relating to his own particular situation.

The executive complex

Many expatriate managers felt that the foreign national managers were susceptible to an "executive complex," characterized by unwarranted pride in their position, title, and office furnishings, a tendency to stay in their offices, to glory in signing papers, a reluctance to get into details or play an active responsible role in daily management problems.

There are repeated examples of this attitude toward an executive position. The American manager of one company made this statement:

> Our managers act as if the actual job of managing is beneath them. They apparently feel that the status of a manager is very high and that once a man is a manager he should be able to give orders and sign papers and deal only with the broad problems. He feels that the detailed daily decisions will somehow be made at levels beneath him and that it is beneath his dignity to get into these daily problems. These attitudes are prevalent with any manager above the foreman level.

Failure to follow through and take responsibility

This criticism is illustrated by the following experience.

Example 2

An executive in an oil company asked the foreign advertising manager to prepare a new calendar for distribution to customers. The request was made in June and a question in July brought assurance that it was coming along satisfactorily. Subsequent checks each month promised progress. When a sample of the calendar was requested in November it became obvious that nothing had been done. The advertising manager then promised to get into it immediately, but in December it became an emergency rush project. A subsequent inquiry made it clear that the advertising manager had simply assigned it to his assistant, his assistant to a clerk in the office, the clerk in the office to an outside vendor, and none of these individuals had been following its progress.

The Winston Truck general manager was frustrated because of the relaxed attitude of the organization toward expediting locally procured parts.

Example 3

Four trucks had been waiting a week for a simple fuel line fitting which had been ordered four weeks previously. The general manager had asked his assistant three times about the progress on this item without obtaining a definite answer. The assistant had reported each time that his man was following the part and that it was coming soon. The general manager brought up this type of problem repeatedly at Saturday morning staff meetings, complaining of procrastination and a lackadaisical attitude.[2]

Too little emphasis on time

The American manager of a plant in Pakistan complained that his managers, even his production control manager, showed

no concern whatsoever over time. They don't seem to worry about schedules; they don't seem to recognize that we have to produce a certain amount by a certain time; they don't seem to be

[2]Winston Truck Turk Fabrikasi, Harvard Business School case.

concerned about the days passing by and very little being accomplished.

This type of comment was heard in every country visited.

Our supervisors love to put things off until the next day. They have no conception of the value or importance of time. They procrastinate and delay doing anything unpleasant, hoping that somehow the task will disappear. They have no feeling that time is important.

Another American manager stated:

We have no problem at all in making deliveries on subcontracts because no one in this country seems to worry about time. Our subcontractors and vendors deliver late to us and we can generally deliver as late as we need to with other companies. No one seems to do much expediting or worry about schedules. When we do need something from another vendor we go into his plant and often find the job covered with dust with no one paying any attention whatsoever to the due date.

Technical falldowns in middle management

The technical skills of middle management were frequently criticized. American managers complained that production control men abroad could not schedule: they developed elaborate planning boards which served little purpose; procurement managers had insufficient technical ability to help vendors improve their quality; plant layout men worked out inefficient layouts; labor relations "experts" wrote contracts that tied their company's hands completely. The industrial engineering groups in many plants were considered weak by expatriate managers. Their complaints were that the process engineering was impractical; time studies and standards were full of errors of judgment: "For lack of adequate leadership time study men go around the plant making time studies which frequently fail to include important elements and they apply allowance factors improperly. Furthermore, they select poor examples for time study, so that their work is useless."

Foreign national managers show poor judgment

Poor judgment was often cited by Americans in sizing up their counterparts, even those at a high level. "They don't think ahead;

they don't see the implications of their actions," said one American manager. "They are like children in that way."

Poor judgment was often cited by home office managers as well as overseas production managers. Judgment was criticized, for example, in ordering unnecessary machines or equipment, in failing to cut expenses during a downturn in sales, or in giving unnecessarily large wage increases.

Paternalistic personnel practices

Foreign national managers are sometimes considered to "go easy on their subordinates and be very harsh on those several levels below them." One manager refused to tell a subordinate that he was not being given a raise, and instead offered to give his own raise to the subordinate. One manager in Turkey said that he would "rather give up his job than fire any manager who works for me." At the same time in most of these companies managers were excessively cruel by U.S. standards, punitive in dealing with lower status individuals beneath their organizational level who had been guilty of some minor transgression.

AN EVALUATION OF
U.S. MANAGERS' CRITICISMS

To the researcher one of the interesting features of these criticisms was that they were so universal, applied in almost every country and in nearly every plant visited. It is hard to believe that all the criticism can be warranted.

Nevertheless, although expatriates often exaggerate the problem, study of the plants and the operating results indicated that there were in fact many evidences of weaknesses in foreign national managers judged by U.S. standards. Low productivity, amateurish or paternalistic industrial relations, nonexistent production control, the "executive complex," failure to follow through, the lack of a sense of the importance of time—all these reported features were found to have a significant basis in fact. There were some notable exceptions—men who were praised and well accepted by the American managers. These men were apt to be at the top of organizations, very westernized in their general appearance and manner. But they were relatively few and far between.

Of course weaknesses of management abroad should come as no great surprise. Lack of experience, cultural differences in values and business emphasis, a dearth of schools of management, an absence of a tradition of business leadership and efficiency all contribute to management weaknesses. Management is a new concept in many countries. Knowing this, it is curious that American businessmen overseas were regularly shocked, surprised, irritated, and disappointed over the performance and behavior of foreign national managers.

The literature is full of analyses of foreign managers, their traits, points of view, contrasts with Americans, and so forth. Five "facts" have become part of conventional wisdom about overseas management:

1.   Management is a scarce resource.
2.   Management is a necessary ingredient for industrial development.
3.   Indigenous management is a necessity for individual company development.
4.   Management abroad is apt to be basically inadequate.
5.   Managers abroad are different.

These "facts" are indeed debatable, but they are common knowledge and the subject of frequent discussion among executives in international companies. One might have expected therefore that individual American managers would be forewarned and less surprised to find "poor managers" in overseas locations. It was clear that anticipation of the inadequacies or cultural differences of management in less advanced industrial countries could not eliminate real problems for American overseas managers.

Several reasons help to explain the Americans' disappointment and irritation. Certainly there is evidence that each man who goes abroad to work must experience the situation himself before he becomes truly aware of the problem and recognizes its impact. Reading about the problems or hearing about them from other managers is apparently insufficient to condition the manager in advance.

Many disappointments occur after the American manager is initially favorably impressed in interviewing or meeting foreign managers. They typically present good credentials from educational institutions; they are apt to speak good English, be well-dressed, appear quite westernized and act confidently. Hence, when the American manager runs into falldowns or problems from men who appeared to be able and well-established, he is likely to be disappointed both in them and in his own previous judgment of their potential.

A further problem is the difficulty of judging performance. Often an American manager, warned that things are done differently abroad, hesitates to condemn his new subordinate for using methods that seem unorthodox to him. Instead he places reliance on the man and when the results are unsatisfactory his disappointment is keen.

The performance of foreign managers in fact tends to be erratic. Abilities may seem entirely satisfactory in certain situations but, given conditions which the foreign manager has not experienced before, his judgment and lack of experience may hurt. The American finds himself surprised and disappointed at the apparent incompetence of his subordinate.

Unfamiliar methods of management often upset the Americans in spite of advance warning. They may be antagonized by Turk managers who shout at the workers; they may be incensed at the treatment of the lower caste Indian workers; they may be shocked and irritated over the apparent blase unconcern of South Americans toward time and appointments; they may be dismayed over the casual attitude of Spaniards toward systematic personnel policies and procedures.

The irritation of the manager when falldowns occur is understandable. The corporate management typically is impatient for improved performance. United States production men are trained to be conscious of costs, quality, and time. They are disturbed when they find that their foreign counterparts are not meeting their expectations.

In fact, foreign national managers are often better administrators than they at first appear. They may appear to be excessively formal, possessed by the "executive complex," casual about time and business deadlines; but some of this may be due to mannerisms typical of their culture, or it may be an attempt to appear in casual command of the situation in front of their American superiors.

Often Americans respond to differences in culture and administrative methods in the form of criticism, which then tends to become self-fulfilling. Several foreign national managers interviewed stated that when they were treated with disrespect and felt criticized by Americans whose business acumen they respected, they began to feel less competent and more sensitive to criticism. Under these circumstances presumably they acted with less sense of security, certainty, and decisiveness, and, in fact, became less competent.

Finally, much of the research and common knowledge about foreign managers does not actually help the expatriate manager. In the first place, as Professor John Fayerweather has pointed out, much of the research is not very "solid." In reviewing an article in *The International Executive,* he stated that "our knowledge of management abroad is short on solid studies and long on journalistic impressions and tourist-anthropological anecdotes."[3] There has been little research that centers specifically on the behavior and accomplishments of foreign executives as viewed within the terms of their own culture. It is easy for Americans to see that foreign managers act and behave differently than Americans, but research that clearly analyzes whether their behavior is more effective or less effective than Americans might appraise it in their own society and culture is rare.[4]

After disappointing experiences with foreign managers, the U.S. manager is forced to confront his own failure as a manager-motivator of men. He must face the fact that the culture is more potent than he is, a fact he may not have really believed until he tested himself against it. Annoyance with foreign managers appears to be coupled with an equally strong sense of personal inadequacy.

Common knowledge and most research studies fail to provide a viable framework for the American manager. He faces difficult problems in making an industrial operation successful when he must deal with so many unfamiliar factors. In particular, he must cope with the fact of relatively inexperienced foreign managers who not only do things in a way to which he is unaccustomed, but often do not communicate very well just what they are doing. Expatriates need better tools and more useful concepts for dealing both with foreign nationals and with their own feelings during the period of management improvement. Let us examine the problems of the American in dealing with the foreign national manager overseas.

PROBLEMS IN DEALING WITH FOREIGN MANAGERS

The American manager abroad confronts a complex challenge in understanding and dealing with the foreign manager. In the first place, he is faced with a different language and a different culture.

---

[3] John Fayerweather, *The International Executive* (Winter 1961), p. 3.
[4] For one example of such research see Mason Haire, Edwin Ghiselli, and Lyman Porter, "Cultural Patterns in the Role of the Manager," *Industrial Relations* (February 1963).

Foreign managers usually have different values, assumptions, beliefs, goals, and so forth than American managers. They perceive their jobs and their lives in business quite differently. They usually have different attitudes toward the parent corporation than the American.

Inevitably, the American is under pressure to develop a going enterprise with all possible speed. His problems may fall within the following four classifications.

Selection

He must size up the men available. This is difficult, for the men who come to him may present variety in dress, appearance, education and apparent experience. These factors must be evaluated. By and large, men who apply for management positions in overseas companies come to the interview with an impressive array of credentials, including considerable education and a list of fine jobs and former affiliations. They usually speak English well.

How does the American go about selecting among these individuals? Since they are possibly a scarce resource, he may have to accept a large percentage of those who apply. On the other hand, experience in the developing countries shows that there actually is a wide latitude of choice, particularly in the early years of national development when educated men often have few good job opportunities other than those in government.

Evidence in this study suggests that in more advanced countries American companies may have more difficulty in attracting a good sample of high-quality men. This may be understood by considering the attractiveness of an Italian company that sets up operations in the United States. Which American executives would leave their posts to work for the foreign corporation? In the more developed economies the men who apply to the American corporation may include some who are dissatisfied with their jobs, who are looking for a higher salary, but who may have marginal ability.

Recognizing better managers

Not only is it a real problem to identify the more able men who seek employment, but it is even difficult to be sure of recognizing the "good" men after they have been working for some time. It cannot be done simply by measuring production or efficiency because in the early phases of a new production operation, all the new managers often seem weak or at least unorthodox. Their low output can be explained by lack of experience.

Sometimes men who are from the "wrong" tribe, caste, school, or locale may have a difficult time through no fault of their own. Their associates may cause them to show up poorly, although, given support, they may turn out to be able men. This was the case of a Turkish production manager who was Jewish and was not accepted by other members of the organization. An American manager saw that the man had sound judgment and backed him up. Eventually he became the strongest manager in the plant. This was equally true of a low-caste Indian with relatively little education who was given an opportunity in a pharmaceutical plant. To the apparent surprise and annoyance of his higher status Indian colleagues he turned out to be an effective administrator. The Americans in both of these cases were not deluded by the prejudices of the foreign managers and succeeded in developing suspected talents. The two foreign managers in these examples, although "outlanders" in the working groups, apparently were less culture-bound and seemed able to adapt more easily to American norms and expectations than their more locally acceptable peers.

It is risky for an expatriate to judge a foreign national manager by the administrative practices the manager employs in dealing with his subordinates, for these practices are influenced by the local culture. They are apt to be quite different from those the American is accustomed to and uses as his yardstick.

In the process of doing business in our own culture we size up a man's integrity and his values over a period of time. This may not be done explicitly, but, in effect, when we decide whether or not we trust a man, whether he is genuinely working for the company's good, whether he will be valuable in times of personal crisis, we make this judgment. The wise manager readily acknowledges the difficulty of making a valid judgment. He allows time for it and cautions himself against too hasty a size-up.

But overseas many managers sized up foreign managers too rapidly to be discriminating. With less knowledge and comprehension, they established more distinct opinions and prejudices. To many Americans the Spaniards were "lazy" because they liked to start work at a "late" hour in the morning and have a two-hour break in the middle of the day in spite of the fact that they then worked well into the evening. The American reaction was that the Spaniards simply "resisted putting in a good day's work." But these working hours have been the Spanish tradition for hundreds of years and the Americans could not properly judge their counterparts' motivation on the basis of practices about office hours. Perceiving the practice as "immoral" or "improper" not only missed the point but created new issues.

Translators

Where there is a language problem, the use of an interpreter sometimes introduced a critical factor. The filtering action of a translator made the possibility of his influencing the interaction between two men almost inevitable. Many American managers have learned to their chagrin that the translator did not comprehend as well as they had assumed. In choosing words that slightly distort the intent, the interpreter could innocently change the nature of a conversation and its meaning to both participants.

Relationships

It is not easy for the American to interpret the response he is receiving. Certain cultures feature an overt politeness, a deference toward authority and higher position which Americans might consider excessive. Some foreign managers spoke to the researcher about their concerns over the way in which the business was being managed but would not consider speaking to their boss about it. This phenomenon of subservience to one's formidable superior is common in certain cultures.

It is difficult for the American manager to recognize how his own administrative practices are affecting the organization. When his managers have a different sense of time, different attitudes toward the company, hold more than one job and yet look to the company for a permanent sense of security, the American manager is often baffled by his apparent failure to motivate them to "go all out" for the company. He wonders how to appeal to his men, whether it should be through making more stringent demands, or whether he should attempt to deal with them on a friendly and accepting basis. In conclusion the manager has had these four problems with foreign national managers:

1. Predicting how effective his foreign managers are going to be.
2. Minimizing operating problems while foreign managers develop.

208 The Foreign National Manager

3. Maximizing the development of the foreign managers.

4. Improving his own administrative practices and coping with his own feelings during this maturing process.

Americans wrestling with these four problems have dealt with foreign managers in quite different ways. During this research the existence of several different "schools of thought" or practices in dealing with the problem was observed.

DIFFERING WAYS OF
DEALING WITH FOREIGN MANAGERS

The first school of thought is represented by this statement: "This is an American business and the foreign nationals have got to learn to do business in the American way. We call a spade a spade in this business; we don't mince words, we expect each one to perform adequately and in the process we all have a pretty good time doing it." Men of this school of thought tend to judge the foreign manager quite harshly at first and to be slow in entrusting responsibility. A manager of a company using this approach in India stated:

The Indians really like to work for us, we can see this, and they say it because they like to have a frank, open approach even though they don't work that way themselves. We let them know where they stand and if a man doesn't have much to offer to a meeting, he simply is not invited to it. We expect good productivity from them as managers and good judgment, and, when they don't show it, we feel that we should not try to be polite, but let them have it right between the eyes when necessary.

The Indians in this plant, however, told the researcher through an interpreter that "the American managers do not trust us. We are not invited or allowed to sit in on their meetings. When we are given an assignment, we are checked on everything—like children; we often think of leaving and quite a few men have left."

Another example of this school was found at an American plant in Turkey where the manager was the only American. He also believed in responding immediately to problems, sounding off (through an interpreter) to "let the Turks know exactly what was wrong and how they should do things differently." The researcher's observation was that the Turks seemed to respect this man's

strength and his willingness to speak out. The American had had a
series of predecessors including several Americans who had treated
the Turks with a low degree of respect, had delegated very little
responsibility to them, and had been reluctant to communicate what
they were feeling about the Turks' performance. In a meeting (with
the American present) the Turks discussed the past years. A Turk
who had been in charge of the plant before the U.S. organization
took it over was hired as assistant to the production manager. He
said:

"This (new position) wasn't hard for me at all. I felt that the
plant was like my child and I wanted to see it produce efficiently
for the benefit of the country. And I was also glad for a chance to
learn from Americans. We felt we could learn from them and
wanted to if allowed to be partners. But I was disappointed in
how they went about it. They had no idea of Turks or Turkey
when they arrived. Back in the USA the executives gave their
men write-ups of the company's procedures and forms and told
them to set it up in Turkey the same way. They did not have a
real understanding of what they were doing—they just copied
California operations. Then the Americans did not really train the
Turks and turn over responsibility to them.

"The Americans isolated themselves with other Americans both
at work and socially, with their own neighborhoods and parties.
They didn't even use our knowledge of the government and officials in dealing with them. The Americans here did not know
how to make anything in a factory except tractors. We asked for
know-how and they gave us know-nothing. We Turks are not
fools. We could have helped but we were not consulted or used.
We have good experience and are capable engineers. And, as
managers, we would have been better than the Americans."

The Turk sales manager agreed and added, "We Turks are more
adaptable than Americans. They feel there is only one way to do
a job. The Americans should have come here being prepared to
adapt to and learn from the Turks, ready to learn and discuss and
appreciate their thinking and not get upset if they worked differently. Then they would have gotten along and done better. One
man even tried to change the way Turkish people go the toilet.
This company was a test case of United States business in Turkey
and its success would have made a big difference. But the idea
has lost much prestige here. The whole trouble was the underrat-
ing of the Turkish personnel.

"We have no organization at present. It needs to be restudied and reorganized. But we have made great accomplishments here in the last six months. We have good cooperation and spirit starting at the very top. Team work has been formed. Before, every department was a different company. Now we consult with each other. There is an increase in morale of the workers, too. And we are getting close to making a profit."

A second school of thought goes to the other extreme. They recommend that "the American, when in Rome, should act as the Romans act." These Americans tend to delegate responsibility to selected managers abroad and then work closely with them on a cooperative basis to work out problems.

Although this sounds enlightened and reasonable, the performances of members of this school have not been without problems. For instance, in a plant in Spain the American management was aware of many shortcomings in the areas of production control, labor relations, inventory control, plant scheduling, and procurement. But they took the position that "the company is profitable, things are going along reasonably well, and as these problems become more important and more evident to the Spanish, we will then act to assist them in improving the operation." This company's staff group, located in Europe, was available to assist the operation, but they made no attempt to intrude themselves upon it. They treated the Spanish managers with considerable respect and even deference and simply tried to make their own services available. It was quite clear, however, that they were tolerating slow progress in developing those business practices that would eventually result in increased productivity.

A third school seems to make good sense in some instances: The foreign managers are treated with respect as long as they seem to earn it. The company does not hesitate to make changes if necessary, but first it attempts to deal with them in an understanding way.

None of these three schools of thought, in the writer's opinion, is generally applicable. In fact, the "school of thought" approach is bound to run into difficulties as the company works in entirely different circumstances, in different countries, or with different managers. The company which ran the operation in India with such a heavy hand had more success with the same approach in South Africa where the local managers seemed responsive to this style and grew under it. But back in the home office, the top production men were beginning to doubt whether the "hard knocks" school of thought was really the best approach. Too many problems were arising throughout the world due to insistence on doing things in the American way.

Many American managers abroad lack a useful way of thinking about dealing with foreign national managers so that they can more effectively adapt their administrative practices to the specific situation at hand.

A SUGGESTED FRAMEWORK FOR AMERICAN MANAGERS IN UNDERSTANDING FOREIGN NATIONAL MANAGERS

Many expatriate managers could benefit from being trained to think more precisely about the ingredients of the situation in which they find themselves. New insights would be more useful than applying predetermined notions about "how to get along abroad."

Three ingredients appear essential in developing a workable way of thinking about the problem: (a) to recognize and isolate how the particular foreign managers, as individuals, appear to conduct themselves and manage; (b) to determine the differences between familiar and unfamiliar practices and determine which ones really hurt managerial performance and which, although irritating, are relatively harmless to the job; (c) to develop better ways of dealing with falldowns, shortcomings, and differences on the part of the foreign managers. These three elements of suggested framework for working with foreign managers are now described more fully.

Understanding the foreign manager better

First it is helpful to develop a more precise understanding of what each foreign national manager is like: to determine his values, assumptions, goals, and ways of working and to identify these characteristics that make up his performance as an administrator. The process of attempting to understand foreign managers is probably more important than the answers obtained.

Three measures can be useful tools of analysis in attempting to identify how a foreign manager works: (a) a measure of two basic values of the man in his administrative practices: the relative weight he places on people versus the relative weight he places on the job;[5] (b) a measure of his beliefs in what constitutes leadership and what constitutes the manager's role; (c) an appraisal of his be-

[5]Robert R. Blake and Jane S. Mouton, *The Managerial Grid*, Gulf Publishing Company, Houston, Texas, 1964.

havior in terms of his native culture. The common element in these three approaches is that the American works to develop a more precise understanding of the foreign environment and managers.

The "managerial grid" is one way of approximating the man's relative concern with people versus task. The man rates himself and is rated by others, using a questionnaire that shows the extent to which he is task-oriented and the extent to which he is people-oriented. Discussing the results can help develop insights into the motivations and assumptions under which he performs. Blake and Barnes describe this method of analysis and its use in an article called "Breakthrough in Management Development."[6]

A second analytical tool is described by Haire, Ghiselli, and Porter in an article titled "Cultural Patterns in the Role of the Manager."[7] The purpose of their research was to examine the cultural patterns exhibited by managers in different countries. They found quite dissimilar patterns in the managerial practices in various countries. The authors wished to gain insights into three areas of personal beliefs of values pertaining to (a) leadership; (b) the manager's role; (c) motivations and needs. They then developed measures of the degree of satisfaction of these motivations or needs felt by the managers. Their analytical approach can be helpful in attempting to develop a more thorough understanding of individual managers. Answers to their questions can help to explain observed behavior and make existing differences reasonable rather than threatening.

A third approach is to examine the foreign manager's behavior in terms of the culture patterns within his own country. Culture study poses many problems for the amateur, for he must avoid jumping to easy conclusions. The list of examples of the impact of culture on various phases of production administration (Exhibit 1) may be used by the American manager to describe the particular culture in which he is operating, and it may help in thinking about the responses of individual foreign managers to their own culture. This topic list is intended to stimulate the manager's keener observation of the culture in which he is operating. Understanding a culture involves a long period of personal research.

A large part of the American's problem in dealing with foreign national managers is learning to understand himself, his own val-

---

[6]Louis B. Barnes and Robert A. Blake, "Breakthrough in Management Development," *Harvard Business Review* (November-December 1964).
[7]*Op. cit.*, p. 204.

ues, beliefs, and culture in more precise and explicit detail. Not only may the values and assumptions of the foreign manager be understood in more detail, but they may be contrasted to the American manager's own particular set of values and beliefs.

Since cultural patterns are easier to talk about than to mull over alone, there may be advantages in studying the culture on a group basis or under the leadership of someone trained in anthropology and the study of administration. But a great deal of progress can be made by an individual in roughing out descriptions of some of the major behavior differences he can observe and in examining some of his own contrasting beliefs.

Evaluating the effects of cultural differences

The second dimension of this framework is the determination of which cultural differences are significant and which, when understood, are relatively harmless to industrial operations.

Which cultural traits are incompatible with industrial efficiency? Does a marked distinction between castes or social or ethnic groups hurt efficiency? How much does a different attitude toward time influence managerial behavior? Attitudes toward subordinates, productivity, delegation, responsibility, involvement — all of these may have an impact on a man's business behavior. How can an American manager discriminate among deviations from conventional American managerial behavior to ascertain which make a difference in his situation?

Certain cultural deviations are more irritating or confusing than actually harmful. Some Indian managers were criticized by Americans because they were unhappy about being asked to move a typewriter from one desk to another. Some Americans saw this as evidence that they were lazy, unwilling to lower themselves, to "roll up their sleeves" and work. But this was not really very important. It simply reflected the fact that in India the higher castes and educated people do not do manual work.

Distinguishing between these deviations to determine which ones are harmful is not easy. There can be no definite rules applied, for what may be effective in one situation may not be so in another.

One useful approach is to differentiate individual foreign managers' divergences from conventional American behavior to ascertain which ones are due to a different (a) degree of Westernization, (b) degree of industrialization, (c) degree of pertinent experience within the company or the industry, and (d) the particular personality and managerial ability. This differentiation is useful, for those deviations essentially due to Westernization do not appear to be as harmful to business performance as those due to lack of industrialization, experience, or personal ability. Yet they are easily confused and sometimes labeled "batty," "nutty," "irrational," "childish," "unpredictable," or "irresponsible," by the nonplussed American manager.

Behavior deviations due to different degrees of Westernization, different degrees of industrialization, and the amount of pertinent industrial experience also have quite differing impacts on a manager's industrial performance. Granting that some of the differences in degrees of Westernization can be important in a man's job performance, probably these factors are not as important as the extent to which a manager has adapted or adjusted to industrialization as such. Distinguishing between cultural differences and industrialization effects can be a subtle task, for the values we assume are "Western" often include the values required of an industrial civilization and are not peculiar to Western civilization.

For example, in South Africa the Europeans are generally Westernized and yet often are weak managers. A chief reason is that they have not yet become "industrialized" in their values or their habits. The typical South African manager has the Western notion that energy and diligence can bring about change, but, on the other hand, he is still new enough to life in industry so that he often has what the American managers there call a "just now" attitude. When asked when he is going to carry out an assignment he may say, "just now," which means that he is probably not going to do it right away and may never do it. His attitudes toward time are not industrially oriented.

This point may also be illustrated by the fact that many men in the United States do not acquire certain industrial values until they have worked in industry. For instance, the industrial value that the interests of job and the company must come ahead of personal friendship is learned as a manager begins to distinguish his personal feelings from rational company decisions. Such an attitude is critical in salary administration, for example.

Men who change to manufacturing jobs after having worked in other fields such as agriculture, government, education, and social services generally have different points of view toward their jobs and work quite differently from those who have been "brought up" in industry. Industrialization brings with it a necessarily heavy emphasis on time, scheduling, precision of coordination, and on not "letting grass grow under one's feet."

Industrialization also involves a focus on the company's success, which sometimes makes the individual's wants and needs subservient to the corporation. Emphasis must be placed on accomplishment, both individual and departmental, in terms of production, cost reduction, quality improvement, and so forth. The managerial emphasis cannot be on such objectives as "developing character," "serving one's fellow man" to the extent that might be appropriate in certain nonindustrial occupations. Finally, there is an emphasis in industry on action. Because of the necessity for coordinating a large number of people, slow decisions and lengthy time delays must always be avoided.

These characteristics of industrialization may be distinguished from "Westernization," and may be found among non-Western, industrialized people such as the Japanese. Conversely, a lack of industrial attitudes and values may be observed among Western folk who have not long been industrialized, as in areas of Eastern Europe, South Africa, Australia, agricultural or mountain areas of the United States, and in people entering industry from other fields in any country.

The distinction between Westernization and industrialization is important for several reasons. First, it appears that industrial traits and values can be assimilated much more rapidly than those of Western culture itself. The industrial imperatives have their own compelling qualities and their rationale is not subtle: He who doesn't deliver on time loses business. He who gives a friend an undeserved raise is pressured for raises by others. Failure to plan and coordinate results end in idle machines and complaints from the boss.

Deviations from Western traits and values are more subtle and probably less easily changed than the industrial imperatives. But, fortunately, they generally do not have as serious an impact on a manager's performance. For example, the fatalistic manager who does not believe that energy can bring about change needs a different kind of supervision, but he can still carry out assigned tasks. Absence of a personal sense of follow-up in a supervisor is disturbing to the American manager, but when he realizes this fact he delegates and supervises differently.

Isolating differences between deviations from typical behavior into separate categories of Westernization and industrialization is not only helpful in understanding otherwise strange behavior but also useful in diagnosing those deviations that are critical to business and managerial performance and then taking appropriate action to overcome these deviations. Many deviations are simply surprising, unique, or annoying, but they are not necessarily harmful to industrial activity.

A third source of deviations to consider in sizing up an individual manager is the amount of pertinent industrial experience he has acquired. A man who has had years of experience in a steel rolling mill, for example, may adjust slowly to the plastic molding or the flour milling business. Technical experience — "feel" for products, markets, quality, and the difficulties of the process — is important in becoming useful in a particular industry. Whereas newness to industry per se may entail problems of time, self-discipline, or working cooperatively with others, lack of experience in a particular industry is evidenced more by deficiencies in knowledge or judgment. A man who has worked in another industry may have excellent possibilities for the future, even though at the moment he may know very little about the particular industry in which he has recently chosen to work. The pertinent industrial experience will come in time. It is important not to condemn a man because he does not yet have it. To sum up, it is an unnecessary error to confuse deviations caused by non-Westernization, nonindustrialization, and lack of specific industrial experience.

A fourth area of analysis of the foreign manager is to examine the individual: his intelligence, mental flexibility and adaptability, emotional stability, attitudes toward others, abilities to adjust in society. A man who is thoroughly Westernized, who has made progress in developing useful attitudes and the discipline of industrialization, who has extensive pertinent industrial experience, but who still lacks the basic intelligence or the emotional stability to adjust within the company organization will not be very successful. In contrast, a man who has the intelligence, the emotional and personal characteristics that help him work cooperatively with others, may lack industrial experience and may not be at all Westernized but may still have an excellent development potential.

The critical step for the American manager is therefore to distinguish the differences or deviations from "normal United States managerial behavior" with which he is confronted by his foreign manager. He may first identify deviations that concern him and then separate the important ones from those that are merely surprising or irritating. He can identify which deviations from "normal managerial behavior" are correctable, which are going to be more difficult to deal with; and he can then determine corrective action.

It is usually unnecessary to press for Westernization. But it is important to seek managers who have made the adjustment to industrialization, or, if this is impractical, to focus training and management development in that direction and teach the pertinent industrial attitudes.

DEALING WITH FALLDOWNS, SHORTCOMINGS, AND DIFFERENCES

Overseas managers have no choice but to staff their plants with foreign national managers. Those who fit the title are generally a scarce commodity. Their relationships with Americans and their effectiveness as managers are affected by differences in cultures, beliefs and assumptions. From the beginning the U.S. manager, under pressure for high performance and profitable results, must cope with almost inevitable falldowns and deviations from acceptable performance.

What administrative practices are useful in managing foreign managers? Are any generalizations possible? The situation demands that the expatriate manager take a position of leadership. But there are many different ways of doing this.

In the writer's opinion many American managers might approach these tasks with more of an attitude of inquiry. There is a tendency on the part of some American managers to stylize each foreign manager, "pigeonholing" him in such terms as "he'll never be any good," or "he is hopeless," "he lives in a completely different world." Instead, an attempt to analyze each manager, to identify specifically how he thinks and works, and to pinpoint the deviations from U.S. norms may isolate the deviations that actually affect his work. The devotion of more effort toward understanding one's managers is an administrative practice whose process may be as beneficial as is its ultimate goal.

Since falldowns and shortcomings will occur, the expatriate manager can benefit by developing his own capacity for analyzing the causes. What element in the foreign national's makeup or in the total situation allowed the man to forget his responsibility, fail to follow through, miss a schedule, not communicate, or not report back? How much of this was due to his lack of industrialization? How much of it was due to his own personal weaknesses? How much of it may have been due to failure of the top management to communicate expectations? The ingredients of the program needed for improvement can be determined from such a thorough and penetrating analysis of the foreign manager.

Acquiring such understanding can be a long and painful process. More dialogue and discussion of differences between the outlooks and approaches of the foreign manager and the American manager can be useful. Men interviewed who had developed such understanding were easily spotted by their attitudes of acceptance and less tense relationship.

The process of listening and attempting to understand how subordinates work is a key administrative device which is often overlooked. Through dialogue both the foreign manager and the American manager can become more aware of their differences in ways of looking at problems and realize that they are each influenced by their culture, values, and assumptions. Making this understanding more explicit can moderate the confusion and frustrations often observed abroad.

This is not to say that the American manager should become a philosopher who muses thoughtfully over the falldowns and shortcomings of his men. His understanding must be exercised under fire, for schedules must be met, costs lowered, quality improved. There are no substitutes for taking action, for pointing up the falldowns clearly, for emphasizing that things must be different next time and attempting to communicate clearly what happened and what went wrong.

But instant remedial action is only part of the prescription for preventing the problem in the future. It will surely happen again as long as a man's basic way of operating or looking at his problem is not changed. This is where the mature and capable American manager is separated from the impatient type who cracks the whip but finds failures repeated again and again until he has fired a series of production managers. This is not really managing; it is taking some action when action is needed, but it is not creative, mature leadership of an organization of human individuals who are capable of self-improvement when the basic causes of their falldowns can be isolated.

Management development programs

Few management development programs were encountered among 48 plants studied abroad. Many Americans spent hours discussing problems and shortcomings among their foreign managers, but little was being done about it in any organized fashion. When foreign managers need to acquire pertinent industrial experience, to find new ways of thinking about time, the corporation, and their jobs, a great deal more could be done with management development programs.

One reason for the dearth of such programs may be that many companies have had poor experiences with them. One plant in South Africa, for example, has had a management training course for many years, but it was recently discontinued. "Temporarily," they said, "for it did not seem to be very effective on a continuous basis and we needed a vacation from it." In a plant in India the personnel manager was holding supervisory training meetings on human relations. But the description by the instructor made it clear that the course was limited to textbook concepts about being nice to people and attempting to work together as friends. In the face of the Hindu concept that each man is caught up in a series of lives, the approach was probably not very useful. Similarly, at a pharmaceutical plant in India the production manager stated that "Our supervisory training program meeting never clicked. We ran out of things to talk about." Another plant in southern Europe had held weekly supervisory meetings but finally stopped because there was "nothing further to discuss." Another company developed a management training program to be used worldwide consisting of a program of lectures and conference leader-type discussion groups. It was presumed that this program could be "taught" to certain members in the home office and then duplicated in various training centers by a man who had been through the program. The notion at headquarters was that the program would "instill" the company mode of operation and "teach" human relations and communications. How naive it is to assume that men's patterns of thought and behavior can be changed by presenting them with a company philosophy outlined in the form of a particular approach in communications, in human relations, in motivation. Differences in Westernization, in industrialization, in human characteristics, in cultures, in particular problems of marketing, selling, and producing in different parts of the world are so vast that it would seem to be folly to even suggest such a program.

Other companies have sent men regularly to the United States for "training." It is the writer's experience that sometimes this is a useful experience but it often does not accomplish much development. In Turkey, for example, it was observed that those men who were sent to work in American factories often came back conflicted between Western procedures and Middle Eastern ways. They imported mirror images of the techniques and approaches used in the American plants but were handicapped in their relations with Turkish subordinates and colleagues when it came to installing them. They often became confused as to what was appropriate. In the United States foreigners may be taught specific approaches, certain ideas, company techniques: "Here is the way to do it, here is the way we have done it in our plants in the States and we have made great progress and profit."

Our view is that quite a different type of training is necessary. Our analysis suggests that foreign managers need (a) to acquire the pertinent industrial experience, in terms of facts, knowledge, and specific problems in the industry, and (b) to learn to recognize the difference between their present assumptions, values, and beliefs and those imperative to industrialization.

Much more training attention could be placed on key attitudes and approaches necessary in successful industrialization: the emphasis on time, schedules, accomplishment, the success of the company, and the importance of work. These attitudes and skills can probably be developed through a combination of locally oriented cases, problems, and analyses of differences in the way people behave. In management development programs there could be more emphasis placed on learning to think, to analyze problems, and to develop specific action plans to carry out improvements. Training should be designed toward learning to understand feelings, beliefs, and cultural assumptions both explicitly and implicitly. In contrast, existing training more often emphasizes learning "principles" of marketing, production, or finance and "instilling" a company philosophy. Problem solving and social and human relations analysis is probably more important than learning certain patterns of doing things.

Management development is especially valuable under a man who treats his managers with respect and at the same time holds up high standards and insists that these standards are met, who involves them, and keeps them closely tuned in with the problems of the day. Such a man understands that the Indians who were left out of the daily top management meetings were slow to develop. They were not consulted and they were not involved with decisions on meeting the plant's current pressing problems.

The fact is that managers the world over are capable of excellent performance. Managers have been found everywhere who showed ability to analyze problems, handle men, organize, plan, and carry out the functions of the corporation in an orderly, aggressive, and responsible style. By learning to understand the cultural and social beliefs of the foreign national managers and the effects of the lack of heritage of industrialization, American managers can become more effective in understanding deviations and in dealing with fall-downs, and thereby they can stimulate substantial improvement in their foreign managements.

11

THE OVERSEAS
PRODUCTION MANAGER

This chapter is concerned with expatriates sent abroad by international companies to participate in the management of overseas production operations. The focus is on managers who are sent abroad for years rather than on staff who visit foreign plants for assignments of several weeks or months.

Men who live overseas on a long-term basis face problems in relationships with foreign nationals, job effectiveness in a foreign environment, and communications and relationships with the home office. They must adjust to new and difficult demands from all quarters. This chapter describes some of the problems of overseas production managers and relates them to the consequent problems of the parent company. Implications are discussed for the selection and development of men for overseas assignments as well as the process of managing them.

The "problem" orientation should in no sense imply that all men sent abroad fail to perform well, that most assignments abroad are unhappy ones, or that expatriate managers always present difficult and absorbing problems for executives in the home office. This is not so. In the process of this research the writer talked with and analyzed the experiences of some 60 overseas managers, (mostly American but also a number of third country nationals)[1] whose experiences were mixed. Neither success nor failure was uniform. But nearly all of the men found the experience of managing production

[1]Such as Englishmen sent to Spain.

operations abroad to be quite different from domestic operations —
more interesting and more difficult.

Needs for expatriates abroad

Practitioners and researchers in international management usually
take the position that companies investing in overseas manufacturing must employ a significant number of Americans (or third country nationals) to manage their plants because indigenous foreign
managers are not adequate for the task. Readers will have perceived
from Chapters 9 and 10 that the author shares this opinion.

Most American companies do not have a fixed policy regarding
the number of American managers needed in their overseas plants.
These companies generally have a policy of using foreign nationals
as managers whenever they are available to the extent that they are
able to handle the job. However, some American companies believe
that because the U.S. company has committed large amounts of
money in a major plant abroad, it should always have a basic cadre
of American top managers in the plant.

A few critics disagree, and their position warrants some explanation. For example, the concept that some Americans must always be
abroad and that it is necessary at least to start out with a number of
Americans is challenged by John C. Shearer.[2] Mr. Shearer's research indicated that Americans cost approximately four times as
much as Mexicans in management jobs in Mexico, and that the excessive cost was not justifiable in terms of efficiency. He stated that
"Few firms get their money's worth." He noted that there were
many "second stringers" abroad due to the scarcity of good Americans and that ineptness in training and selection combined with
increased compensation had the net result of high cost of administration and low administrative competence.

This research concurs with Mr. Shearer's observations about the
relative inefficiency and many problems involved with American
nationals abroad and with his conclusions regarding the frequent
failures to develop competent foreign nationals. Nevertheless,
granting the many problems in "mixed" administration, Mr. Shearer's conclusions do not appear practical. It takes many years of mis-

[2]John C. Shearer, "American Overseas Managers—Necessities or Luxuries," in *Management in the International World and International Analysis.* Princeton University, Industrial Relations Section, 1960.

takes and supervised problem-solving for a foreign national manager to learn to work effectively within the U.S. company structure. An earlier chapter in this study suggested that many indigenous top managers brought into overseas operations failed because they were not sensitive to company pressures and background factors in company policy.

Although it is true that Americans have no monopoly on "integrity" and "trustworthiness," prudence will ordinarily require the parent company to place the management of expensive foreign manufacturing assets in the hands of a man who has thoroughly proved himself to his company. Many American companies have been able to turn over their foreign operations to foreign nationals only after years of developing and testing the foreign nationals to the point where they have demonstrated the competence to handle the job. Thus, while the ultimate aim of a completely locally operated firm makes good sense, the fact of the matter is that for many years a large number of expatriates will continue to manage corporate activities in foreign countries.

The purposes of this chapter

As the number of plants abroad has increased and the existing plants have expanded, the net result has been a continuing need for significant numbers of Americans abroad. It is this need, which prompts a great deal of thought and soul searching at the home offices of most international organizations, to which this chapter is addressed.

In every home office the researcher noted that the questions and problems the home office managers were most likely to bring up reflected their genuine concern with the selection and management of Americans overseas. The concerns had to do with:

1.   Who to place in overseas jobs.
2.   What knowledge, skills, and attitudes were necessary and useful abroad.
3.   Where to obtain men with these attributes, both in terms of age and experience, whether from within or without the company.
4.   How to select such individuals.
5.   How to orient them.
6.   How to train them.
7.   How to manage them—in terms of the authority, responsibili-

ty, staff services, and information given, and in the amount and type of reporting and controls required.

8. How to develop these men further.

9. How to handle administration of their salary, benefits, changes of assignments, or other elements of personal management.

It was clear to the researcher that many of these decisions have been made either without clear criteria or on the basis of "company wisdom" in the form of general rules of thumb; for example, one company stated, "We always select men who have deep and extensive training in one particular department because they will be on their own abroad and it is very important that they have one area of functional management in depth rather than a lot of smatterings which the more general managers may have." Another company's conventional wisdom was that "Since work abroad is demanding, it is an ideal way in which to develop our people. Therefore we send men abroad for a limited length of service with the ultimate objective being to return many of them to domestic operations."

This research indicates that there are many valid alternatives in the handling of these eight decision areas. In every company studied there were both problems and successes. No company proved the validity of one clear rule or approach.

Many observers and researchers have offered suggestions on this subject, often describing the particular personal qualities they believe are necessary for successful overseas work. In fact, there has been scant rigorous research on this subject. There are many contradictions in the literature and few clear areas of agreement. Most of the work has simply observed men abroad and attempted to define those qualities that seem to make them more or less successful.

Is there such a man as the ideal overseas production manager? A definitive answer is not within the scope of this chapter. The goal here is to describe the problems met abroad, to analyze the impact of these problems in terms of the requirements for men working abroad, to review the literature, and to add some hypotheses that grew out of this researcher's experience. Our conclusion is that a clear definition of the qualities needed by overseas production managers is unobtainable at present. There are too many complex variables involved. It is more a matter of configuration than of qualities. A realistic comprehension of the difficulties inherent in the problem and some of the variables involved is much more useful than the search for the ideal overseas manager. A good starting point is the observable problems of expatriate managers.

PROBLEMS OF THE EXPATRIATE
MANAGER OVERSEAS

The problems encountered can be grouped in three main categories:

1. Problems of living in a "different" environment.
2. Problems of career and relationships with the parent company.
3. Problems peculiar to managing overseas operations.

We will examine these in order.

Problems of living in a "different" environment

Leaving familiar and comfortable housing in suburbia, friends, supermarkets, and packaged foods, and customary forms of recreation, the American manager and his family move abroad. They typically find themselves in some sort of apartment housing in a "Little America" enclave, surrounded by friends, a plethora of servants, strange foods, and few of their customary leisure time pursuits.

"Culture shock"[3] is a typical reaction. The experience of Americans in Turkey is illustrative.

Example 1

The Americans, accompanied by wives and families, moved abroad in the late winter of 1955, two months after being notified of their new assignments.

For all the men and their wives, most of whom had never traveled abroad, the new location provided innumerable shocks and surprises. The women were upset by the lack of familiar household items (milk, Kleenex, frozen foods, soft toilet paper, canned vegetables, coffee, etc.), by the need for boiling all drinking water, the poor sanitary conditions, the drab appearance of the houses and apartment buildings, lack of television, intermittent electricity and water supplies, and "substandard American schools." Their living quarters were considerably less comfortable and pleasant than those they had enjoyed in America; they missed their relatives and friends; the language barrier and unfamiliar customs made simple shopping chores complicated and time-consuming; the meat obtainable was of an "inferior quality."

[3] See Cleveland, Mangone, and Davis, *The Overseas Americans*, McGraw-Hill, New York, 1960.

All these problems — and more — combined with the original distaste for the country due to poorly maintained and dingy buildings, the smells, and the strange often unkempt appearance of the residents, resulted in a long and unhappy period of adjustment. Repeatedly during the first six months the men would return to their flats at the end of the day to find the wives in tears, homesick and lonely, and filled with genuine loathing of their new location.

After the first six months most of the families had a servant and access to supplies from the United States and the women's lives became somewhat more normal. "We began to live again."

The Americans in Istanbul tended to live together in colonies for they found Turks living nearby seemed to resent their higher standard of living, and they felt more comfortable in American neighborhoods. With frequent informal social get-togethers for bridge and mutual discussions of their problems as expatriates they managed to make life tolerable.[4]

Career problems and relationships with the parent company

Although the overseas salary question is often cited as a problem source of the first magnitude, most of the Americans abroad were receiving extra benefits and allowances for living costs and salary was usually not a substantial problem. In fact, many considered the additional salary benefits one of the chief reasons for working abroad.

To some third country nationals, however, salaries were a real problem. For example, the salary scale of an Englishman sent to India by an American company was based on his pay at the company plant in England. This was relatively low compared to the American scale. His salary scale might have been adequate in England, but, since he had to pay for scarce, expensive housing in a foreign colony and buy nonlocal foods, he suffered a financial hardship. He considered this unfair and also felt that it was inequitable to be paid so much less than the Americans in India.

American companies usually have dealt with these problems in an aggressive and careful way. Worldwide studies have been made and salary policies have been well formulated. Hence serious prob-

[4]From California Farm Implement Turk, Harvard Business School case.

lems in this area are becoming rare in internationally experienced companies.

But less tangible career problems have been important: concern over being forgotten at the home office, worries about where the next post would be, the feeling of impermanence that often creeps into overseas work, and difficulties in feeling the rewards of personal achievement when relatives, neighbors, college friends and peers are not nearby to register their approval.

The concern of being forgotten at the home office is present even in domestic branch plant operations. It should be no surprise when one considers the long distance and the irregular contacts typical of the foreign operation. The man works hard, performing what he considers a good job, but often he feels that since his boss and the men high in the ranks of the company are not there to personally observe what he is accomplishing and witness the obstacles he must handle, his work is little appreciated. The difficulties he has to master in the foreign country are, he feels, often underestimated. "Any slight mistake or problem or difficulty is heard about in the home office," one man said, "but they have no idea how much we have to overcome just to keep operating here at all."

Lack of appreciation of one's overseas experience is particularly poignant to the man who is assigned to a foreign post for a relatively short time (such as two or three years) and who expects to go back into the domestic operation. The fears of many of these men have proven justified. In this study some careers have been followed over a six-year period, and there is no question that the men returning to domestic divisions from foreign operations are frequently placed into domestic slots in which their authority and responsibility is much curtailed from what it was abroad. Some domestic jobs have been chosen with little apparent realization of the growth opportunities these men have had in foreign operations. This problem is recognized by enlightened personnel men who wonder what to do with someone who has been a key manager in a substantial overseas operation and then returns to the domestic scene where he becomes much less important.

Fear over being forgotten is often mingled with worry over where the next assignment may be. Some companies have set up independent international operations to deal with this problem by having international personnel managers who survey the needs of the total international operation. On visits they can talk with individuals about their careers and their next possible avenue of advancement.

Such a solution is not so easy for companies that have only a few

overseas plants and an organization that is more domestically oriented. A factory manager in India said, "I was told when I came
over here that they just wanted me to straighten things out here and
get some improvements in labor relations. That was three years ago
and I still don't know how long I am going to stay and just what I
am going back to when I get through." An American plant manager
in Turkey had been gradually promoted until he finally managed
the whole Turkish operation quite independently from the home
office. After seven years in Turkey, feeling that he had lived abroad
long enough, he asked to be sent back to the United States. He was
subsequently placed in charge of managing a relatively minor department in the home office. He found this so confining that, after
four months, he left the company for which he had worked twenty
years.

American home office executives do not always recognize the
amplified feelings of insecurity and concern over the future managers experience abroad. Managers in domestic operations often have
the same type of career problems, but in domestic work they are
closer to their superiors and to other men with whom they can talk
over their problems. Overseas they are removed from such sources.
They wonder what has happened to them; they wonder what their
next job may be; they wonder if what they are doing is going to be
appreciated.

The question of appreciation is more important than it first appears, for the overt appreciation demonstrated by a promotion in a
domestic operation is apparently only part of the reward system
which tends to motivate. This research suggests that a man's sense
of achievement is based not only on what he actually accomplishes
but also on what he feels that his friends, neighbors, relatives, and
college classmates believe he has accomplished. This is an un-
proven hypothesis, but there is some evidence that when men are
abroad they feel that what they are doing does not count as much as
it does when they are at home in full view of those whose appreciation they respect and value.

The reaction is credible because a man's sense of worth or self-
esteem is influenced by responses from others as well as by his
own evaluation of his own performance. In this sense a manager's
promotion from one position to another abroad often does not reward him as it might because he feels that no one at home values
the progress he is making. "Progress" counts more when it is ac-
knowledged by those whose judgment counts. The accolades of
Turks do not ring in one's ears as do the accolades of neighbors and

friends. (There are exceptions, of course, to this generalization. The man whose sense of success depends on measuring accomplishment against his *own* standards may be especially valuable on overseas assignments.)

Managers abroad also have problems in dealing with the home office staff, for they are men who are far removed and visit only occasionally but need to have a sense of control and involvement in a foreign operation. When the personal needs of staff men encounter the needs of men abroad, the traditional line-staff tugging and hauling often results. The overseas men feel that there is too much control, too much interference, too much reporting; and the home office men feel frustrated by their wish for more information, involvement, and command. The resulting tangled relations often give the man abroad the uneasy feeling that he is not appreciated and that men close to the top brass at home may be submitting derogatory reports. Such concerns may be compounded by difficulties of communication mostly by letter and cable, with managers on both sides of the ocean frequently feeling that their needs and points of view are not understood.

Thus a man abroad works with a feeling of impermanence, a concern about being forgotten, overlooked, or improperly judged by men who are in a position to vitally affect his career. Although one might expect overseas managers to feel that visits from the home office were threatening or interfering, this is generally incorrect. By far the majority of overseas managers interviewed complained of the infrequency of visits of men from the home office. Not feeling fully appreciated, they comment that "If headquarters men would only come around more often, they would understand a lot better what is being accomplished."

The particular problems of managing abroad

There are many problems peculiar to the management of international production, most of which have been discussed in earlier chapters. At this point we can generalize that the problems particular to the international situation create demands for special knowledge, skills, and attitudes on the part of the men abroad who have to handle them. Four of these demands stand out.

1. *The production manager must cope with economic and political problems that are often far more complicated and involved than*

those he encounters at home. The domestic branch plant manager may occasionally get into zoning problems or local ordinances such as building codes, smoke abatement, or pollution, but by and large he does not need to spend much time on political problems. The overseas manager must deal with the economic and political problems of foreign exchange, import licenses, bureaucratic paperwork, the acceptance of his company by government officials, obtaining permission to expand or move, requests to increase local manufacturing content, and so forth. Some economic and political problems may be handled by the managing director rather than the production manager, but it is generally the production manager who must handle many of the problems himself or deal with men in his organization who are involved with them.

2. *The overseas manager must deal with local foreign managers who have backgrounds, languages, cultures, attitudes, values, and points of view different from his own.* The relationship with these foreign national managers has been discussed in earlier chapters. Suffice it to say that they can be very frustrating and difficult. The delays, language problems, and difficulty in making oneself clear to the foreign national are all challenges to managers abroad.

3. *The U.S. foreign manager needs to learn how to adapt his technical and managerial know-how to an unfamiliar environment.* The production manager may have developed systems in the United States which, for example, are adequate for maintaining control of parts inventories, but when he has few men in his orga. ation whose inventory count can be depended on (or when he has men who, as one production manager put it, "would prefer to give me an inventory figure that they think will make me happy rather than one which they have obtained by counting the parts"), he needs to work out a new control system. Under these conditions know-how from the United States is not directly applicable.

Expatriate managers need to develop new techniques and to adapt the old ones so that they are appropriate to the values and skills available in the foreign country. Some of the problems of adapting know-how in the management of production control, labor relations, the work force, procurement, and choice of process and equipment have been discussed in earlier chapters. At this point it may be concluded that it is usually a mistake to attempt to export equipment, processes, or specific management systems and procedures expecting to apply them directly abroad. Creative adaptability is required of overseas managers. The process of getting concepts and techniques understood and applied abroad requires more personal involvement and less delegation than would be necessary in the United States.

4. *The overseas manager must cope with the cultural differences between the area in which he is working and his own culture.* Positive interaction with an overseas culture is often helped by awareness of the features of one's own culture. This is discussed further later in this chapter. Awareness and sensitivity to sentiments are perhaps even more necessary and valuable abroad than at home because the overseas manager depends on an accurate perception of how he is being received. Abroad the overt symptoms such as facial expressions and the tones of words are unfamiliar. Somehow the American abroad must determine what is appropriate, what is relevant, and how to "graft" what he has previously learned into a new situation.

SOME ADVANTAGES OF WORKING ABROAD

Because the challenges abroad are so demanding, the expatriate manager may feel particularly rewarded when problems are successfully mastered. Broadening of the manager's sensitivity, his understanding of the entire production operation as a system, his ability to work independently — these experiences are cited as advantages of working abroad. And many men assert that the greatest satisfaction in overseas work is increased autonomy — "a chance to run my own show."

It was evident in the companies visited that the opportunity for personal advancement and promotion has been generally greater abroad than in domestic operations during the last ten years. The additional financial remuneration has been mentioned. Finally, the opportunity to travel, to work in a variety of cultures, climates, civilizations, and locations are features ranked high by most of the men interviewed.

These advantages in overseas work are usually recognized and appreciated by the men abroad. No general aura of complaint has been observed in this research. Most of these production managers have either chosen to be abroad or have accepted it in good spirit. Most of them appear to be satisfied and challenged with what they are doing, but they are facing an enlarged scope and intensity of problems which require additional abilities.

PERSONAL ABILITIES REQUIRED ABROAD

What do overseas assignments demand in terms of personal abilities? Several features emerge from observation and analysis of the experience of the 60 men interviewed abroad.

First, *organizational ability* is inherent in starting new foreign plants and coping with growth amidst foreign culture and economic parameters. The overseas administrator (especially in a developing economy) must develop and build an organization, often without benefit of much prior expertise. There is usually no "book" to go by.

Second, these managers need the ability to *improvise and integrate*, imaginatively applying what they know to the demands of the new situation.

Third, the ability to *plan* assumes increased importance because of the economic and political uncertainties in many overseas locations. Planning is necessary in order to anticipate contingencies and develop flexible approaches to meet a variety of possible circumstances. Typically, less experienced foreign managers are not able to do much of the planning.

Fourth, as pointed out earlier, the *increase in breadth, scope, and responsibility required* abroad is usually quite substantial.

Jobs abroad generally require different abilities at different times. Early in the history of a production operation men are needed who can personally demonstrate a large variety of operations and, operating in relatively unstructured situations, can build an organization. At later phases specialization may be required in such areas as systems and procedures, cost cutting, obtaining new sources of procurement, dealing with labor relations after the "honeymoon period" is over, and so forth.

Probably the most important overall requirement for overseas operations may be summarized as an expanded need for basic administrative abilities (in contrast to technical skills or knowledge). There is more necessity for building an organization, for developing men, for planning, for organizing, for "running the whole show" than one would find in domestic operations. These same skills are contributed in domestic organizations by a variety of different individuals, but abroad they are apt to focus on a few expatriate managers. There are few in the indigenous foreign national management cadre who have developed the experience and ability to plan, organize, and build the organization for the future.

We now turn to problems in evaluating the performance of overseas managers in meeting these demands. In order to improve the means of selecting, training, and developing expatriate managers it is necessary to learn to recognize success.

THE EVALUATION OF PERFORMANCE ABROAD

Part of learning more precisely what makes a successful manager is, of course, determining criteria for evaluating his success. Study of the performance of overseas production executives suggests 11 criteria or dimensions which may be useful in analyzing the job a man has done.

1. *The success of the institution managed.* The profit, growth, overall development of the institution being managed, whether it be a department or an entire overseas plant, is one way of deciding whether a manager has been successful. His success must be measured in terms of progress made compared with the difficulty of the problems encountered.

2. *Harmonious and effective relationships.* Such relationships should be primarily with the local managers, but they should exist in the international organization as well.

3. *Ability to "stick it out."* The manager's ability to see through crises, hardships, difficult and frustrating situations with a sense of optimism, determination, humor, and perseverence.

4. *Ability to plan, organize, and control.* The man's effectiveness in doing an orderly and intelligent job of planning, organizing, and controlling his operation.

5. *Understanding of the company's operating environment.* The executive's ability to develop an operating understanding of the economic, cultural, and political environment is another key to his success. He must become proficient in the intricacies of the company's organization and objectives on an international level. He must also recognize that the understanding of any environment is subject to continued growth and improvement.

6. *Development of people.* What kind of a job has the manager done in developing his subordinates: Americans, third country nationals, and foreign nationals? What influence has he had on the improvement of the men in his organization?

7. *Involvement in the job.* Whether the executive likes the job, wants to stay in international work, and has become personally involved in the experience in a particular location are sometimes

clues in evaluating his performance. If he is "fed up," wants to come home or move to a different country—these may be clues that his experiences have not been satisfying and that his performance abroad may be suffering.

8. *Crisis behavior.* How well has the man handled the various internal and external crises that have confronted him? Has he panicked, or has he taken hold in such situations? Has he recognized the main fundamentals of the problem? Does he recognize when he needs help in a crisis, differentiating such times from those when he may solve the problem best by himself?

9. *Personal growth.* Are there indications that the manager has grown through the experience abroad and that he is now prepared for a more demanding assignment?

10. *The quality of the man's influence.* In evaluating an overseas executive's performance it is useful to look at the amount and the quality of the influence he has had. Has he influenced the organizational interrelationships around him so as to further the development of a team of mature and confident industrial managers?

11. *Impressions made on local elites.* John Shearer[5] and other authors have pointed out the difficulties many American overseas managers have had in becoming socially accepted by the local elite with whom they deal.

The evaluation of executive performance is difficult enough within one's own culture and society, but when a foreign environment is involved, it becomes even harder to decide just how good a job a man has done. The preceding measures of performance cannot be applied in absolute terms.

One result of the difficulty in evaluation of performance is a subsequent constraint in deciding what personal characteristics the "successful" manager has. This, in turn, makes the processes of proper selection, training, and supervision of overseas production managers even more elusive.

For instance, it was observed in this study that a smaller propor-

[5] *Op. cit.,* p. 223. One source of the problem in many of the developing countries is that the Americans, because of the key positions they hold and their apparent high standards of living, are thrown in contact with local elites who are at the top of the ladder socially, financially, and culturally. Often the American executives are not as socially sophisticated or as well educated as the elite with whom they find themselves, and they do not stand up well under the scrutiny of the educated foreigner. The net result, according to foreigners who discussed this problem with the researcher, is that the foreigner tends to be disappointed in the "rich" American manager who has so much power. The reduced respect derived from this disappointment influences the relationships and is disturbing to both parties.

tion of overseas executives appeared to be successful in the under-developed countries than in developed countries. Some men were more adequate in some countries or particular environments than they would be in others, and it was more difficult to appear "successful" in the underdeveloped countries. Personal performance must be studied in relation to the problems the men have to face. The different kinds of problems faced evidently require different qualities in executives.

There are no clear, clean, or simple standards that apply to all situations. In a new organization in a developing economy the major problems may be simply getting started, putting together an organization, developing some sort of simple systems and procedures whereby the product can be manufactured. At a later stage more specific skills (such as productivity and cost control) may be required. In a location where relations with the government had been difficult and demanding, the managers' ability to learn to work effectively with local government officers would have to be a major criterion for selection.

Different jobs, countries, and time periods all place their particular requirements on the executive. We must conclude that there can be no simple means of evaluating performance or of describing particular qualities that are necessary for success abroad. To be realistic, home office managers responsible for overseas assignments must study the particular requirements of each position.

A SUMMARY OF VIEWS AND OPINIONS IN THE LITERATURE

In spite of the inherent difficulties, many authors have attempted to describe qualities of the successful overseas manager. Although these are based on relatively subjective analysis, businessmen may be interested in the characteristics selected. A synopsis of what each of the authors has suggested may help find potentially useful suggestions.

Harlan Cleveland and Gerald Mangone in *The Art of Overseas-manship*[6] suggest the most important managerial ability is in building institutions — planning, organizing, and working with people to create an institution that will continue after the manager has moved on.

[6]Harlan Cleveland and Gerald Mangone, *The Art of Overseamanship*, Syracuse University Press, Syracuse, N. Y., 1957.

John Masland[7] analyzed a number of men who were successful. He found variations in administrative techniques in successful managers. One man, for instance, a colonel who supervised the building of a dam in India, was very direct and was inclined to "call a spade a spade." Another was extremely polite and cordial in his relationships. Masland felt that both of them were successful. After analyzing traits of these two men and finding many similarities, he isolated "Factor X," which he described as "a sense of mission," "a desire to go abroad and do a job."

Torre[8] states that adjustment and successful performance abroad are related to several elements: (a) the ability to cope with local conditions; (b) an ability to live successfully in a small, intimate American community; (c) the ability to get along with the indigenous people. He notes that Americans abroad often disappoint the local elite.

Eugene Miller[9] states that the opposite of ethnocentricism is necessary. He feels that an ethnocentric individual will not be successful, but one whose parents have both had well-rounded educations is apt to be more successful.

Edward Hall in *The Silent Language*[10] states that because the rules of behavior abroad are unstated, it is difficult to teach men abroad what the culture demands of them. The job, according to Dr. Hall, requires an ability to absorb unfamiliar elements of a new culture. Dr. Hall cites some factors that should be avoided in selecting overseas personnel: (a) emotional dependence on parents; (b) emotional dependence on living in a particular area; (c) any tendency toward racial prejudice. He points out that often rather eccentric people who have not adjusted well in their domestic societies are effective abroad.

John Fayerweather[11] asserts that the successful overseas manager will (a) understand his own position and objectives, (b) understand the point of view of the foreign national manager, (c) be flexible and self-disciplined in order to modify his position to fit the circumstances, and (d) understand the basic value concepts of the foreign culture.

[7]John Masland, *"The Art of Overseasmanship,"* ed. Harlan Cleveland and Gerald J. Mangone, pp. 96, 97, Syracuse University Press, Syracuse, N. Y., 1957.
[8]Mottran Torre, "Selection of Personnel for International Service," U.N. Research Project, 6(2).
[9]Eugene Miller, "Send the Right Man Overseas," *Think* (April 28, 1960).
[10]*Op. cit.*, p. 45.
[11]John Fayerweather, *The Executive Overseas*, Syracuse University Press, Syracuse, N. Y., 1960.

Cleveland, Mangone, and Davis[12] list factors they feel are necessary for overseas success: (a) technical skill; (b) sense of mission; (c) cultural empathy; (d) a sense for politics; (e) organizational ability; (f) resourcefulness; (g) buoyancy; (h) emotional stability and the ability to "snap back"; (i) previous experience at lower management levels and with a variety of foreign nationals; and (j) intellectual curiosity.

This writer suggested in 1960[13] that these factors appeared desirable: (a) broad training and experience, both technical and cultural; (b) an ability and willingness to demonstrate; (c) teaching ability and interest; (d) personal adequacy, which would make a man able to accept cultural differences without decreasing his decisiveness; (e) many skills (that is, not a specialist); (f) a "staff" approach rather than a "line" approach with foreigners, working in a self-effacing manner and wanting others to receive credit for the work; (g) sufficient respect for the foreign nationals to allow the man to be "tough"; (h) a sense of idealism and dedication.

When John Shearer[14] spoke of the need for abandoning the combination approach toward staffing overseas businesses with expatriates and foreign nationals, he was especially concerned with the "inferior" quality of the men being sent abroad. He pointed out the "available" Americans are apt to be "second rate" and sometimes their desire to go abroad is due to the fact that they have not been successful in this country.

Stieglitz[15] states the necessity for cultural flexibility, a desire to go abroad, "company religion," a liberal arts background, early overseas exposure, and the advantages of getting training on the job. By "company religion" Mr. Stieglitz means that a man must have a strong sense of loyalty to a company and a consequent desire to do a good job, which can carry him through hard times.

Kiernan states that what is necessary is the ability to persuade, and the ability to be a "diplomat."[16]

Lingle[17] of Procter and Gamble asserts that it is desirable for an

---

[12] *Op. cit.*, p. 226.

[13] C. Wickham Skinner, "Wanted: Frontier Managers," *Virginia Law Weekly Dicta* (April 1960).

[14] *Op. cit.*, p. 223.

[15] Harold Stieglitz, "Effective Overseas Performance," *Management Record* (February 1963).

[16] Paul N. Kiernan, "What It Takes To Be a Successful Manager," *International Manager* (August 1962).

[17] Walter L. Lingle, Jr., "The Development of Managers for Overseas Operations," *Management Record* (September 1962).

overseas manager to have concentrated training in one department, that most good overseas managers must be developed through long experience with the company.

Keld Rosager-Hansen[18] analyzed some of the traits of a number of successful production executives, concluding that the men who were successful generally (a) had small town origins, (b) desired to be "practical and decisive" rather than "scientific and consultive," (c) emphasized the importance of planning and delegation, (d) had come from domestic operations, (e) did not desire permanent positions abroad, but enjoyed their stay abroad. He concluded by stating that the extra pay offered for men going abroad could attract the wrong people.

Exhibit 1 summarizes the literature and catalogues desirable traits under six categories: motivation, relationships, administrative skills, attitudes toward oneself, adaptation ability, and past experience. This exhibit lists the conclusions from the literature just cited in abbreviated form. The diversity of qualities recommended is quite revealing. Its message is that since all the experts cannot be "right" if their opinions conflict, perhaps no answer has yet been found.

Exhibit 1 demonstrates that the literature presents some negative aspects: it lacks semantic precision and scientific approach, and it presents some internal conflicts. For example, some authors favor broad training and varied experience, whereas others specify experience in only one department and living in a small town during childhood. There seems to be a conflict, too, between idealistic motivation and the desire to go abroad for higher pay.

Semantic problems abound in the literature. What is a "diplomat," for example? What does it mean to be "tough-minded" and have a sense for politics? Indeed, the phrases "cultural flexibility" and "cultural empathy" are difficult to pin down.

The literature—including this research—is based more on personal observation than significant scientific testing. But in a recent book Torre[19] gives a wide variety of means of selecting and training U.S. managers for work abroad. He discusses the use of psychological tests and describes them as "rather nonconclusive."

We also note that many of the attributes described in the literature do not check out with this writer's observations in the field (based on my subjective interpretation of the same words). For

---

[18]In an unpublished report submitted in partial fulfillment of MBA degree, Harvard Business School, 1964.

[19]*Op. cit.*, p. 237.

EXHIBIT 1
Contrasting Opinions of Personal Ingredients for
Overseas Management Success

Motivation	Relationships	Administrative Skills	Attitudes Towards One's Self	Adaptation	Past Experience
1. Sense of mission	1. The ability to get along with others	1. The ability to plan and organize	1. Emotional balance	1. The ability to adapt to local conditions	1. Multicultural early exposure
2. Company promotion	2. A sense for politics	2. Institution building	2. Buoyant, snap-back, ability	2. Adapting to living in small American groups	2. Not tied to one U.S. area
3. Desire to go abroad for the sake of the opportunity	3. Cultural empathy	3. Technical skills	3. A small quotient of emotional dependence	3. Reducing one's prejudices	3. Educationally well-rounded parents
4. A family de-sire to go abroad	4. Sensitivity	4. Many skills versus being a specialist	4. Understanding one's own objectives	4. An ability to be patient	4. Broad training and experi-ence
5. Teaching	5. Showing re-spect for the foreigner	5. Being tough-minded	5. Understanding one's own points of view	5. Cultural empathy	5. A liberal arts education
6. A liking for demon-strating	6. An ability to accept per-sonal differences	6. Persuasion	6. Self-discipline		6. Many years of experience in one depart-ment
	7. Diplomatic	7. Not being scientific or consultive but being practical	7. One's own goals		

7. Idealism

8. Dedication

9. Enjoying one's stay abroad

10. Excess or higher pay

ability

8. The opposite of social provincialism

and decisive

8. Planning on a large scale

9. The ability to delegate

8. Independence from a particular area or climate

7. Basic experience with the company for which one goes abroad rather than being hired from the outside

8. Good experience in the domestic home office operations

9. Small town childhood

241

example, "cultural empathy" usually implies a man's ability to understand and adjust to a foreign culture. But one of the more effective overseas executives studied, Mr. DeSalle in Turkey,[20] did not appear to adjust to the culture. In fact, he objected to most everything Turkish and told the Turks this directly. He was in no sense diplomatic and clearly preferred not to mince words but to deal with situations quite directly. It was interesting, however, that the Turks seemed to respect him and like him; indeed, they responded to him more favorably than they did to some of his more tactful colleagues. In this context the ability to be smooth, diplomatic, and accepting did not seem to be important. Mr. DeSalle's main weakness appeared to be derived from his lack of management experience and ability in planning and building an organization.

A major failing of the literature is that it seems to add up to the necessity for "being a good executive." The ability to be a "good executive" is not enough, though, because many men who have had good records as able executives in the home office were no longer successful and able when they went abroad. There is virtually no differentiation in the literature as to companies, products, time phases, functional areas of business, management levels, a country's stage of development, whether the job is line or staff, and so on.

From the literature and personal observation it is necessary to conclude that we still do not know very much about the qualities that are necessary for being and becoming a successful overseas executive.

It would be unfair to dismiss all this work as merely contradictory without noting that there are three general characteristics of the successful overseas manager which emerge from a composite of the literature with some consistency:

1.   The men abroad who are described as successful seem generally happy, outgoing, "bouncy," receptive, and intuitively sensitive people.

2.   The successful men abroad usually appear to have a genuine desire to accept an overseas opportunity and to take on a challenging job, whether the challenge be the company opportunity or the possibility of making a personal contribution abroad on an idealistic basis.

3.   Perhaps most important is the necessity for *organizational ability*, in relation to both "line" and "staff" positions. This neces-

[20]California Farm Implement Turk, Harvard Business School Case.

sity for planning, organizing, and working with foreign subordinates by both line and staff managers so as to increase their confidence and competence seems to ring through much of the literature.

COMPANY APPROACHES IN MANAGEMENT SELECTION, TRAINING, AND DEVELOPMENT

Most companies handle the problem of staffing the overseas organization on a "catch as catch can" basis. Most of the men interviewed in the companies abroad had come from the domestic organization. Many were selected by international managers who had known them in the United States. In most cases the men who were asked to go abroad were given the opportunity to turn down the appointment without penalty[21] if they wanted to do so. Thus most men go abroad, nominally at least, on a free choice basis. In cases where men felt virtually forced to go abroad the results have usually not been good.

The problem of obtaining men from the domestic operations is a difficult one. At one company, for example, the new international organization has been decentralized into several major geographic areas and managers of these geographic areas are competing with each other to obtain men from the domestic divisions to go abroad. In many companies where the domestic operation has been under competitive pressure or pressure to expand, there has been a shortage of able men who can be made available. As a result, company executives felt that certain of the men who are available for assignments abroad either have been or will be bypassed for promotions because of their own inadequacies.

The researcher's observation is that a number of the men sent abroad (particularly in the production area) were technically competent, seemed to know their jobs well, know the product, and know the process, but they had not been able to adjust to increased competitive demands and the increased product turnover in the domestic plant. They have been recommended, therefore, as "good, solid individuals who know their jobs well" and would be quite adequate abroad.

In four different circumstances, men sent abroad on this basis

[21]However, several men interviewed stated that, while the company spokesman said the move could be rejected, the word got around if a man turned down a move and it was harmful to his reputation in the company.

have not worked out well. The apparent key reason was their inability to do the job of planning and organizing abroad any better than they were able to do it at home. They knew the product and the process, but abroad they needed to independently get things organized in an orderly fashion, to train managers, to work in the community and with politicians in handling local economic and bureaucratic problems. The job turned out to be larger and more demanding than it had been in the home office. The assumption that product and technical knowledge is sufficient is frequently not valid.

Another problem in obtaining men from the domestic operation is that frequently the man expects to return to the domestic operation within several years. He wonders where the job abroad is going to lead him; he wonders if he has been forgotten; he feels like a temporary employee in an overseas organization. Extra pay and special benefits can entice men to go abroad for the "wrong" reason, or they can cause difficulties when the expatriate returns to the domestic organization.

There are some real advantages to procuring men from within the company. They already understand the company's process and technology; they may personally know the men in authority in the home office; they probably have a sense of company loyalty; and overseas they may be oriented to the possibility of obtaining experience useful for the future. In this sense overseas work can be good company training.

Obtaining men from outside the company has obvious problems. Men who are sent abroad immediately after being hired are frequently on their own with relatively little day-to-day contact with the top international officers. They are likely to run into problems due to their lack of feel or knowledge of the company policy and the company culture, what its values are, what is acceptable and what is not. Men who are obtained from outside the company generally need a long period of orientation in the international home office or domestic plants before they are sent abroad.

There are advantages in obtaining men from third countries, such as an Englishman sent to run a plant in Nigeria. A principal benefit is that these managers often can offer a background of more travel and cultural interaction in their lives than Americans, who, by and large, have not traveled and worked abroad nor had as much contact with "foreigners." Frequently foreign nationals seem able to adapt abroad better than Americans. In addition, there is often the advantage that in using third country nationals the company becomes more truly internationally oriented. The U.S. company is less criticized thereby for excessive Americanization.

The selection of foreign nationals is normally difficult, however, because of the problem of judging credentials and getting to know the man well; it is harder to analyze a man from a foreign country in an interview. Hence there seem to be some advantages in employing only third country foreign nationals who have already proven themselves.

In the final analysis, the problem is more one of availability than selection. The combination of qualities necessary is such that very few men can be expected to be equipped and ready to go abroad. Both cultural and general education is usually needed.

Companies have yet to realize the extent to which their overseas performance is hurt by mediocre expatriate and home office managers in the area of manufacturing. Few international companies have mobilized management development efforts to the same extent and scale as they have for domestic operations. The author has not yet run across a company program for managers focusing on the management problems of operating in different environments and in strange cultures. Corporations may eventually get together to train the men necessary, for few men seem to "just grow" into the total configuration of skills, knowledge, and attitudes needed.

CONCLUSIONS

The following conclusions on the selection and training of men for overseas work are derived from this study.

1. There is a good deal of confusion, conflict, vacillation, and differences of opinion not only in the literature but among the companies over how to select men for overseas jobs. No truly "solid" answers have been developed.

2. The source and selection of men for overseas work must depend on the type of work involved. The aim must be to match men's abilities and attributes with the particular job requirements. This can be attempted more precisely than is usually done. Jobs can be looked at in terms of their technical content, the administrative ability required, the difficulties of working with foreign executives, and finally in their breadth or scope, such as in terms of the

political and economic problems that must be handled. There is a need to be more realistic about the difficulty of job requirements.

3.   There appears to be a real advantage in establishing an end-point for any job considered "temporary." If a man is probably to be in India for three to four years he should be told this, and the end date should be rigorously held rather than making the man suffer from the company's need for flexibility.

4.   There are a number of "buffering factors" which have helped to make men abroad more successful than might have been expected from the "catch as catch can" methods of selecting them. Company friendships and knowledge have helped support men abroad, as has the familiarity with company practices, which do not vary a great deal from one country to another, including the United States. These factors help minimize strains and adjustments. We have observed that interpreters will shield executives to some extent from their own communications mistakes by making their words more palatable to their listeners.

5.   There appear to be certain advantages in hiring younger men directly out of college and training them for international work. Young men who have had some initial training in the home office and then have gone abroad have typically worked out well. They knew from the start that they were to go abroad and indeed had chosen that career path.

6.   Many companies have found a real advantage in maintaining a permanent international division corps. The adaptation required for overseas assignments, the possibilities of building up experience and knowledge in international work, the increasing need for men who are willing to specialize in international activity, the long break-in time—all these factors suggest that the more permanent international staff is going to become a necessity.

7.   There is a need for more clearly developed personnel policy for many companies. Sometimes there is sheer indecision or vacillation in regard to the permanence of staff, the source of staff, and the length of assignments abroad. This causes uncertainty and unnecessary problems in manning the overseas operation.

8.   It is clear that different qualities and different skills are necessary for different companies, countries, and situations. There is no substitute for company analysis of the demands of each job.

Out of the literature and the experience of observing Americans who have gone abroad we can now suggest some hypotheses that may be useful for researchers to study and for companies to try out.

Let me suggest these following hypotheses for further exploration.

HYPOTHESIS 1.   Companies will benefit from a permanent international staff.

HYPOTHESIS 2.   Organizational ability—the skills and attitudes requisite to building effective organization—is perhaps the ability most necessary for successful work abroad. Due to weaker lower and middle management it is necessary to organize at lower levels as well as top levels.

HYPOTHESIS 3.   It is important to send men abroad who are neither very strongly task-oriented nor very strongly people-oriented[1] but at the same time are not poorly motivated in either of these areas. In the language of the "managerial grid," what is needed perhaps is men who are "5 by 5" rather than "9 by 9" or "1 by 1." A strong people satisfaction orientation is better than a weak one and a strong task orientation is better than a weak one, but with the frustration of life abroad, the necessity for accomplishing a great deal but at the same time often going at it slowly, and the possible threatening effect of the overaggressive manager on foreigners—all of these factors suggest the advisability of selecting men who are fairly but not extremely strongly motivated.

HYPOTHESIS 4.   We need more understanding of cultural sensitivity and men's abilities to adapt to a new culture. The necessity for understanding culture in a cognitive sense is not at all certain, but the attributes of sensitivity and absence of strong prejudices, the ability to talk out their prejudices and differences, seem to be more clearly needed than cultural knowledge itself.

HYPOTHESIS 5.   A critical ingredient of success abroad is the ability to judge oneself on the basis of one's contribution to the needs of a particular situation.

A man who judges himself rather than needing outside approval examines each situation in terms of the organizational tasks and the individuals' needs and sets the accomplishment of these tasks as his standards. In examining the situation he reacts with cultural sensitivity. Since his achievement needs are for his own personal satisfaction rather than for building his image with his neighbors, he can function effectively away from home.

HYPOTHESIS 6.   There is no one list of qualities of the successful overseas executive. The total configuration of executive qualities, skills, attitudes, and environments are much more relevant than any checklist of specifications or common ingredients.

If the final hypothesis is valid, then it would be true, as suggested earlier, that the problem of the overseas production manager

---

[1] Blake and Moulton, *op. cit.*, p. 211.

has been discussed for years asking the wrong questions, questions to which there are no answers. It is time to stop looking for simple answers and accept the full complexities of the possibility of myriads of effective combinations of qualities which, although rare in the natural state, may be encouraged to crystallize. Our efforts in practice and research could then be directed toward discovering the conditions and the processes by which the development of overseas managers takes place.

12

CONCLUSION

The purpose of this book has been to describe and analyze problems encountered in managing international manufacturing subsidiaries and to suggest approaches and points of view useful to headquarters and overseas managers. The focus in this final chapter is on broad conclusions of a fundamental nature growing out of the discussion in earlier chapters.

The principal findings of this study are summarized in three parts: (a) the nature and consequences of the problems encountered; (b) the causes of the problem; and (c) recommendations.

THE NATURE AND CONSEQUENCES OF THE PROBLEMS ENCOUNTERED

The nature of the problems encountered can be described as

1. Relatively loose and inefficient production operations, ranging from low labor and equipment productivity and utilization to excessive inventory control and imbalance, and irregular flows of material from vendors.

2. Strained and difficult relationships with government officials and foreign national managers and occasionally with labor organizations.

3. Strained and difficult control and communication relationships between headquarters and overseas managers.

This study of overseas plants has pointed up a multitude of problems and inefficiencies. Since these problems have been set forth in

earlier chapters, it may suffice to recall the worker-supervisor training difficulties, procurement shortages, inadequate scheduling, excessive inventories, improper organizational emphasis, unjustified
equipment investments, the harried expatriates, frustrated local national managers, and irritated headquarters executives. In spite of
generally ample operating margins observed in developing economies, there were needs for improving total productivity and providing
better customer service in most overseas manufacturing plants.
Maximizing output using scarce resources of equipment, material,
and working capital was usually of more significance than labor
productivity. Major problems developed where manufacturing investments were made to implement corporate objectives and plans
which were inconsistent with the needs of the host government.
This occurred in several plants set up in Turkey dependent on the
importation of parts, and it was equally true in assembly operations
in countries whose governments regularly applied pressure for increasing the local content of the product.

In countries where the government both controlled prices and
required local manufacturing instead of importing regardless of
economic effect of scale, production became a key factor in the success of the enterprise. In a few situations the U.S. company had
entered into local production after its competitors, its plant cost
more, and its market was smaller. With narrow production margins,
production efficiency became critical for survival. Finally, in a
number of plants in locations such as Nigeria and Pakistan, foreign
competition came in after the plant had been established and reduced the operating margins drastically. Hence yesterday's profits
are no measure of tomorrow's.

The allocation of responsibility, authority, and control between
home offices and overseas plants adds a further difficult dimension
to international production. Often seen as a struggle for power, an
issue of centralization versus decentralization, the issues are in fact
more fundamental. They are rooted in differing values and objectives between men separated by wide geographical distances and
under considerable personal pressure.

The evidences of headquarters/overseas conflicts are many, ranging from complaints and tensions at home and abroad, a frequent
major difference of opinion over policy, and running battles over
the extent and content of controls and reporting.

When the production manager's problems in overseas manufacturing are contrasted with his capability to handle them, there is a
consistent picture of overstress. The analogy is that of the three-ton

truck with a four-ton load. In total, the problems of operating overseas manufacturing facilities tend to be broader in scope and more difficult than those in strictly domestic operations. The overseas managers must deal with national economic and political problems as well as the usual domestic technological and work force problems. They must cope in a cultural environment which differs from their own. The net result is that everywhere a sense of struggle can be felt, a sense of the managers fighting for survival.

The sense of tension and overstress was also observed (although generally to a lesser extent) at the home office headquarters. There managers attempted to achieve some degree of control and influence across thousands of miles, dealing with a considerable array of different cultures, political situations, and environments. The need for specific knowledge, "feel," and sound judgment in these jobs is great. The result is that many headquarters and overseas managers of international manufacturing operations feel overloaded and often challenged up to their personal limits.

It is interesting that the economic consequences of the problems encountered have usually not been severe. The exceptions have been in the cases of shutdowns due to foreign exchange or procurement difficulties and in the few cases of extreme incongruencies between the aims and policies of host countries and the international corporations.

The chief reason for the lack of severe consequences of often mediocre production management has been the relatively substantial operating margins supported by high demand and low labor costs. Manufacturing operations overseas have typically been profitable. Because of generally ample operating margins, there has been little necessity for concern over the productive operation of the plant. And in fact corporate success in most international enterprises to date has not depended on production efficiency.

In all the overseas locations visited there were signs that production operating margins were shrinking. Rapid domestic growth from import substitution, the most typical pattern of economic development, has its built-in limits. Competition increases both locally and on a worldwide basis. More American firms are establishing overseas operations, often in competition with German, Swiss, French and English plants. In fact, as pointed out in the first chapter, the American share of overseas markets has been declining in spite of our tremendous expansion abroad. Increasing competition is coming, too, from Japanese firms and from local manufacturers in many of the countries in which American companies have been operating.

This increase in worldwide competition reduces gross margins and increases the necessity for emphasis on improving manufacturing productivity. It seems a safe prediction from the pattern to date that the manufacturing function in operating international firms will be more vital to success in the future than it has been in the past.

CENTRAL SOURCES OF PROBLEMS IN INTERNATIONAL MANUFACTURING

Problems encountered when a corporation with headquarters in one nation operates a partially or wholly owned manufacturing plant in another nation can be traced to one of three central facts of international manufacturing:

1.   Problems arise from operating in an environment differing from that of the corporation's home nation.
2.   Problems stem from the delegation of management tasks to foreign nationals.
3.   Problems are caused by the geographic separation of the plant from the corporate headquarters.

Environmental problems in manufacturing abroad

It is obvious that a company manufacturing abroad operates in a different environment than it does at home. But not immediately evident is precisely how the foreign environment actually affects plant operations or requires managers to modify domestic production management practices. In fact, the effects of environmental differences are often subtle and far-reaching.

The environment in which the production system operates affects costs, availability of materials and equipment, skills and attitudes of workers and managers, acceptable quality and price of product, to mention only several broad categories. It therefore seems gratuitous to state that a production system should be designed for its environment if it is to operate productively. This may be a truism, but its implications are not always fully understood. The following examples in various plant functional areas may illustrate this point.

A common mistake in choosing equipment and processes is to copy them from another plant, typically a domestic plant. In so doing the company ignores a different cost mix, and often a different product specification, lot size, maintenance capability, scale of production, and labor and supervisory training demands as well.

In different environments different parts of the organization become more or less critical. A specially tailored organizational structure can place emphasis where it is needed. For example, assigning a key function as a full-time activity of one manager who reports to the top executive gives it attention and raises its status. But it is expensive to give each function its own executive and every function cannot report to the top. Hence organizations must be designed to fit the local situation.

One environment may place a particular premium on effective management of the maintenance function if, for example, spare parts are limited in supply, skilled mechanics are rare, and the economics or technology requires the use of closely linked equipment. In this way tire plants in India are especially dependent on capable maintenance management.

Problems stemming from delegating
management functions to foreign nationals

Inherent in manufacturing abroad is the necessity of entrusting much of the management of the plant to foreign nationals. Daily decisions in production scheduling and control, procurement, and supervision of the work force must be made by foreign nationals, regardless of their capabilities. In domestic branch plants new lower and middle managers can be supported and closely supervised by the requisite number of more experienced men from the parent corporation. Abroad, cost, distance, and nationalistic pressures often combine to make it nearly impossible to rely on headquarters expatriates to train a competent local team.

The central problem in foreign national manufacturing is usually inexperience — inexperience in manufacturing in general, in the particular industry, and with the specific company. Of course no single nationality has a monopoly on effective management of manufacturing plants. But there are ingredients in the experience of a competent manufacturing manager which take time to acquire and assimilate. Even a trained and experienced manager requires time to learn new customs and policies when he goes to work for a different company. If the new company is a foreign-based firm, the amount to learn is naturally much greater.

Similarly, the requirements for new learning are enlarged if the manager's experience has been in another industry. They are further expanded if he must adapt to industry from a prior post in government, military, or other nonfactory occupation. And if the candidates are from a non-Western culture, the cumulative requirements are greatest of all. This is because certain elements of Western culture are usually assumed in the management of an international firm, particularly its emphasis on time and assumption of personal responsibility. Pictorially, the adaptation requirements are shown in Figure 1 with each adaptation building on those below it.

With all these adjustments to be made by foreign national managers, it is no wonder that expatriate production managers are typically disappointed over their performance. Foreign managers are usually criticized by headquarters and expatriates. Many of these criticisms are imprecise labels open to various interpretations and meanings. Many represent the frustrated complaints of expatriates who have been unable to communicate satisfactorily with their subordinates or counterparts, do not understand their behavior, and therefore condemn their performance. Such criticisms are natural, but they are also unfortunate, for, although sometimes justified, they accomplish little but building resentment and mutual dissatisfaction. Hence it is not surprising to find foreign nationals equally critical of U.S. managers.

To move beyond mutual criticism, managers of foreign manufac-

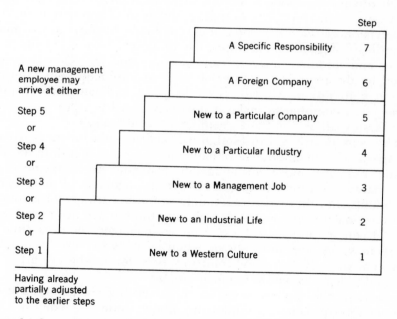

Figure 1. Seven steps in a foreign manager's adaptation to his job in a U.S. foreign-based company.

turing need special skills and insights in selecting, managing, and developing their foreign national managers. Some suggested approaches in acquiring these skills and insights are discussed later in the chapter.

Problems derived from the fact that owners and plant are located in different countries

There are two kinds of problems included in this category. The first has to do with the compatibility between the international corporation and the host government and conditions in the foreign country. The second consists of problems of administration at a distance across international barriers.

Problems often erupt because the plant's policies and operations may not serve the international corporation and the foreign nation equally well. For example, the foreign government may require the use of local materials which are expensive or off-grade and increase costs to the point where the firm cannot compete in the nearby export market.

The local plant must fit into total corporate strategy and conduct its operations to benefit the corporation as a whole. Each company has objectives and policies that make up its total strategy for growth and competition, but the local plant must also shape its policies and practices to be congruent with the needs of the nation in which it is located. This fact is frequently repugnant to corporate managers who resent government interference, but it is a fact that cannot be avoided. For example, the nation may insist that the plant manufacture 90 percent or more of its needs, whereas the international corporation may wish to consolidate the sourcing of certain items in one location in order to gain economies of scale. International manufacturing requires the constant reconciliation of these points of view.

Something must give in these conflicts. Sometimes governments can be persuaded but, more often, the international corporation must adapt. A number of U.S. firms have pulled out of countries rather than accede to government demands felt to be unreasonable. Such steps have sometimes proven shortsighted. In the long run most of the countries involved had markets which continued to grow and the government was forced by unsatisfactory results to moderate its economic policies.

Geographical decentralization across international boundaries also introduces problems of organization, control, and communication between headquarters and branch plants. The problems center around who determines manufacturing policy, how control is obtained, and the headquarters services needed abroad.

Circumstances peculiar to the locality, nation, or culture must be taken into consideration at the corporate policy level. Hence manufacturing policy questions (such as whether the plant should expand, diversify, make a larger fraction of its total product) can rarely be answered unilaterally by the corporate headquarters. Nevertheless, policy and corporate know-how must be transferred across political and cultural interfaces so that the corporation and its plants benefit from each other, cooperate, and prosper. Unfortunately tensions between headquarters and overseas plant management are more common than genuine cooperation. Both parties have typically felt the need for information and control, and distances and disparities of immediate interests introduce continued difficulties.

RECOMMENDATIONS

The following suggestions for overseas managers and headquarters are in two groups: the first is related to the three problem areas previously discussed; the second relates to several central concepts and assumptions which cut across the whole field of international manufacturing.

Building a production system to fit the environment

The first recommendation is to design the total production system to fit the environment rather than either "doing it the U.S. way" or abandoning the development of the overseas production system to relatively inexperienced foreign managers. The first extreme clearly fails to tailor process, equipment, work force management, controls of production, procurement, and manufacturing organization to the cultural, political, and economic environment; the other extreme fails to attempt to design a system adopting accumulated company experience to local conditions. A flexible, situational point of view is required.

Such a point of view depends on managers who possess a keen sense of perception relative to environments that differ from their own. One starting point is a thorough analysis of the environment. Failure to take the culture into account has resulted in many baffled managers and antagonistic foreign nationals.

The cultural system is more difficult to delineate than the economic, political, or technological environment, because values, beliefs, and philosophic assumptions are somewhat intangible. But they are nevertheless as real as more easily measured factors such as interest rates or foreign exchange controls.

The overseas manager who is interested in the study of cultural anthropology[1] is fortunate, whereas a manager with scholarly expertise is not essential. The wise overseas manager avoids labeling as "right" or "wrong" values and beliefs resulting from people's responses to their environment and history. A listing (Exhibit 1) of some major environmental factors and examples of their primary and secondary effects may be useful. Some of the elements of cultures are shown in Exhibit 2, with random examples of possible responses and effects on the production system.

The necessity of designing a production system appropriate to the economic, political, technological, and social facts of the environment should now be clear. When this is not done carefully, the unrealistic mismatching of equipment, policies, and organization results in excessive cost, lost production, antagonized government officials and factory workers, and constant "firefighting" by harried executives.

The task of matching the system to the environment is naturally complex. Even with the present techniques of analyzing environments and synthesizing production systems, managers are seldom equipped for the task. Imperfection and numerous falldowns are inevitable in even the most carefully planned international manufacturing enterprise. But the impossibility of a perfect matching of system and environment should not imply that efforts in that direction are wasted.

A production plant may be viewed as a system. The system is composed of *workers* and *equipment* carrying out a *process* of transforming *materials* into a marketable *product*. The ingredients of the system are guided and coordinated by a set of *policies and rules* designed to optimize productivity and profit. When one part of the system changes, therefore, adjustments may be necessary in other parts of the system in order to keep it in balance.

The following guidelines for achieving congruence of a firm's production system with a foreign environment may be tried:

1.   Describe the environment in as precise and explicit terms as possible. The outline in Exhibits 1 and 2 may be useful in this task.

---

[1]The study of man relative to the characteristic features of the behavior of a group of people who share the same environment and traditions.

EXHIBIT 1
The Effects of an Environment upon a Production System

Environmental Factor	Some Primary Effects	Which in turn may affect
Economic		
Cost of:	Inventory, choice of	Scheduling, labor
Interest	equipment	skills, supervision
Materials and	Procurement organi-	Make or buy
supplies	zation	decisions
Labor	Equipment	Training, wage
	decisions	system
Equipment	Technological	Capital versus labor
	strategy	intensity, number of
		shifts, tooling
Taxes	Net profit	Return on investment
Utilities	Plant location	Choice of process
Local availability of:		
Foreign	Ability to import	Make or buy,
exchange		scheduling
Capital	Ability to borrow	Inventory policy
Workers	Selection, training	Labor relations
Subcontractors	Investment require-	Technical skills
	ments	required
Materials-	Plant location	Equipment,
supplies		maintenance
Technological level		
Skills and	Equipment and	Training, supervision,
knowledge	process	maintenance or-
of labor		ganization
Supervision	Worker productivity	Labor relations
Engineers	Technical indepen-	Costs, quality, reliabil-
	dence of overseas	ity of process
	plant	
Middle	Numbers and skills	Needs for head-
management	of expatriates	quarters staff
	needed	services
Communications	Customer, distributor,	Plant location, local
services	and vendor relations	offices
Vendors' skills	Quality, delivery	Amount and type of
		vendor assistance
		needed
Utilities	Reliability of service	Standby equipment
Transportation	Warehousing, inven-	Planning, forecasting
	tory requirements	
Equipment,	Plant downtime	Planning inventory
spare parts		
availability		

Environmental Factor	Some Primary Effects	Which in turn may affect
Marketing situation		
Purchasing power	Size of market	Scale of plant
Competitive prices	Operating margins	Cost control system
Distribution channels	Delivery requirements, customer service requirements	Scheduling inventory controls
Political		
Laws pertaining to foreign investment	Taxes, incentives, risk	Start-up process
Governmental attitudes toward foreign industry	Government cooperation	Middle management organization
Permits, licenses, paperwork	Need for men trained to handle gov't liaison	Lead times, schedules
Government regulation of:		
Manufactured content	Equipment needs	Costs and capital required
Prices	Operating margins	Manufacturing strategy
Working conditions and fringe benefits	Labor costs	Equipment strategy
Foreign exchange	Make or import	Increased local flexibility
Quality	Reduced freedom to change produce specifications	Quality controls
Government involvement in company relationships	Short term decisions	Increased concern with precedent
Employment of foreigners	Management development	Headquarters assistance
Process and equipment	Use of second-hand or local equipment	Maintenance
Plant location	Labor supply, transportation	Choice of process

EXHIBIT 1 (continued)
The Effects of an Environment upon a Production System

Environmental Factor	Some Primary Effects	Which in turn may affect
Expansion	Expansion timing may not be ideal	Excess capacity or limited capacity
Profit repatria- tion	Financial policy	Modify objectives of local plant
Competition	Umbrella over prices	Dependence on government
Distribution	Channels established by government	Finished goods stocks
Suppliers	Government monopolies	Quality and delivery from vendors
Political strength of economic inter- est groups, unions, farmers, business	Political climate re: Taxes, regulation, unions, importing	Procurement, labor relations
Social		
Educational levels	Selection	Training
Urban/agricultural populations	Continuity of em- ployment	$ invested in training
Population mobility	Plant location	Housing needs
Attitudes toward business	Quality of managers available	Headquarters assistance
Union strength	Supervisory tech- niques	Grievance procedures
Position of minorities	Interpersonal relations	Hiring practices
Democratic institutions	Worker attitudes	Supervisory practices

Facts can be collected from many sources: historical and anthropological literature about the area; discussions with personnel from other companies; marketing and staff personnel in the foreign country; and government sources, both U.S. and of the foreign country and legal representative overseas.

These data should be assembled and analyzed under the direction of the manager who will be responsible for the overseas operation.

2. Contrast the environmental conditions with those at another company production plant whose operation is familiar and consid-

ered successful. Identify differences, using specific data and examples to highlight the differences.

3. Identify the foreign conditions that are essentially static or persisting and those that may be subject to change.

4. Identify and describe the company environment, its technological requirements and basic policy constraints, which must be considered as "givens," not subject to significant latitude or management choice. They include specifications on materials and products, identification of segments of the process which cannot be subcontracted and/or require critical company control and know-how, proprietary information and key policies relating to products, ownership, quality, and finance, which the company considers inviolable.

5. Design the production system. This step requires synthesizing a practical and concrete plan from a combination of facts and variables. The decision sequence should lead from markets and strategy to product to process, thus making the most basic and critical decisions first. The production system can then be built around the process, for after the process is determined, equipment, organization work force, procurement, control and planning systems, and so forth, can all be designed to fit the process. The key environmental forces — marketing, economic, political, and social — affect all the production system decisions; hence each decision must be checked not only for internal congruence with the rest of the system but externally with each environmental factor.

A conceptual scheme for such an analysis is shown in Figure 2.

The approach shown could be followed in the original design of a production system or in the appraisal of an existing overseas manufacturing operation. Eight sets of decisions are shown, taken in order, from top to bottom. In general the arrows indicate a logical flow of thought and decisions: those on the same line can be worked out as a set, in parallel; decisions on a lower line should typically follow all those on higher lines.

The simplicity of this format is not intended to suggest that the process itself is simple or that there are short cuts that guarantee good results. Instead, the diagram's purpose is to indicate an orderly approach to a problem of considerable complexity. This approach suggests a useful framework in which to think, rather than offering "answers." The detailed adjustment of a production system to a particular set of circumstances is beyond the scope of this book and, indeed, the state of the art. What we are saying is: try to understand the five segments of a company's environment (Figure 2)

EXHIBIT 2

Elements of a Cultural System as They Affect Production Management[a]

Differences in these cultural factors –	. . affect a people's values and habits relating to–	For example, the local employee might feel that–	. . and this would affect approaches in these (and other) areas of manufacturing management
I. Assumptions	Time	Time is not measured in minutes, but in days and years	Production control, scheduling, purchasing
	One's proper purpose in life	The only purpose which makes sense is to enjoy each day.	Management development
	The future	The future is not in man's hands.	Short- and long-range planning
	This life versus the hereafter	Life and death are completely ordained and predetermined.	Safety programs.
	Duty, responsibility	Your job is completed when you give an order to a subordinate.	Executive techniques of delegation and follow-up
II. Personal beliefs and aspirations	Right and wrong	I give the boss inventory counts which please him.	Inventory control system
	Sources of pride	A college degree places one higher in society for life.	Selection of supervisors
	Sources of fear and concern	A man laid off finds it hard to get a job regardless of the cause of layoff.	Layoff policy
	Extent of one's hopes	Without the right education and social class, advancement is limited.	Incentives, motivation

			Labor relations
III. Interpersonal	The individual versus society	The individual's own needs must be subordinated to the whole group	
	The source of authority	My men don't like the new process. It won't work.	Quality control
	Care or empathy for others	I'd rather give my salary raise to my foreman than have to tell him he is not to receive one.	Merit reviews
	Importance of family obligations	I had to stay home because my father was sick.	Absenteeism
	Objects of loyalty	Friendship is more important than business.	Work-group relationships
	Tolerance for personal differences	If you don't agree with your boss, he will be insulted.	The decision-making process
IV. Social structure	Interclass mobility	I'd refuse to work for a man without a trade school certificate.	Promotion from within
	Class or caste systems	Men with my standing don't move heavy objects such as typewriters.	Job descriptions – flexibility of job
	Urban-village-farm origins	The company must take the place of the village in caring for its people.	Fringe-benefit program
	Determinants of status	Elderly people have wisdom. They deserve the most important jobs on big machines.	Equipment selection

[a]C. Wickham Skinner, "Management of International Production," *Harvard Business Review* (September-October 1964).

Sequences and Environmental Influences in Production System Design for an International Manufacturing Plant

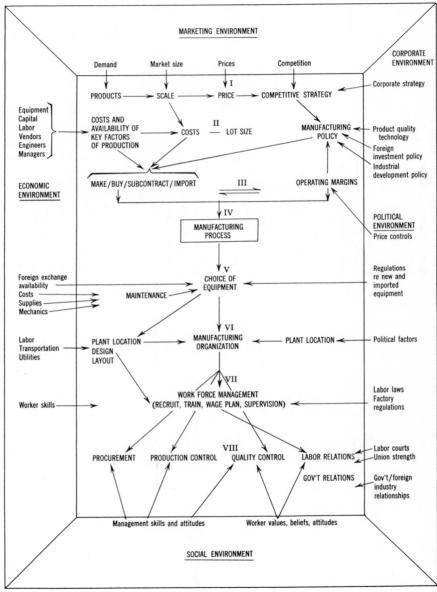

Figure 2

as well as possible and design the system around the processes which best fit the local circumstances and the company's experience and abilities.

Managing foreign managers

A second set of problems arises from the necessity of delegating management responsibilities to men whose culture, education, and business training is generally different from that of managers in the parent company. National pressures for reducing the number of "foreign" managers sent overseas from the parent corporation are universal. Hence staffing an overseas plant with experienced expatriate managers, seasoned and trained by the company itself, is seldom possible, if advisable. In any case, worker supervision, with its impact on productivity, morale, and labor relations, must be performed by local nationals. Similarly, daily procurement and production control management decisions at all but the very top levels are necessarily handled by local managers. Development of foreign national managers often progresses slowly. Yet, surprisingly, few companies have recognized the high costs of mediocre manufacturing performance due to slow middle management development.

Neither the approach of "When in Rome do as the Romans do" — adapting to the foreigner, accepting his methods of managing, and delegating fully — nor the approach of "This is an American company. They must learn to do things our way" has proven clearly effective in managing foreign managers. The problem is too complex to yield to such simple, ideological concepts.

What can we learn from our experience? Certain ingredients appear critical in the more successful experiences observed:

1. An ability to recognize and identify how particular foreign managers, as individuals, behave and work.
2. The skill of separating from conventional or expected behavior those deviations that are actually important to job performance and those that are merely surprising or annoying.
3. Specific techniques for dealing with the important shortcomings and differences so as to bring about changed behavior on the part of one or both parties.

The first ingredient may be intuitive, but for many overseas executives some specific approaches for analyzing individuals' behavior would probably be useful. The managerial grid[2] is one example of

---

[2]Blake and Moulton, *op. cit.*, p. 211.

such a technique. A questionnaire[3] developed by Mason Haire is another potentially useful tool. [This analytical pattern examines managers' beliefs and values about (a) leadership, (b) the manager's role, (c) motivations and needs, (d) the degree of satisfaction of these motivations or needs achieved by the managers.] Finally, a study by managers in terms of Exhibit 2 in this chapter may also lead to useful insights. Some companies use group discussions and training sessions to help their managers develop skills of understanding. The common element inherent in each of these approaches is of course that the expatriate (or headquarters executive) attempts to understand his managers instead of criticizing them.

Evaluating the significance of the differences in managers' behavior from conventional or desired patterns is a second ingredient. Again, the successful overseas manager questioned and searched for understanding instead of simply condemning. Many expatriates tend to criticize foreign managers for differences in dress, religion, beliefs about the future, optimism, democracy, the uniqueness of each individual. Such differences, mostly due to lack of Westernization (Step 1 in Figure 1) are, on analysis, relatively immaterial to managerial performance in spite of the annoyance and exasperation they may cause. For example, the fatalistic manager may not realize that his own energy can bring about change, but with close and persistent supervision he may still become efficient at carrying out assigned tasks.

Differences due to lack of industrialization (Step 2 in Figure 1), although more serious, are also somewhat more susceptible to change. The industrial imperatives of attention to time, cooperation, self-discipline, and consistent application to details are built into the very nature of manufacturing. Many managers who come to industry from nonindustrial occupations — government, education, military — have much to learn and old habits and outlooks to change.

A third important area of analysis is the pertinent industrial management experience a manager has had, that is, experience in the particular industry such as pharmaceutical or food processing (Steps 3 and 4 in Figure 1). Experience in a copper mill may be scarcely applicable to a job in a food processing plant.

In summary, the significant "foreign" differences are likely to be due to inadequate industrial experience and disciplines rather than lack of Westernization, even though the non-Western traits may be more obvious and more resistant to change. The expatriates who

[3] Haire, Ghiselli, and Porter, *op. cit.*, p. 204.

approached management development by attempting to identify deviations from genuinely important habits, attitudes, and beliefs were more apt to net good results than those who labeled unfamiliar behavior with such terms as "impractical" or "irresponsible."

The expatriates who were most effective with foreign managers replaced superior-subordinate relationships with teaching and coaching relationships. The practice of listening as an administrative technique was useful not only for developing managers but in communicating acceptable and accepting attitudes to them. The expatriate who operated as coach and teacher involved himself in all aspects of the job—observing, listening, explaining—and so gained information, which he applied in training the foreign manager.

Several headquarters staff groups were effectively involved in the early years of their foreign plants. Their role, too, was one of coaching and training; they became involved in local operating problems and details. The "rule" that "a manager should stay out of details" was consistently invalid and indeed misleading overseas when a plant was staffed with managers engaged in this complex process of adaptation.

Managing problems arising from the fact that owners and plant are in different countries

Analysis of corporate experience abroad suggests two conditions that should be appraised before a company decides to invest in a manufacturing plant abroad:

1. The company's needs and plans for the plants should be congruent with the long-range requirements of the host nation.
2. The company's anticipated investment and returns should be realistic in terms of the competitive conditions existing or forthcoming in the industry in the host country.

The first condition involves manufacturing considerations concerning products and markets served, plant location, equipment and processes, make versus buy—local versus import, labor relations—personnel policies, use of expatriates, and local financing of work-in-process.

The second condition depends on the corporation's realistic assessment of the competitive situation in the local industry. Careful examination of the operating margins available and projected (i.e., the difference between prices and costs of materials, labor, and manufacturing equipment) will determine whether the spread is adequate to cover marketing and administrative costs and profit. Its breadth indicates the possibility of competing successfully and reveals the emphasis necessary on each part of the production system, (e.g., labor cost control, production and inventory control, quality, maintenance) if the system is to be viable.

Usually the international corporation must do most of the adapting in order to create compatibility between corporate strategy and local conditions. It has proved valuable to accept that foreign government objectives and competitive conditions are difficult to change. The expatriate company operates in the spotlight of the foreign nation's public opinion and government attention. The role of a "foreign investor" is fraught with delicate relationships. Sensitive nationalistic feelings often create political and public relations pressures.

Achieving effective administration of the international manufacturing corporation is more difficult because the ownership and plant location are in different countries. Organizations have crossed international boundaries for centuries. Consider the management problems of Roman emperors, worldwide religious orders, colonial systems, and the British Admiralty. In commerce, the East India, Hudson Bay Trading, and Balfour-Guthrie companies operated profitably long before the post World War II flood of U.S. investments abroad. These enterprises paralleled modern international corporations in their need to achieve effective operating controls and policy direction from a remote headquarters.

In overseas manufacturing the overall problem boils down to three key issues: the nature of home office control; the nature of home office support; and the nature and type of the communications between the home office and overseas plants.

Home office control. The debate over "centralization" versus "decentralization" is seldom meaningful in conducting international manufacturing operations. Because situations differ in terms of the key variables in manufacturing, the nature of the environment, and the developed abilities of local executives, appropriate controls and influence from headquarters vary from plant to plant. It is therefore a mistake to attempt "a philosophy" or take a position on how much or what type of controls "our company" should exert. Unfortunately, however, many companies attempt to apply one universal approach to home office control.

It is more logical to examine each situation in terms of critical variables: the competitive situation, the aspects of manufacturing most vital to success (e.g., procurement, workforce productivity, equipment maintenance) and the strengths of the overseas management relative to the task. Headquarters which functioned to fill the gap between tasks required and skills available abroad were the most effective. The support and control indicated in each situation was provided with the particular administrative method that was appropriate to the job at hand.

In planning headquarters administration in relation to the needs at each foreign plant, it is necessary to determine where and how decisions should be made, ranging from broad policy and planning to specific operating decisions. The "where" and "how" affect the amount of headquarters control. But the concept of "headquarters control" is too vague to be very useful. More precise terms are needed.

In fact, "headquarters control" can be divided into two key facets: *involvement* and *command*. It is possible for headquarters to be highly involved but to exert only minimum command over a foreign plant if it keeps in close contact with progress and problems, and its charter allows it to offer advice which the local plant is free to accept or reject. No one combination of involvement and command can be "right" for all situations. Exhibit 3 specifically represents a range of possible combinations of involvement and command. This matrix is not intended to be definitive but to demonstrate the possibility of different headquarters/plant relationships in each functional area of manufacturing.

It is recommended that each company should explicitly decide what combination is best suited for each functional manufacturing area: manufacturing policy, procurement, workforce management, equipment and process, labor relations, and controls of production. With rapid change so prevalent, these decisions should be reviewed annually as a matter of course to ensure that the chosen point in the matrix for each area (and the entire set of administrative practices which follows from each matrix point) is in keeping with the actual situation.

SOME CENTRAL CONCLUSIONS AND OBSERVATIONS

As one stands back from the experiences of observing and analyzing foreign manufacturing subsidiaries of American corporations, several impressions and concerns begin to emerge as central to the entire process of international management.

EXHIBIT 3
Selecting the Appropriate Degrees
of
Headquarters Involvement and Command

	DEGREES OF COMMAND				
DEGREES OF INVOLVEMENT	A. Observe and advise if requested. Approve capital budgets	B. Observe and offer unilateral advice. Approve capital budgets	C. Command per B plus approve annual budgets on capital and operating expenditures	D. Command per C plus require policy plans and decisions to be submitted for advance approval	E. Command per C plus requiring approval of any deviations from budget and any changes in operations or procedures
I. No headquarters involvement. Reporting is only on broad overall basis and infrequent.					
II. Involvement in general policy, objectives, strategy, long term planning. Receives frequent information on overall results.					
III. Involvement per II plus more detailed reports on results. Participate in short range planning. Participation in general approaches for achieving aims, i.e., organization, general systems.					
IV. Involvement per III plus participates in procedures, specific approaches, and local controls. Reports more detailed and frequent.					
V. Involvement per IV plus regular deep involvement in specific operating decisions, schedules, manpower, expenses. Constant information required.					

First, grossly overgeneralizing, results show that U.S. overseas plants are typically not well-managed. They lack sharpness and attention to details; their productivity is far from ideal; the possibilities for improvements are readily visible. Managers abroad, expatriate and indigenous are under several stresses—and this sense of struggle is seen at headquarters. There is no lack of concern or effort, but the rate of improvement is slow and tedious.

Why is this so? Why is the industrial expertise which has helped make the U.S. nation affluent not being effectively transferred abroad? The self-interest of all involved would be furthered by better international production management, yet results are poor and progress is creeping.

Several observations throw light on these questions. The first is simply that corporations and managers are inevitably still inexperienced in this work. There is little body of knowledge available to apply to provide a framework for more effective thinking about the subject. All involved have much to learn.

Second, it must be clear that the task is very difficult. The manufacturing job is complicated by environmental factors, foreign managers, and corporate headquarters needs and demands. It is a complex mix of technical, political, social, corporate, and economic issues and constraints.

Third, the job is further complicated by rapid change in most countries, in most technologies, and in most corporations. For these reasons, the lack of crispness in overseas plants operations and the sense of struggle observed universally are in fact nearly inevitable. In fact, the researcher could not help but admire most of the managers met in all countries, for they are struggling with problems of great magnitude and perplexity and they are generally progressing.

But progress must be speeded. Competition is increasing; operating margins are often shrinking; and standards of living on a per capita basis in many countries is still dangerously low. The U.S. corporation has been playing a key role in economic development abroad, but the contributions made barely scratch the surface of what is needed. The key question is simply: how can international production management progress be accelerated?

One conclusion runs through most of this book. It is that a great deal of the progress of international manufacturing turns on the abilities and functions of the corporate headquarters group. In virtually every subject we have looked at—from work force management to procurement to foreign manager development—the performance to date and the source of future improvements rest largely on the headquarters. The picture abroad is generally one of inexperienced indigenous managers and overloaded or inadequate expatriates; at home the corporate plants were far better managed and manufacturing expertise bountiful.

It is tempting to reduce this problem to that of transferring U.S. corporate technical and managerial know-how abroad. If we could learn how to do this better—working through and across cultural and geographic barriers—progress, seemingly, could accelerate. The process of teaching, communicating, and learning is, in fact, vital and relevant to the problem.

To see the problem in only this dimension introduces several assumptions which are not only misleading but appear to be quite wrong. The first erroneous assumption is that the know-how or expertise to be transferred is in fact existent and available. The second is that it can flow from headquarters to overseas plants.

It is the conclusion of this study that the necessary know-how and expertise are not available in corporate headquarters and will not be developed there, naturally coursing out to the foreign plants. The expertise needed, in its full sense, is new.

What kind of a wage plan will work best under certain conditions of environment? How do Moslems or Hindus or Africans perceive the role and task of a supervisor? When a culture confronts the imperatives of industry for the first time, no one knows what is going to work best. The suggestions, frameworks, and charts suggested earlier are crude attempts to suggest some new ways of thinking about the problems—but they contain no answers and little expertise.

The assumption that U.S. headquarters can and should transfer their know-how abroad lies at the heart of many of the problems observed all over the world. American headquarters personnel simply do not have the training and equipment and knowledge to establish truly effective production systems in most parts of the world. No one has this skill in sufficient quantity. Assuming otherwise breeds much of the sense of struggle and miserable productivity seen abroad. For the foreign managers assume the Americans have it, and the top corporate officers assume the same. All involved are disappointed and perplexed.

Does this imply that the headquarters staff should stay at home and let the overseas managers flounder? In some functional areas where problems were assumed to be local in nature this was a general pattern. But the floundering of overseas managers was unfortunate in nearly every situation. The headquarters must contribute and help—but with what? Not with existing expertise ready to apply abroad.

United States corporations do have a great deal to offer. But it is not ready-to-wear systems and procedures and processes. It is a state of mind, a concept of production as a system, a sense of zeal to find answers and to achieve ever-improving total productivity.

Few Americans were able to offer this kind of approach to overseas plants. They tended to be so bound up within their own cultural assumptions and corporate wisdom of proper ways to manage their plants that they either set up systems that were incongruent to the environment or created massive resistance.

Even if we can begin to see the task of improving international production management as one of mutually developing new concepts and systems rather than exporting know-how abroad, the problem will not be solved quickly. For the skills, the knowledge, and the judgment required by overseas managers and headquarters staff are new in concept and in combination. Research is urgently needed to learn what must be accomplished and how to accomplish it. Certainly training in technology and management is entirely inadequate to the task. For in addition, men who can transcend cultures and strange environments need training in certain rudiments of cultural anthropology, political science, and economics.

Our conclusions need not be disheartening. The new kinds of training for these jobs is important and necessary, but it is by no means impossible. A wider view of the requirements of U.S. corporations is needed quickly, however, if we are to reverse our present results.

It is too slow—considering growing competition, nationalistic pressures, and explosively low standards of living in many locations —to let U.S. overseas plants slowly learn from experience. The headquarters corporation can contribute—once they have properly trained men and replaced commonly held mistaken assumptions about the role of the home office in exporting culture-bound expertise.

New concepts and systems tailored to local conditions can develop from trained men working with local managers. When the goal becomes the creation of appropriate procedures rather than the transference of alien procedures, the tone of the international relationship can be new and its results more fruitful.

INDEX